Doreen Bates was born in 1906 and died in 1994. Brought up in South London, she attended Croydon High School and read history at Royal Holloway College.

Doreen joined the civil service as a trainee inspector of taxes in 1927 and met a more senior colleague, William Evans, with whom she formed an intense, mutual emotional bond. He was married, but childless, and Doreen came to long for a child fathered by him. This longing was fulfilled with the arrival of undiagnosed twins, a boy and a girl, in 1941, whom she, along with their father, nurtured while at the same time pursuing a professional career in the stressful conditions created in London during the Second World War. She wrote this remarkably vivid diary documenting her life during this time.

Any proceeds from the sale of this diary will be put towards the charitable work of the Frederick Foundation, a charity set up to support the development of a Stroke Unit at the University Hospital, Ibadan, Nigeria and an academic link between Ibadan and Oxford University Medical Schools.

Doreen Bates

DIARY OF A WARTIME UNMARRIED MOTHER

Edited by 'the twins', Margaret
Esiri and Andrew Evans

AUSTIN MACAULEY PUBLISHERS™

LONDON · CAMBRIDGE · NEW YORK · SHARJAH

A CIP catalogue record for this title is available from the British Library.

ISBN 9781035840854 (Paperback)
ISBN 9781035840878 (ePub e-book)
ISBN 9781035840861 (Audiobook)

www.austinmacauley.com

First Published 2024
Austin Macauley Publishers Ltd®
1 Canada Square
Canary Wharf
London
E14 5AA

We'd like to acknowledge the great support of Lucy Caldwell.

A Foreword to Diary of a Wartime Unmarried Mother

– Lucy Caldwell

I first met Doreen Bates in the winter of 2019, as Diarist 5245 in the Mass Observation Project. I was beginning to research life in Belfast during the second World War – she was posted there as a Tax Inspector in the spring of 1941, just in time to document the aerial raids of April-May 1941 which became known as the 'Belfast Blitz'. The entries I read were fresh, fulsome, candid and unsentimental – she had a journalist's eye for the salient detail, and a painterly delight in the mood-impression that a slant of light or a scudding cloud could give to a scene. In one passage, I followed her as she walked up my parents' street, past the house in which I would spend my own childhood, under the very same beech trees – planted to commemorate the victory over Napoleon at Waterloo – by which I too would walk, half a century later. I was intrigued enough to follow her out of Mass Observation and into her own first volume of diaries, published in 2016 as Diary of a Wartime Affair – and I was smitten. These personal diaries, beginning in her late 20s, and taking us through the heartache of a decade-long forbidden love affair, and to the birth of her much-wanted children, brim with soul, passion, candour and wit, giving vivid insight into the life of a woman unvanquished by her time, a woman who leaps from the page so strikingly you feel your pulse beating in time with hers. I felt I'd met a kindred spirit – I knew she had to be part of the novel I was writing.

This novel, These Days, interweaves real with imagined stories about the Belfast Blitz. The easiest thing for me to do would have been to make up a fictional Tax Inspector – call her 'Eileen Yates' – with a line in the Acknowledgements crediting my source material. But Doreen felt so real to me, so alive, and – there's no other way of putting it – I seemed to feel her insistence that she be part of my book in her own right, in her own name. So I wrote her in, sticking as scrupulously as possible to her dates, her facts, the details of her meals, her outfits, her evening walks, the weather. I made her an older colleague of my protagonist Audrey – the sort of woman, I thought, whom Audrey would regard with awe and admiration, the sort of woman who could show her – show all of us – that there are always other choices, other ways of living.

One of the tensest moments of the whole process came for me when the novel had been formally accepted for publication. Up until then, you work with a wild kind of amorality, your only loyalty to the story itself, doing whatever the book needs to work. Now your awareness must turn outwards, to its readers, to the world into which it will be published. I had used Doreen – instinctively, blithely – as a character, and now I had to inform the editors of her diaries and her Estate what I had done, and to send the full manuscript in the hope of their approval. The relief and wonder when I heard back, not just from the publisher or their rights teams or their lawyers, but from 'the twins' themselves – with whom she is of course pregnant in my novel, though she doesn't know until she is in labour that she is carrying two babies – was indescribable.

And so began a very special friendship, and a series of conversations, both public (via the WarTime NI podcast and the Linen Hall Library's online lecture series) and private, about women's lives, about writing the twentieth century and about vanquishing stereotypes and shame; and it was my privilege to be an early reader of the diaries that form this second volume, Diary of a Wartime Unmarried Mother.

Here, once more, is Doreen's hunger and capacity for life, her alertness and susceptibility to nature, and to culture. She writes of the jubilant birds on a day of brilliant sunshine on wet roads, of wandering into the woods to find: "The wood anemones were just coming out, the pussy willow was a fuzz of grey silk and gold thimbles; bluebells and dog's mercury were making the ground green; the elms were misty red with blossom." She is overcome by Citizen Kane, also by Beethoven's Romance at the Proms. She is engrossed in the final chapter of Stephen Spender's Life and the Poet in bed one morning, fobbing her toddlers off with bacon rinds from her breakfast as they play in the cot beside her. Here too is her radical empathy. Here she is on 1st June 1942:

I couldn't sleep for thinking of Cologne, which was raided by over 1,000 RAF planes for 1 and a half hours on Saturday night. I couldn't help thinking of the Koln I knew in 1935; the 2 gentle middle-aged sisters who kept the house where we stayed; the little waiter who insisted on our having 3 eggs for supper; the puppet theatre with its crammed audience of children, wildly excited by Hansel and Gretel, kept in some order by the commissionaire who shouted at them and loved them; the grave sweet 13th century carving of the Virgin and the huge wooden figure of St Christopher in the cathedral. It is these who suffer more than the men responsible.

One of the joys, for me, of the first volume of diaries were the moments where Doreen wrote about – say – her hair being just greasy enough to be manageable, but not yet looking in need of a wash, or of having painted nails that had lasted longer than expected without chipping. Such details are gold dust for a novelist – they bring a person, a social milieu, to life, and they don't tend to be the things deemed worthy of being recorded. This volume, too, is rich in material detail – of clothes: "a new green tweed costume with silk blouse and new green shoes" – and of food: "a salad with egg and tomato and a blancmange with cream," "tea and cider and a huge piece of homemade cake and apple jelly," and "the almond icing" on a Christmas cake "made with soya bean flour and flavouring." The candour of her appetite is another joy, particularly when she talks, with relish, about making love:

As the twins were asleep in their pram we had a quick tea and then went upstairs and fucked for an hour. […] I hadn't had a flicker [of desire] ever since they were born and thought perhaps it had cured me! But it hadn't! We both found it as lovely as ever. […] We began with me on top and had cigarettes – in spite of the budget – then turned over and finished.

And again:

A red-letter weekend! E came down to Collingbourne and we had a lovely, lovely fuck!

Some of my favourite passages in the first volume of diaries were those where Doreen, miserable and impossibly in love, a situation condemned by the church, by society, by her own family, nevertheless finds sanctity in their love. Here is one such passage from the 18th December 1935:

In a shadowed corner E held me in his arms and kissed me. This is the third church he has loved me in – Church Street, Fingest, Hughenden. There is something so beautiful about doing this in a silent church. It sanctifies it, as it were – makes it sweet and holy and purifies it of connection with Eastbourne Terrace or biological mating or suburban respectability. It makes it as-it-were an offering – a tribute – a testimony to the creator who could imagine his creatures rising to such heights of feeling.

In this volume, too, she writes that: "I cannot think it is wrong to cooperate in such joy," and describes their love-making in spiritual terms: "He was sweet on Saturday night. I rarely remember such ecstasy. It changed key in the middle – "modulation" he said – into a kind of holy rapture – like Pentecost."

But for all this surety, the certainty of this grace, the life that Doreen has chosen is not an easy one. The trials that her unorthodox lifestyle create are here; the effort of will that it takes to keep a disapproving mother on her side, to lie to the neighbours about her situation, to have the twins' ration books registered under their father's surname. There are flickers of despair, too, at the situation with K – the twins' father's wife – who, four months after they have been born, is yet to be told about them. "I get so impatient with K – which is unfair because E has not given her the opportunity of being anything but an obstacle." When K is finally told about the babies' existence, in early February 1942, Doreen, poignantly, always willing to see the best in people, notes that K is "much concerned about the twins, that they should have no father." In these diaries, people are good – they try to do the right thing. Doreen's sister Margot goes to the ballet with K to discuss "the present ménage", and people try to come to accommodation with things, for the sake of the twins.

The threat of societal sanctions, though, is ever-present: she is called into her supervisor's office for an interview about her "extra-matrimonial activities", and told that they are usually grounds for a woman to retire from the Civil Service, although each case is considered on its own merits, and she is therefore obliged to give them an assurance that her "activities" are now over. She responds, tartly, that although having twins made it less likely she should repeat such activities, she would not change her lifestyle, and not even necessarily stop at twins.

Such flashes of her strength of character are electrifying – like the Harley Street doctor who tells her that he likes intelligent questions and doesn't often get them, to which she responds, "I like intelligent answers and I don't often get them from doctors," or the more troubling account of an encounter with an American GI on a lonely road – she on foot, soaked, a broken buckle on her shoe, he mulishly determined that she have sex with him behind a hedge. "It would take only five minutes," he insists, but she keeps her head and dissuades him, telling herself later that he was "a nice lad" and that she hadn't felt any fear at all.

If the first volume of diaries has the compulsion that comes from the arc and the agony of an impossible love affair, and if, occasionally, in this volume the reader feels the grind of life with young children, it is leavened by the poignancy of knowing that here we are reading about the happily-ever-after. This is the life she has longed for, and this is the reality of life, in all of its intimate detail – looking after children with tonsillitis and bad fevers during air raids, their soft bodies "appallingly vulnerable"; charting the increasingly complex worlds of their fantasy games.

Time and again she yearns for more – she goes to a show of watercolours and drawings at the National Gallery which "made me itch to try to do likewise – how inadequate is the time at one's disposal for all there is to do." The day after her 40th birthday she writes that:

Time is inexorable though my only regret is that there is so little time to do all there is to do – having children, rearing them, travelling, reading books, listening to music, gardening, watching birds, flowers, trees, doing research, teaching, writing – and all the hosts of things I want to do.

She writes frequently, poignantly, of her desire for another baby: "…but E keeps evading and it is easy for him to do so."

I remember a particular, peculiar sensation that would come over me while researching the Belfast Blitz – the dizzy feeling that none of it had happened yet. There is a sharp ache that comes from reading these diaries, knowing the future that Doreen wonders about – the ways in which her beloved children will grow up, and the children they will have, and all they will do. The days are slow but the years are fast, and they spin on, Christmases and birthdays, concentrated orange juice and rusks and clutched handfuls of posies, chills and fevers and potty training and temper tantrums, litters of puppies, wooden-soled sandals and sardine sandwiches, trains and timetables and tax returns, haircuts and vicar's tea-parties and collections of milk tops and matchboxes, books and plays and Proms, the hedges bare and the hedges green again, and a new carpet of bluebells in the woods. "Suddenly," the final entry reads:

I felt quite overwhelmed with happiness – seeing Andrew and his father crawling about on the floor – Margaret with her bright face in the glow of the lights and Sallie on the floor. The whole scene fixed itself in my mind and I watched. I knew I should look back on it in the future as one of the loveliest moments in my life. And then it dissolved like a cloud picture – E went off on the train; the twins were tired and I put them to bed.

Life, real life, does not happen apart from the boil-washing of rompers and the nightly trials of bedwettings, or in spite of it. This is life – this is what we get – this, here, now, and any meaning, any immanence, or transcendence, cannot be outsourced, or postponed, but is to be found within the mundane and the quotidian.

This seems, to me, to be the most important message of these diaries, the final reason that Diary of a Wartime Unmarried Mother, edited, in an act of great love and generosity, by its grown-up protagonists, deserves to take its place as one of the essential diaries of the twentieth century.

Lucy Caldwell, November 2023

Table of Contents

Introduction

This diary carries on the story of a young woman whose previous 8 years of diary were published as 'Diary of a Wartime Affair' by Penguin Random House in 2016. Doreen Bates, its author, was born in 1906 and was the first person in her family to go to university (Royal Holloway College, where she read History). She was working in the Inland Revenue in London at the time when she started writing her diary.

As recorded in 'Diary of a Wartime Affair', Doreen developed an intense mutual attachment to an older, married (but childless) male colleague, referred to in the diary mostly as E, and came to long for a child fathered by him. Eventually, this longing resulted in the birth of undiagnosed twins, a boy, Andrew, and a girl, Margaret, in October 1941, in the middle of the Second World War. The present segment of her diary commences when the twins, Andrew and Margaret, are 3 months old and she has returned to full-time work. She had employed a live-in nanny, referred to here as Hobday (or Nannie), who had gamely taken on the task of helping to look after twins rather than the single infant she had expected to be responsible for. They set up home in a rented small house in Addiscombe, South London, not far from where her mother and sister lived at Riddlesdown, near Purley, in Surrey.

Doreen derived enormous help in embarking on her new life as a mother from her younger, unmarried sister, Margot. Her mother, Rosa, was deeply opposed to having anything to do with the babies' father, towards whom she always had feelings of intense hostility. Yet she was strongly drawn to the twins and eventually helped considerably with their upbringing. However, her opposition to E posed great difficulty for Doreen as she wanted E to have a role in their upbringing too. At times, she thought she might have to cut E out of their lives but (fortunately for us, the twins) this did not happen.

In the 5 years of this diary, the war continued for most of the time with heavy bombing driving Doreen to evacuate Hobday and the twins early in 1944 to a tiny cottage she purchased in Wiltshire where she managed to join them every single weekend despite the chaos of wartime travel. She gave up the tenancy of the Addiscombe house and lived with her mother and sister during the week.

The twins were the main focus of Doreen's life during the 5 years of this diary even though she was working full-time for the Inland Revenue and taking much interest in cultural happenings such as picture exhibitions and concerts as well. She had already mastered the work required of her in her office and was able to carry it out very competently. Her observations of the twins' development show just how absorbed with them she was. And her deep affection and enlightened interactions with them, the latter exceptional at that time, are plain to see.

After the war, Doreen found a house in which to bring up the twins near Oxted in Surrey. It was near a station on the railway route to London via Riddlesdown so, despite lacking a car, she was able to reach both her mother and sister as well as her work in London quite easily. Hobday left shortly after they settled in Oxted (she had recently married) and Doreen then employed, consecutively, two unmarried mothers, each with their own child, to act as nanny/housekeeper. There was also a 'sitting tenant' in the house, an elderly retired nurse, so the modest 3-bedroom house was very cramped. Nevertheless, she managed to create a stable, lively and happy environment for them all, which was all the more remarkable for the challenging circumstances—emotional, social and financial—in which she lived.

Her relations with E continued and formed the central emotional attachment in her life, apart from the twins. E, who was once reluctant to have children, was completely won over by the twins to the extent that in 1944, he remarks to Doreen that 'The supreme experience in life is to see one's children'.

1942

Doreen and the twins while toddlers

Thursday 1st January 1942

First, the twins: Yesterday Dr Elder came and vaccinated them on the left shoulder. He said they were flourishing and was most impressed with Andrew's development. Up to now, the vaccination has not affected them. They are sleeping one each end of the cot and each has a red ribbon around the left arm to remind us to be careful in picking them up. They were bathed on Wednesday. Margaret still has spasms of fright in the bath as if she is uncertain she is safe, though she enjoys it between. She is less confident and active in the water. Andrew loves it all the time and makes great efforts to stand up. He doesn't laugh in the bath but seems quite intent on what he is trying to do.

Andrew resents attention to Margaret. She is less inclined to be jealous. He makes obvious efforts to communicate by words, raising his head and trying intensely. He pokes his tongue in and out as he does so and achieves quite a variety of sounds at times. He doesn't seem to talk to himself much but usually makes his efforts when someone is looking closely at him. E[1] saw them yesterday after 13 days and noticed a lot of change in both of them; more active, more concentrated.

---

[1] William (Bill) Evans, the twins' father, referred to mainly as E in this diary

It has been a very full week. On Monday afternoon, ES[2] came in. I felt some constraint at first but liked him more than I expected. I felt he was fundamentally dismal and this made me feel guilty. I asked him if he could come out to Addiscombe if he had time. He said he would think it over and he did, in fact, meet me at London Bridge on Wednesday afternoon and we came down to tea. Margot[3] called on her way home. I was glad as they like each other; also, I didn't want too long alone with him. He was very sweet with the twins. He still likes me, though he didn't say so and I suppose it was perhaps cruel to invite him. Hobday[4] made a fine dinner which was some small compensation.

Yesterday was a lovely day. I had it instead of Boxing Day and met E at West Croydon at 9.00. We went by bus to Caterham. It was cloudy, though once we saw patches of blue sky. There was still ice on big puddles but it was not so cold and there was no wind. An unusually good day for a walk. First I looked in a book shop and bought 2 Puffin books—'Animals of the Countryside' and 'Orlando's Night Out'. We had a coffee and then climbed up to Tillingdown Farm and walked round to the old house on the hill overlooking Godstone. Something—perhaps a bomb—had happened to it; the roof was almost gone and the windows gaping. The beeches were beautiful and tits, chaffinches and blackbirds were poking in the dead leaves. It was so lovely to see it again after being in Ireland[5] that I had to cry. It is so charged with associations—with Margot and E, with Wyndham[6] and Rosa[7]—that I could hardly bear it.

It was a lovely day with a lot of our old nonsensical bickering and playing. It is strange that when I am not with the twins I don't feel at all different but just as irresponsible and light as I was before. We both enjoyed it. It was the first walk since last February when we had 3 walks, lovely, but overshadowed by my move to Ireland.

E had decided, I think as a result of our discussions on religion and the twins, to reread the Bible all through and had got to Genesis 24. He had a lot to say, as it had struck him fresh.

---

[2] ES was a former colleague of Doreen's with whom she became emotionally close about 30 months earlier

[3] Doreen's sister

[4] Nanny/Housekeeper, sometimes referred to as 'Nannie'

[5] Doreen had been posted to Northern Ireland for several months in 1941

[6] Doreen's father, who died in 1939

[7] Doreen's mother

Saturday 3rd January 1942

I returned to City 6 today and found a stack of work and a note from Loach[8] asking me to see him next Thursday at Somerset House! Had coffee with E. He had read some more Genesis and been lent Moffatt's translation of the Old Testament. He said he had a message for Andrew—a quotation from the meeting of Esau and Jacob—"I looked upon thy face as it had been God's." Up to now he sees the fruit of his seed and it is good. They are lovely children, so lovely that I hold my breath. Such loveliness—and the happiness of contemplating them seems so precarious. It is a vision, a miracle, that can hardly persist in such a world, but one must have faith.

Rosa came this afternoon and I rejoiced to see her playing with the babies— laughing with them and helping with them. I went to the library and left her alone with them.

Monday 5th January 1942

I shall be glad to get my room to myself tomorrow[9]. I lunched with Le Huquet[10] who was cordial. It is astonishing how news of the twins have spread— she heard of them from people I don't know at all!

Tuesday 6th January 1942

I have done more work today than I have for months, having a quiet room and piles of it to do! I nearly forgot to have tea with E. It has been very cold but fine. I was supposed to lunch with McCreath[11] but he didn't phone me—I don't know why as I know he put it in his diary; possibly he is ill. E met Margot and had a serious discussion. I saw her in the train this morning. This is a pleasant institution. I talk and knit and we always get to London Bridge unexpectedly quickly.

Wednesday 7th January 1942

While I was dressing, I looked at the twins. Margaret was asleep. Andrew was awake, lying on his back, quite content. I looked at him and he smiled and tried to talk, waving a hand over his head to help.

---

[8] Senior colleague

[9] At her office, in the Income Tax office, City 6

[10] A female colleague

[11] Another senior colleague

Friday 9th January 1942

Yesterday morning I had my interview with Loach. I was surprised to find him quite cordial. He said Bradford[12] had told him to have a 'winding-up' interview. He was instructed to tell me the 'official theory'. A woman had to retire on marriage and also on 'extra-matrimonial activities'. I said this theory was not made public. He said, "No, because the Board in practice considered each case on its merits, and mine was rather unusual." But what it boiled down to was 'once and once only!' I said that having twins made it less likely that I should repeat it but I should not necessarily stop at that. "Was he telling me definitely that if I did it again I should be dismissed?" He said it was all rather in the air but he would say I should gravely prejudice my position. (As I was going he returned to this point and said, "Don't do it again, but if you do let me know at once.") He pointed out that I had made it more difficult to put me in a district. I admitted this but said I would do my best to minimise difficulties. He asked how I liked City 6 and I said I thought I should when I had cleared up the mess. He said I could not expect 'permanent immobility'. I replied that I did not ask for any privileges whatever which anyone else could not have, but he promised to try to keep me in London while I had 'a very young family'. He would give me all the consideration he gave to a married man—i.e. take into account his domestic circumstances.

He enquired how the twins were progressing—whether they were quiet at night—looked at the 3 best snaps—asked me whether I felt fit. I said yes—never felt fitter and he said one would expect that. I had undoubtedly chosen the other parent carefully—from that he talked about Rebecca West and HG Wells (whom he knew)—he could not see how she could have—but it was an intellectual attraction obviously! I deduced that he put me in a class with her! He told me that the Board's attitude to the permanent retention of women on marriage had been modified[13]. He would be prepared to say if I had applied he thought it quite likely even now. There were not many Higher Grade women (2 in fact) and promotion to HG could, he thought, 'be taken to indicate that a woman was outstanding and of particular value'. He asked about my family and domestic circumstances and I told him when I saw him early in February about going to Belfast I did not know I was pregnant. He said he had concluded this after comparing dates, but at first he assumed I had not been quite candid. I thanked

---

[12] A senior manager in the Inland Revenue in charge of staffing

[13] Earlier, women were required to leave the service on getting married

him for his consideration and we parted on what appeared to be most cordial terms.

Before going to Somerset House, I had used the opportunity to buy 2 rattles at Hamleys. They are bone, to cut teeth on, fast colours and can be boiled. They cost 6 shillings each. E is giving Andrew his and I am giving Margaret hers.

Sunday 11th January 1942

The coldest day this winter—the milk was frozen in the bottle at tea time, though it had been standing in the hall since morning. E came over to tea to see the babes. Andrew had been a bit off colour but they were both recovering from the general upset due to the vaccination. We gave them their rattles. They noticed the sound and looked at the rings, though each seemed more interested in the other's. No doubt they will learn to manipulate them. When they both went to sleep about 5.45, E said, "The show seems finished—I might as well go!" and later, "I can't imagine how anyone can be jealous of children." He is so sweet with them—if only he could live with them. K[14] has a great exam on Jan 23rd and we both want her to pass. With her temperament, he is afraid to give her a shock before it, so he is postponing telling her [about the twins] till after it. There is always something, though I am sure he does not intend to let things slide.

Thursday 15th January 1942

Andrew has been off colour, whether from his vaccination or from my cold I don't know. He wasn't hungry as usual and had diarrhoea. Margaret seems to have quite got over the vaccination. Her scar is smaller than his and she is so happy—just smiles and plays when her tummy is full. He talks and sometimes smiles. He likes attention even more than she does. Hobday sings to them and recites to them. Andrew prefers tongue twisters (like Theophilus Thistleton, the thistle sifter) and Margaret prefers songs and rhymes.

Monday 19th January 1942

Still freezing, and tonight snowing. Lunched with E. He had bought the Mothercraft Manual on Saturday and written a lovely inscription inside the cover. It is silly, but though I know how he feels it means a lot more when he expresses something in words. I had a glorious glow inside all the afternoon. He came down to see the twins this evening. Andrew talked and laughed to him and

_____

[14] E's wife, Kathleen

loved to hear him say a tongue twister about Poppy. Margaret quite ignored him but played a game of peep-bo with the light. When Nannie took her, she rewarded her with a magnificent smile. He noticed a lot of development—much more precise use of their hands, more variety of vowel sounds from Andrew, a few still rather accidental vocal noises from Margaret and a much clearer sense of the direction of sound from both. He had made a graph of their weights and put in the average from the Mothercraft Manual.

Monday 26th January 1942

A hammering headache due to the cold wind hampers this note but I must put something down. On Saturday, I read a small part in Family Reunion. The play read very well and I was reinforced in my opinion that one gets nearer the play's essence in a reading than in a full production. The psychological distance is reduced by the absence of footlights.

Yesterday Hobday made me go out. It was a shining morning with brilliant sunshine, wet roads and jubilant birds. I went to Purley[15] and Margot and I took Susan[16] over the downs—the first time I have been since I left Belfast. It was lovely and just the same except for extra barbed wire. She was going to a lecture after lunch so I played Bach, Haydn and Mozart for 1and a half hours and then went to Kennington to see Rosa's sculpture[17]. It was good and she was pleased. We had tea and I came back to Addiscombe early.

A year ago today E and I mixed the twins at Elsie's[18] room in Pimlico, and I got my transfer to Belfast. What a year! I have had a better week, getting straighter at the office, going to bed earlier and no visitors till E came to dinner yesterday. The twins have usually slept till 7.00 am, though it was 5.45 when Margaret woke today. They are growing and developing. Andrew has more varied noises and makes them consecutively in sentences or long harangues, usually after meals. They require less effort, less concentration, and he is eliminating irrelevant movements. He kicks and waves his arms less when he 'talks'. This was after a few days' rest when he made almost no sounds. On Wednesday, he suddenly and easily produced these long sequences of more complicated sounds. Margaret kicks more vigorously, with evident enjoyment.

---

[15] The house where Rosa and Margot lived

[16] Their bitch

[17] Rosa was learning sculpture and making a head of Wyndham

[18] Elsie Fisher, a friend Doreen first met at College

And it is a form of response to other people's talking to her. She almost never 'talks' (though she occasionally emits, suddenly, a shout), but if one speaks to her when she is lying quiet she smiles and begins to kick. Yesterday they showed more interest in each other. Margaret sat on my lap and definitely smiled at Andrew, sitting on E's. He noticed this and 'talked' to her. She was more inclined to try to talk back than at any other person. When E first came, Andrew didn't remember him and realised he was 'different', and cried and wouldn't talk. He clearly knows Hobday and me and doesn't much mind other women. He evidently sensed that E was different. Margaret was friendly and smiled at him.

I have made an approximate budget and find I am overspending between £30 and £35 a quarter. This is what I had estimated. It is clear that this can't go on. In about 18 months, I should be quite on the rocks. I have said no more to Rosa. I am waiting (still) for the result of E's disclosure to K. She didn't get through her exam, so by postponing the discussion we have gained nothing except the certainty that her failure cannot be attributed to me and the twins. I felt rather dismal yesterday and today, partly the weather, partly the strain of this eternal waiting, partly because Andrew would not at first talk to E. I get so impatient with K—which is unfair because E has not given her the opportunity of being anything but an obstacle. She doesn't even know he has children. He said he did not want an arrangement by which he wouldn't see them at all. I get so edgy and weary with this uncertainty—nearly 4 months since they were born—nearly 11 since I knew they were conceived and still he puts off speaking.

Thursday 3rd February 1942

Appalling weather again. A heavy snowfall yesterday and during the night made the roads dangerous. The snow remained hard till lunchtime and then the air grew warmer and it melted fast, turning the roads into seas of brown mud.

Last night I went to Purley. I decided to talk business with Rosa. I explained that I could not afford to run Purley and the Addiscombe house. She was inclined to say I ought to have thought of that before, and she was definitely against any combined household, let alone at Purley. She is probably right—if 2 households can be managed. I felt a pig, but really she does not consider how much it costs to maintain her standard even with her excellent management. E did not say anything to K; she had a cold at the weekend.

I am overwhelmed with work again and seem to make little progress. The book on genetics from the library is most interesting but E took it yesterday.

Thursday 5th February 1942

What a week! Yesterday it turned milder in the afternoon and the snow melted but today it has snowed without ceasing all day with an east or north wind. I have been in each evening since Monday and have seen quite a lot of the twins. Yesterday I held his rattle before Andrew. He looked at it and put out his hand. After a few attempts, he took hold of it. He managed this twice. He seems happy and laughs more readily than before, though he still looks serious in between.

E said today that K's health is bad—she sleeps little and has a good deal of pain (usually indigestion). He said he was not afraid of her but of the effect of the news on her.

Saturday 7th February 1942

Still bitterly cold, a biting east wind driving snow all day, ground hard as iron. It seems impossible to keep warm. I had coffee with E. Last night he told K about the twins. She was better than she had been and stood up to it better than he had expected. She said she had wanted a girl of her own, but felt she would not survive and thought he might want her. How odd to suppose that any woman was valuable in general or to him in particular more than a child. She regretted her inability to express what she felt. She was much concerned about the twins, that they should have no father. E wants Margot to see her and he thinks if she could see the twins it would be better, and, ultimately, me too. He seems to have done this difficult job as well as it could be done. It remains to be seen how she reacts. I was relieved that it was begun, but more shaken up than I expected. I feel that whatever merits or claims anyone else has—K or E or me or Rosa—the primary consideration is the welfare of the twins. But it is not easy to be hard—even as hard as necessary.

I went to lunch at Purley today, in a snowstorm. Afterwards I went to Coulsdon to look at a second-hand cot for £3.05d. They were very nice people—had lived in India till 10 years ago, then at Bexhill, then with friends in Essex. The cot belonged to their boy, now 7. They gave me tea and I paid for the cot but forgot to give my address. When I rang up to give it, he asked me whether I would like a high chair for 7/6d. I said yes, so they will send it all. It is as good value as one can get nowadays and second hand goods with pre-war material are better than the shoddy expensive stuff in the shops.

Thursday 12th February 1942

I began my leave yesterday and the weather so far has been good, cold but bright. Yesterday morning I went to Croydon and bought 9 yards of 4 different ginghams to make summer clothes for the twins. They were attractive colours and good of their kind but they were 1/9d a yard (pre-war would probably have been 10d), and cost 2 coupons each yard. Also went to the library and enjoyed myself for some time. I looked at 'History under Fire' with photographs by Cecil Beaton. Hobday brought the twins to meet me and we continued to push the pram back. The cot and chair had arrived and in the afternoon Hobday sandpapered and varnished the cot. I did some ironing and in the evening went to Purley. Margot was depressed about her job. I felt I couldn't bother her about money and my difficulties. She is lunching with E tomorrow to discuss K and what line Margot shall take. This morning I went to the dentist—one filling, which was unpleasant, but I suppose a small price for the additional strain on my calcium supplies. It is over a year ago since my teeth were examined and there is a superstition that you lose a tooth for each baby. I only hope their bones and teeth will not be deficient.

I went to the cinema with Margot on Tuesday evening to see 'Citizen Kane'. It was one of the best films I have seen. Its integrity is impressive—no concessions to sentiment, box office, no exaggeration, so logical and fearless and uncompromising. The theme, that goes right against popular belief—that wealth does not bring happiness. The presentation was intriguing. The newspaper magnate has just died. A reporter is out for a story and interviews people who knew him. You get different glimpses through various individual eyes from which you can construct the essentials of his life—the guiding principles and decisive events, that no one or newspapers knew. Humour (the singing lessons he forced his second wife to have), pathos (the spectacle of the wife trying to rise to the prima donna he expected her to be, and failing ignominiously in her own eyes and everyone's but her husband's), his failure at politics on the eve of election. A good film; it contradicted the whole atmosphere of the Davis Cinema, though it is now getting a bit shoddy, owing to the impossibility of renewing its plush and gilt in wartime.

E came down this afternoon and enjoyed the babes. If only K would have the courage to let him go to them! He is lovely with them. Andrew liked him today and Margaret was her usual friendly self and a bit more.

Friday 13th February 1942

I met Rosa in London and we walked through St James Park and admired the ducks. The lake was mostly frozen over but a whole shoal of ducks was sleeping in the sun. We had a coffee and went to the Leicester Galleries to see the Epstein sculptures. The central thing was an alabaster carving of Jacob and the angel. It is a massive 'ugly' thing—of colossal power and strength and suggestive, evoking thoughts one would not expect. It has extraordinary vitality of a sub or superhuman kind. Jacob is standing upright, locked in the angel's grasp, seeming at the same time to be defying him and supported by him. His own hands hang down almost wearily, his head tilted up, in powerlessness or in union? The angel is massive in strength and size, struggling against, and yet with, Jacob. A marvellous ambiguity and an unsolved equation. No message, but yet just shouting (for me) that through struggle, through pain rightly understood and withstood, man attains super humanity.

The bronzes were as subtle as always. Another study of Haile Selassie, head bent, "Emperor in exile"; 3 studies of Leda, at 4 months, 6 months and 18 months. These particularly interested me because of the subject. Ishmael, a fine tragic head, a Negro study for a slave; Maisky, a peculiarly subtle head, superficially less violent but concealing the oriental cruelty—the cat and the mouse; a study of Mrs Epstein and one of himself in 1916; a resurrection figure that was lovely; a Burmese girl, a negress, a lovely girl's head smiling— "Melinda 2." Rosa was especially interested in the technique and made a lot of notes.

Wednesday 18th February 1942

Still bitter, cold NE wind, and a grey day. It was hard to get up and face the cold wind in time to get a new season ticket and catch the 8.43 after a week's leave (I can't remember when I had as much as a week on end—must have been August 1940, at the beginning of the blitz). Hobday gave me breakfast in bed nearly every morning and then I luxuriated reading till 9.45, getting dressed in time to give one of the twins the 10.00 am bottle. When I got back to the office, I quite liked it. Wilson (an SI[19]) was on relief clearing up Holden's work and turned out to be a cheery soul. Atkinson[20] was away for a day and he pulled my leg about my being his deputy and temporarily in charge of a City district. He

---

[19] Senior Inspector, a rung above Doreen, who was a Higher Grade Inspector
[20] Head of the office staff

had never before worked under a female etc. There was the expected accumulation of work and Whitton took me round to Ibex House, our new 'dispersed' office. It is 5 minutes east of Walsingham House, on the 6th floor. The building is like an enormous liner, all windows and promenade decks. The rooms, in spite of having lost some panes of glass, are beautifully light and some are bigger and better, but the fairly small room I shall have to share with Holden and Milner will be most inconvenient. There was a lovely smell of tar which I discovered came from the stain they were using for the doors. On the way back, Whitton took me up French Court Alley to smell its smell—most unusual as it is where spice is stored. I lunched with E and caught the 5.48 back to feed the twins. Andrew was roaring after his bath and looking adorable.

On Monday, E had a day off and I met him at East Croydon. We went on a bus to Old Coulsdon. It was bitterly cold. The church—one of the oldest in Surrey—still stands withdrawn from the road, with its lovely little Early English choir. E was too cold to be interested, even in the queer acrostic memorial in slate and alabaster to Grace Rowed and Thomas Wood (no apparent connection between them), with its queer spelling. E has to be comfortable to like looking at churches. How well I remember Washington church when his feet were wet and rain was running down his spine. He was quite piteous.

E told me about RA Fisher's book on genetics. The main conclusion seemed to be that Andrew got his one X chromosome from me and would resemble me more than E—which is manifest nonsense. We found Chaldon church locked, as usual, and, having looked through the window, walked back over Farthing Down. The exposed top of the Down, now covered with trenches, was the coldest part of the whole journey. Then, in a leisurely way, back to Baring Rd and we spent from 3.00 onwards playing with the twins till they went to bed about 7.30.

Yesterday morning I got up late as before and did the ironing. After lunch, I went to the clinic with Hobday and the twins. It was pleasant—a good institution. They had the concentrated orange juice from America for the first time. The twins love it and it came just in time as they had the last orange on Monday. They were weighed and their health was enquired into, and the voucher for cheap Cow and Gate milk supplied. I got one of the 6d books about baby care. When I offered 6d, I was told, "You don't pay. The Borough gives it to you for having a baby!" Hobday was at first sniffy about taking the babes to the clinic, but now she goes every week regularly.

Friday 20th February 1942

Still cold, but less cold, and yesterday the sun shone. The evenings and mornings are getting lighter. Today I got Daltons Weekly to look for a house to buy. Yesterday at lunch E said he had 'intended to contribute when the twins became more expensive—give Andrew a microscope, perhaps,—but if I couldn't manage he would contribute a small regular amount'. I think the best thing to do is to try to buy a small house if the furniture can be fitted in somehow. E would lend me the deposit to leave me enough for moving, legal and immediate furnishing expenses. E said he would prefer me to settle finally 'in his direction'—in fact, within walking distance of his place. I was thrilled at this. He really seems to think K may get reconciled and friendly if we are patient and give her time.

Margot came tonight and we had tea by the fire. I gave her toast and lemon cheese (a great treat). The twins were tired and shouting for food when I got back. We overslept this morning till 7.25 owing to having sat up late reading Margery Allingham's 'The Oaken Heart'. We read it aloud—or I did—while Hobday knitted, and we enjoyed it very much.

Sunday 22nd February 1942

Still bitterly cold. Today it has made me furious—so pitiless and inexorable and impersonal. I have thought many times of the German soldiers in Russia with pity. I did not get up till 10.45, partly to save heating. Consequently I had hardly a minute. It was lunchtime when I had finished giving the babes their bottles and tea time after the next feed. Just now I listened to the concert—Handel, Delius and Mozart—all lovely. Rosa came yesterday to dinner and brought Susan and stayed till about 9.15. Elsie came down at last. We all, I think, enjoyed the reunion. The twins were good, and Elsie was impressed. We talked about clothes, food, her job, the government and the war, art in general and sculpture in particular (she had been to Epstein and to see the new Rembrandt, so she and Rosa had a long discussion!) I enjoyed it very much. I love having people to meals and to talk. Rosa was very sweet and offered to machine the twins sleeping suits. She was much more rational and even suggested combining when the twins are 3 or 4, when their characters are formed! She doesn't want me to settle far away from her.

Thursday 26th February 1942

E went to Worcester on Saturday to get on with his uncle's business; came back on Tuesday and phoned me at 4.00 to say he could have tea so I saw him for an hour. Yesterday he went to Chichester to see the other uncle—more enjoyable, the old man is much more congenial to him, but a duty visit all the same. Today we have had a lovely time. I met him at Clapham Junction at 10.15. We decided at once it was too cold for walking and E had decided what to do— the National Gallery. We went straight there and looked first at the Rembrandt. It is lovely. It is Margaret Tripat, 74 (11 years before she died). She looks older than the other portrait of her by him, but beautiful. Has any painter made old age so beautiful? We then saw the Artists to the War exhibition and thought we would just look at it. We spent every minute of our time in it and then saw only half of it. It had a double interest, the aesthetic one and the informative. I learnt more about how the forces work than I had before. We both liked Graham Sutherland's picture of blitzed buildings. He and his subject fit somehow. Eric Kennington's portraits of airmen and sailors were impressive. Some of the airmen made me shudder—so ruthless, almost brutal, perhaps spoilt forever by their job—indispensable and necessary possibly, but appalling that it should be necessary.

We had a quick lunch in the canteen which was crowded—3 sandwiches (sardine, chocolate, vegetable), all good, and a cup of coffee. Then to the concert—a Debussy quartet and a Cesar Franck quartet which was enjoyable. Then to catch the 2.24 to Croydon to see the twins. They had just had their bottles and Andrew was quite ready to play, though Margaret was rather sated. They have clearly begun teething. On Monday, I gave Andrew his bottle after I had gone to bed and he held it quite firmly in his 2 hands. Two thirds of the food was in it and I let him hold it for only a few seconds, but he has now quite grasped the use of hands. He will take hold of a finger and carry it to his mouth to chew. Margaret has succeeded in uttering, after her morning feed, about 3 words, but unlike Andrew she doesn't like notice and goes quiet if one encourages her. He likes to make an impression and clearly uses his noises for communication. Margaret doesn't—her few are apparently self-expression, not requiring a hearer.

Saturday 28th February 1942

At last, some improvement in the weather—not warm, but less cold and glorious sunshine in the day with misty moonlight when I took the washing in at

7.30.

Yesterday I took another day off and Margot had one of her 2 half term days. I met her at East Croydon and we spent a lovely day just poking about doing odd jobs. A coffee to begin with warmed us up. We went to Klitz, the house agent and got orders to view 3 houses. The first, by Selsdon Station, £675, a big, roomy old house with lots of cupboards and a long garden. It had been blasted and had perhaps one third of its windows left and a small crater at the end of the garden. It would have needed at least £100 spent on decorations, repairs, power points etc. We ruled it out. We walked home and had tea and Rosa came with me to look at 2 more. One turned out to be not for sale, a mistake of the agents. The other was up a rather steep hill—had a lovely view over Croham Hurst; had lost 3 or 4 windows at the back, had a garage and tiled bathroom, an Ascot heater, 2 larders but no dresser, and a fair garden and was £825. One has to think of it as an investment and to consider the possibilities of re-sale or letting if I am transferred. Margot and I agreed it was good. Rosa didn't like the blasted windows and got a 'cold' feeling in one bedroom. I went home to dinner and Margot sang. A lovely day, though I was very tired.

Wednesday 4th March 1942

At last, it is milder, and yesterday, which was the second of Margot's 2 days of half term holiday, was glorious—sunshine and mild. They went by bus to Brighton where they got a new Puffin for Andrew, 'On the Farm'. Andrew has been a bit off colour owing to teething—has little appetite and some tummy ache, but he is quite happy if he can sit on one's lap and 'jump'. If one supports his weight, he will 'walk' right up one's chest, putting one foot before the other quite correctly. Margaret is now 'talking'. She began quite unexpectedly one Sunday when Margot came—a little shallow at first. Slightly pathetic sounding from such a fat wench, quite different from Andrew's efforts. Much easier—she got out her sounds with no difficulty or effort, no waving of arms or legs, but an impression that she could have done it weeks ago had she felt inclined.

We move to Ibex House next Friday.

Sunday 8th March 1942

Since Wednesday, the wind went back to the east and it was grey and bitterly cold, but today the sun shone. It was so lovely that Margot and I did not stay in but took the twins for a walk round Addiscombe. For the first time, they lost weight.

I had to register yesterday. I went to the Moorgate Labour Exchange at 9.20 on the way to the office—was asked full Christian names, date of birth, married or single, present employment, full time or not (!!) Did I pay National Health; was I executive Grade—no, technical and she looked rather mystified. The woman next to me was a secretary at Price Waterhouse. Hobday also registered and produced a letter from me explaining that she had sole charge of the twins and without her service I could not do my job.

Saturday 14th March 1942

At last, a really mild spring day; wet pavements, soft wind, sunshine and blue sky and a barrow of daffodils and anemones outside Cannon St Station at 1.00.

A rushed and unpleasant week. First, the office has moved to Ibex House and we lost virtually a couple of days, so that my clean slate has degenerated again. Moreover, Wilson wastes a good deal of his own time as well as, now, Milner's and mine. The wind was easterly and fresh on Thursday, our first day, and just blew straight in on to my head through the thin cotton covering of the missing window panes. We have to carry a pass, signed and countersigned, and stamped and overstamped to get in and out of the building, which buzzes with ATS[21] and War Damage Commission. It is nearer for lunching with E but at least 5 minutes longer to London Bridge (either over London Bridge or Tower Bridge) and Cannon St.

The twins are better and have more than picked up their lost weight. Hobday took them to see the Dr at the clinic on Thursday at my request. She said they were flourishing and the loss in weight didn't matter. They are now having more to eat, rusks and bickie pegs. Margaret has sat in the baby chair. Andrew is too small and threatens to slip through. She now has as much variety as Andrew in 'talking', and she tries to crawl for 5 minutes a day. Andrew will not crawl or attempt to—he just rolls himself over on his back, but he enjoys trying to walk at any time, even in the middle of a meal or immediately after a 7oz bottle. They wore their new clothes today, Margaret in rose pink, Andrew in pale blue—very sweet.

I went to Purley on Thursday and yesterday I met Rosa and we looked at a Selsdon house. It was lovely—beautifully fitted and decorated with boiler, Ascot gas heater, gas copper, New World stove, Frig, a lovely dresser, hot towel rails,

---

[21] Auxiliary territorial Service

2 built-in wardrobes, tiled kitchen, bathroom, WC, etc., but the owner is asking £1100. It is high for a small house but it is probably good value at £1000. It is too dear for me. The Mount Park house which Klitz advertised for £775 (having told me £825) is the best and most possible so far.

Thursday 19th March 1942

It has been mild all the week with soft wind, brilliant sunny hours and warm spring showers, but today we had a thunderstorm while I was dictating.

I caught an earlier train each morning till today when I met Margot. She was having tea with K today and I postponed going to Purley till tomorrow. On Monday, E came to look at the Mount Park Ave house and see the twins. He thought the house quite good and is going to look at it tomorrow. E was a bit suspicious of the new decoration, which might hide serious shaking in the blitz. The ceilings have been cracked and there are 3 windows boarded but we could not see any other damage.

It is difficult to concentrate on work with 3 in one room. Most times of the day there is someone taking interviews (on odd days we have not even the right to use the interview room), dictation, Atkinson or one of the clerks coming in to see someone about something, not to mention Wilson talking to himself, or us to each other, or telephoning. Output and quality of work is bound to decrease and it is clearly a very false economy. City 10 are worse off as their rooms are over the shunting yard and they have no glass at all in their windows and no heating whatever.

The twins are lovely; they both progress on their backs by wriggling forward on their bottoms. Margaret has been doing this for a week and Andrew did it today. He has a very bad temper when he wants attention or helping with one of his activities (walking for instance), and doesn't get it. He screams himself hoarse. He experiments with his mouth, blowing bubbles, cooing, 'talking', quacking and squeaking, laughing and shouting; much more variety than Margaret, who is much more placid in temper and 'talks' in a lower voice and smiles very readily.

Saturday 28th March 1942

I have been very busy and very tired, hence this neglect. Mary[22] came for the night on Monday, E for Tuesday evening; I went to Purley on Wednesday; on

---

[22] Mary Roney, a friend from College days, who became a solicitor in her father's office

Thursday I went to the London AIT[23] meeting and last night I was at home. This afternoon E came and we struggled to put the Morrison shelter up, so that now I can scarcely hold a pencil. It was very dirty and rusty but the directions are very clear and we made no mistakes. A few of the bolts were defective but most of it was quite well made, though rusty. Putting the top on was the worst thing. It weighs 2 tons and it was in an awkward position and nearly crushed our toes or fingers several times. It is now fixed up. There is no room for anything else and it makes an exceedingly large dinner table.

We had our first mishap this week. On Monday morning, Andrew fell off Hobday's lap and banged his head on the floor. He slept for 6 hours, was sick and very pale, but the Dr, whom she called, said no bones were broken and he should be kept quiet and would probably be all right. He was better when I got back, but on Tuesday I couldn't help thinking of awful concussion tales. I just longed to go home at midday.

On Tuesday night, Hobday and I between us managed to burn poor little Andrew's bottom. It blistered and, though quite superficial, was a long and nasty place. Hobday called the Dr again on Wednesday morning and he said it should have hot fomentations every 3 hours day and night. On Thursday night, he seemed very subdued and worn out and we were both a bit worried, but yesterday he seemed better and today quite himself again. These mishaps have not prevented him from gaining 11oz this week. He has, however, had his 'walking' cramped by the bandage, but he puts up with the dressing without a sound. Margaret is fine and today just showed her first tooth. She is enormous and weighs 16 lbs and a quarter oz—well above average. They both deliberately swing their rattles and have begun groats and a cereal in their bottles.

All this week has been Warship Week in London and the atmosphere has been festive—bands playing, voices broadcasting, from nowhere, in various streets; guns firing from the Tower; bombers roaring overhead in the brilliant sunshine; not conducive to hard concentrated work.

Monday 6th April 1942

Another busy week and we have tried to go to bed earlier. Today I went to Purley and, as it was blowing a gale with driving showers now and then, we had our picnic at home and walked on Riddlesdown this afternoon. The wood anemones were just coming out, the pussy willow was a fuzz of grey silk and

---

[23] Association of Income Tax Inspectors

gold thimbles; bluebells and dogs mercury were making the ground green; the elms were misty red with blossom and the chestnut buds sticky and splitting. It was pleasant to see every bit of field—even the slopes which Laing had plotted for building—ploughed and green with the sprouting seed. So hopeful to see spring about her annual business, oblivious of the insanities of men at war.

On Saturday, E showed me an announcement in *The Times* that John Wyn Griffith[24] was missing from night operations. I have been haunted by the thought ever since—the waste of 20 years' devotion and work, the frustration of such potentiality at best, the appalling surprise for Griff and Mrs Griff.

Mr and Mrs Saker[25] came to tea yesterday and stayed from 3.30—8.10! They saw the twins in the garden having their orange juice; having their bath and in bed. They clearly enjoyed themselves. He offered to reduce the rent by £10 a month and I said I would think about it but £20 a month off is the least I could manage.

Saturday 11th April 1942

Andrew's leg has almost healed. He weighs 15lbs 2oz and Margaret 17lbs 4oz—both doing exceedingly well. They are both very lively in their bath now—splashing and experimenting with the water. Andrew concentrates hard, looks serious and never laughs, but Margaret is more careless, laughs and smiles and is faster in her movements, though sometimes she is lazy and just wallows. On Tuesday, I noticed that he spontaneously played with his toes. They both continue to play with their fingers and are beginning to like their rabbits—they hug them, suck their ears etc. For some time, both have liked their rattles and wave them about with great enjoyment. Andrew's 'talk' is getting more like words. He makes a few consonants—d, t, hard g—"didn't, didn't didn't"—"eggal, eggal, eggal." Margot, who looked after them all day on Thursday on her own, was intrigued to find that if one took his bottle away he shouted, "Hey!" like Wyndham used to in similar circumstances!

E has got to have an operation for rupture—probably goes into hospital next weekend. K came to lunch with Rosa on Thursday. I don't know quite what to make of her.

Thursday 16th April 1942

Brilliant sunshine all this week with a gusty east wind which spoilt it. We

---

[24] Son of a former boss of Doreen's

[25] Mr Saker was Doreen's landlord

have shaken down into one room at the office and the amount of talk—some sensible and useful shop, some stimulating and valuable in a broad sense, some just sociable bicker—is astonishing. And apart from talk there is dictation, phone and interviews.

Mr Saker has reduced the rent to £90 pa. On the whole, I think I shall be better off staying here than trying to equip a house now, and there is a shortage of small houses. I must reconcile myself to living in a terrace at Addiscombe with smuts! There are advantages, however—the clinic, the lower season ticket price, and Hobday knows the shops well.

Friday 17th April 1942

The cold wind continues. Mr Hobday[26] is here on 48 hours leave. He looks brown and is now back at Canterbury after a week or two at Sheerness with Canadians. He found them nice except that they are inclined to get drunk too much. The typists are growing 2 boxes of seeds—tomatoes and cabbages—in their room; couldn't waste the sun and light! Hobday and I planted seeds in the bed she dug up—radishes, spinach, lettuce, carrots and turnips (these last for the babes).

Sunday 19th April 1942

Such a lot. We have had 2 lovely days, sunny and fresh, with less wind and last night I saw the thinnest strip of new moon in the west. E has got a slight rupture and he finds the belt pad thing he is to wear till he can have his operation very trying. It makes his skin sore and presses on his bones and is most fatiguing. He finds it tiring even to get to Camomile St for lunch. However, on Friday he said he would work at home on Saturday morning and if he did this he might be able to get over in the afternoon to see the twins. I was a bit doubtful whether he would manage it but decided to wait till 4.30 pm before having tea. I was sitting on the seat in the garden in the sun finishing Julian Bell when he came. He said, "You've made me walk all around Croydon, and finally I went to the chemist at the corner! In Addiscombe, they say 'foreign correspondence'." He told me on Thursday that the spring had got into his blood, so as the twins were asleep in their pram we had a quick tea and then went upstairs and fucked for an hour. It was the first time since the twins were born. Last time was at Rina's at the end

---

[26] Hobday's 'partner', married to someone else, but he and his wife divorced and Hobday then married him

of May last year. I had not been conscious of desire. I was surprised to find that E wanted it. I haven't had a flicker ever since they were born and thought perhaps it had cured me! But it hadn't! We both found it as lovely as ever—he had been bubbling up for 2 days and on Friday night had even made some gloriously coarse verses. He said not one person in 10,000 could do so well for me. We began with me on top and had cigarettes—in spite of the budget—then turned over and finished. He said, "Strange to go so long and when it comes it is like a tornado." I wanted to start another baby but he said no—just for its own sake.

Monday 20th April 1942

Another perfect sunny warm day. Margaret is like a Red Indian. Andrew was slightly burnt again. Wilson (who lives at Horsham) had a tale about a friend who lives at Ferring (Worthing). They are removing the barbed wire on the shore, blowing up mines and making slipways for barges. The inference is that we are going to invade France shortly.

On Saturday, since I was not having coffee with E, I went to look at the Tate Gallery acquisitions on exhibition at the National Gallery. The plum consists of a wall full of Blakes. They are overwhelming in their power. I was most impressed with Newton, the Creation of Adam, Nebuchadnezzar (which was appalling) and the Wise and Foolish Virgins, which I would like to have. The design and line was so lovely. The 5 wise on one side and the 5 foolish opposite, with an angel floating up in the sky overhead, blowing a trumpet.

Tuesday 21st April 1942

(The pictures continued): there was a lovely glowing Matthew Smith (peaches) which I preferred to his more common pictures of people. The Johns were interesting—more varied than I expected, with drawings (familiar); a portrait of Yeats; one of an old lady (both early portraits); a Canadian soldier (later oil) and a landscape (the little railway). Gwen John had 2 cats and a nun, both so characteristic of her assured, quiet style which does not hit one in the eye but grows more and more impressive; 3 very queer Mexican pictures, some lovely mushrooms by Sir William Nicholson which I saw at the Leicester Gallery; a row of plants on a window ledge by Winifred Nicholson (which I liked better than most of hers), 2 Beerbohm drawings, a collection of pre-Raphaelites, mostly Rossetti, which seemed utterly remote in feeling—much more so than the Blakes; an Ivon Hitchings (Autumn) and a Piper (Road Transport) I liked from a distance—they were both staggeringly improved when I saw them by chance from the opposite side of the room; 2 Gertlers (the Servant Girl and Flowers and a violin) I liked as usual, and felt pleased with myself for picking them out at once.

Sunday 26th April 1942

On Monday last week, we went with the family to see the last Disney. He doesn't stand still. He is clever at exploiting the common sentiments. The audience rises as one man to the storks and the baby elephant. But Disney doesn't just do this—Dumbo's vision when he is drunk. The dance of the pink Elephants is purely abstract—colour, shape, movement, rhythm combined with pattern, but the audience swallows it.

The twins took a jump again this week. Margaret gained 9 oz and Andrew 6oz. Andrew is good at banging on the table with his rattle or a teaspoon. Margaret uses a teaspoon only to put into her mouth and wouldn't bang. She sits up well by herself, better than Andrew, who forgets to balance in his anxiety to do things.

Sunday 3rd May 1942

Today is lovely—only a slight breeze, sunny and warm! I am writing this in the garden with the twins wriggling on the eiderdown with bare legs. Andrew, as often most noisy, giving vent to parrot screeches and trying to heave himself up. Margaret quiet but very pleasant, singing a quiet song now and then. She sits up well by herself now and, if given a rusk or biscuit, puts it directly into her mouth and eats it. She has developed a lot lately—seems to take things in much more, looks fixedly at anything strange and turns her head at almost any new sound. We have noticed her turn to listen to a blackbird, to me singing, to the wireless, to Andrew, to the chink of china and glass, or the click of the door. On Wednesday, Hobday turned on her alarm (a buzzer, not a bell alarm) and she listened with concentration for a second or two and then smiled broadly. Andrew didn't like it and puckered up his face to cry. His joy is still standing up and 'walking'. He clearly recognises Hobday's rhyme about walking, even when said by E. E came yesterday and stayed till about 6.30. I rang Rosa up in the morning. She seemed in a not very amiable mood and asked if E was coming and when I told her she was 'grieved'. The more she likes the babes the less she likes E to have anything to do with them. It made me depressed—hopeless about the two of them so that I almost wished he were not coming. Yet, when he loved me my heart just leapt to him.

Rosa and Hobday took the twins to be Polyphoto-ed on Thursday and Rosa and Margot stayed to dinner. Andrew loved Rosa's fur cape and snuggled his face against it and went to sleep coming home. They went by bus for the first time. Rosa (according to Margot) was impressed by the admiration they excited and she herself announced as an oddity (but with some satisfaction) that someone assumed they were hers.

Thursday 7th May 1942

Andrew has been suffering from heat and his teeth today but by 10.30 tonight he was better. He suddenly began on Monday to say a few consonants by themselves—tk and ke. It is strange, this maturing. They spontaneously, with no prompting or teaching, begin to do a new thing, like the bud of a flower suddenly opening when it is ready to do so.

The Times said today that Griff[27] had been appointed public relations officer to the BIR[28], a most unaccustomed access of sense. With his BBC and literary contacts, he should be ideally suited for the job. We wondered who would be chosen to assist him.

Two very trying, though interesting, interviews yesterday: Thames Steam Tug, the biggest of their kind; the secretary called and was charming. He said they had 600 barges, had lost some in the blitz; had others damaged; had a lot on hire to the Admiralty. Now the Admiralty has taken the lot and is altering them, presumably for use in invasion. They must be done in 6 weeks. He thinks it won't be more than a diversion. The other was Mechano—branches in Marseilles, Paris and Istanbul—to talk about bad debts, mostly Chinese and Indian.

Sunday 17th May 1942

A chilly week, though yesterday it turned warmer and today it has been lovely—sunny, with big billowy clouds and a soft breeze. It was beautiful in Ashburton Park when Ella[29] and I took the pram to Woodside. The trees had come out and children were picking buttercups, dressed in summer frocks. Ella met E and me at Cannon St yesterday and we all came down to dinner. E had

---

[27] Nickname for Wyn Griffiths, Doreen's former boss

[28] Board of the Inland Revenue

[29] Friend from College days

bought a 'knock it' at a Waterloo toy shop. It was much too advanced for the twins but Andrew loved the red hammer and banged deafeningly with it on his little table. Margaret merely tried to put it in her mouth. In the afternoon, we went out to get the blocks he wanted. They are 1inch cube and dyed with vegetable dyes so that they can be sucked and are beautifully finished so that they can't splinter. They were both interested and Andrew played with them for quite a long time, picking up one in each hand and then 2 in one hand. They are just the right size for him to grasp.

It was lovely to see Ella. Her story would make an incredible novel. It gets stranger each time we meet. She loves the twins. She advised a co-ed day school and not an elementary to start with, though she agreed with it in principle. E and I had had an argument at lunch this week. I am all for it in theory but I fear that in practice I am inconsistent. I just want them to have the best of everything and not to have any experience that would make things more difficult. He thinks they should go to an elementary school. The only argument he will accept against it is the greater risk of infection but this is not great.

Susan had 7 puppies—5 on Tuesday, 2 on Wednesday. The vet found 2 more. 4 dogs and 3 bitches, 5 brown and 2 white. Curiously enough, exactly like her mother, Sally, she is quite all right and is a good mother. I am having a bitch. I have not seen them yet but they are coming home on Tuesday I have been reading Gesell's book on 'Developmental Studies of Infants and Little Children' and found it most interesting. I liked his attitude—so alive and full of ideas and yet cautious, with no axe to grind or bee in his bonnet, and not so full of detached scientific zeal that he loses sight of the individual. E is reading it now. He has been badgering me to read a book on banking. He tries to blackmail me into doing it by saying that it would make a lot of difference to the twins if I get my SI[30]. I am certain they wouldn't promote me now whatever I did or didn't do. I have read some of it but I get bored when there are so many other things to read or to do.

Sunday 24ᵗʰ May 1942

A stormy weekend—strong wind, heavy downpours of rain, brilliant periods of sunshine. 'Rough winds do shake the darling buds of May' runs in my head as the branches of the laburnum in full blossom and the red may just coming out toss against the sky.

---

[30] Promotion to the next grade, Senior Inspector of Taxes

E expected to go into hospital this weekend for his operation but up to midday yesterday he had heard nothing. He came out to see the twins on Friday and bathed Margaret. He gave them a little trolley filled with bigger and brighter blocks than those he gave them last weekend. They were both very interested and each took them off the trolley holding one in each hand. Margaret liked 'crawling' and pushing the trolley in front of her. Andrew is developing the use of finger and thumb. I find it very moving to feel his little hand growing surer each week as he explores everything within reach, his touch growing more and more subtle. He is inclined to put his hammer in his mouth and once, at least, he hit his thumb with it. He looked surprised but did not cry, though it must have hurt. It is funny to see him shut his eyes before he hits with it, anticipating the bang. Margaret is doing a little banging but still not much. Her talking has improved a lot and she sits quite safely now and turns round without falling. Andrew is safe with just a little support. They both love to stand. Though Margaret does not concentrate nearly so much as Andrew on doing things she can be absolutely intent. When E played 'hares in the park' with her (her favourite game), she watched his face with complete attention waiting for the climax. Physically, they seem to be very good and mentally they are, I think, well up to average. E pulls my leg because I am so afraid of making unjustified assumptions. I over-compensate for the bias of a parent, I suppose. He unblushingly thinks they are both geniuses. He brought their Polyphoto yesterday. The photos of Andrew are excellent but those of Margaret not good. Her attraction depends largely on her colouring and expression and she did not feel like smiling once! Tonight she tried to catch the water dripping in the bath. It is the first time I have noticed either of them do this.

When I had coffee with E yesterday, he said he had had a move to City and London Valuations—not very interesting but he will like being in charge. The office is at Empire House so lunching will be a bit further. However, we expected he would get a move not later than next December and he wondered whether it would be a provincial district so I am relieved. Rosa came to dinner and stayed for the afternoon. She did some embroidery on Margaret's jumper—most effective. She thought Andrew was getting more like Wyndham. She loves the twins but feels cheated because she can't boast about them.

Tuesday 26th May 1942

It is just like being on the top deck of a ship in a gale to work on the 6th floor of Ibex House. Today it has been cold with the wind roaring and whistling round the windows and rain leaking through the inadequate covering of the windows with no glass. My table was swamped this afternoon.

Andrew has taken to spitting—real, wet spitting—presumably to learn Ps and Bs. Margaret manages a spoon very well and holds a cup by the handle—also her bottle. This evening she looked at the lilac (white, mauve and dark red) and smiled. Her 'talking' was more purely communicative than I have ever heard it. They both pick up a block in each hand now and bang with it. I have seen them bang one on the other, but not both separately on the table yet.

Monday 1st June 1942

A glorious first of June for once. At last, the weather seems more settled—glowing sun and light air. I wore my red frock and went to lunch with E without my coat—"approach of the Scarlet Woman," he said, and liked me. He is to go into hospital for his operation on 10th June—Wednesday week. We worked at home on Saturday (I did mine in the evening) and he came to Addiscombe about 11.00 and stayed till 7.00. He played with the babes, bathed Andrew, fed them at teatime with bread and milk. Carole from next door came in after dinner and he was intrigued to see how much the twins liked her. They take very little notice of each other (though more than they did), a lot of notice of grownups, especially those they know, but more still of Carole, a child of 4. Their faces light up when they see her and they both 'talk' animatedly to her.

We are trying to get a second playpen with a floor for 35 shillings and he wants to buy it—"That's my department," he said today.

Last night Hobday woke me and said the siren had gone. She blacked out the lounge in case we had to use the Morrison shelter. I don't know what I should do in a raid now—I just felt sick and my heart pounded at the thought of the twins. After 15 minutes, the All Clear went and then I couldn't sleep for thinking of Cologne, which was raided by over 1000 RAF planes for 1 and a half hours on Saturday night. I couldn't help thinking of the Koln I knew in 1935; the 2 gentle middle-aged sisters who kept the house where we stayed; the little waiter who insisted on our having 3 eggs for supper; the puppet theatre with its crammed audience of children, wildly excited by Hansel and Gretel, kept in some order by the commissionaire who shouted at them and loved them; the grave sweet 13th century carving of the Virgin and the huge wooden figure of St Christopher in the cathedral. It is these who suffer more than the men responsible, and deliberately responsible, for Belgrade and the rest. 25 German planes raided Canterbury last night.

Raper[31] flew from Belfast to Liverpool on Saturday and came to see me on Friday. He has all the news of Belfast—said the 2 convoys of American troops had been a magnificent sight. On each of the 2 occasions, a German reconnaissance had been over. The biggest ship they came in was the Aquitania. It was lovely to hear that one ship at least one knew before the war was still afloat. He told us that the better uniforms and higher pay of the American soldiers caused bad feeling, though the British are being moved out as they arrive. He had had a weekend in Dublin recently. There is partial blackout, fewer buses and trams, but he spoke with enthusiasm of the mixed grills and cream. Mrs Raper has a job in the postal censorship. She started a baby about Christmas but something went wrong after a month and they have decided to wait till after the war.

Friday 5th June 1942

This week has been a heat wave, glorious sun with misty mornings. Everyone has appeared in summer frocks, and woollens have been carefully preserved for colder weather.

The twins have been basking in sun suits in the garden. Margaret feels the heat more than Andrew whose energy seems little if at all reduced. The hot weather is trying when it suddenly comes and our room at the office is appallingly hot for working. It has windows facing south and west so it gets the sun all day and there is nothing to do but pull the blackout against it. Fortunately my work has abated a little.

Mr Hobday came on Monday and finishes his leave tomorrow. He has had another 9 days. Since I came to Addiscombe on Nov 1st he has had 32 days (in 2 spells of 7 and 2 spells of 9) + 3 weekends (Friday-Sunday)—a good deal more leave than I get if one includes his free time as well! I remember in the last war Daddy got 3 weekends and 4 days embarkation leave in 2 years!

Margot went to the ballet with K yesterday and saw Coppelia which was new to her. She said she felt that K was limited but Margot could widen her view if she worked hard and skilfully. She still wants to revert to the pre-war 1930 position but seems to be prepared to see the twins if I wish it. She is absolutely

---

[31] A colleague when Doreen was working in Belfast in 1941

fixed, apparently, in her resolve to continue the present ménage. E is to go to hospital next Wednesday. He had hoped to get his move cancelled.

Sunday 7th June 1942

The twins are now 8 months old. The play pen came yesterday—seems good value. It is well made of excellent wood and has a floor. Now (if one could get one) it would be at least £5. The babes quite like it. Margaret sits up very well and can be left quite safely sitting. Andrew topples over easily so we usually leave him lying against a cushion. He loves to drum his heels on its floor making a great noise which disturbs Margaret and shakes even her end of the floor. He also likes to turn sideways holding on with the bars with 2 hands and 2 feet like a monkey. Today he has been lovely.

Tuesday 9th June 1942

E came to dinner yesterday to see the twins before going into hospital tomorrow. They were in the garden in their play pen. They were lively and played with him till bedtime. He bathed Andrew who splashed with his usual enjoyment but seemed tired and exhausted afterwards. They both went to sleep quickly. We tried not giving them a later bottle, but they both woke up at 1am ravenous and we had to get up and give them bottles. It was lovely to see them grow satisfied as they sucked. I can't imagine anything more appalling than to have nothing to feed a hungry baby on.

Holden came back yesterday so we are now working 4 in the room. This morning I had a joint interview with EA on Modiano; in the afternoon I tackled the job which had been hanging over me for a long time—getting my EPT[32] instructions up to date after 16 months. I lunched with E and felt rather unpleasant as I walked back. One isn't conscious of fear or worry about his operation so much as dislike of K. She will love looking after him and will do it well and I envy her (though I should do it less well). I wish I could get over this; it is a bad state of mind.

Friday 12th June 1942

I lunched with E on Wednesday and said goodbye. It was a lovely lunch hour, though he was going to hospital in the evening. He said quite deliberately, though with the obvious effort necessary to describe feelings, that to be with me was as

---

[32] Excess Purchase Tax

lovely as it had always been—the half hour or so after the twins were in bed on Monday and we drank tea in the dining room and talked was 'pure joy'. It surprised me to notice how happy his words made me feel—a warm glow which persists even now. He said he could not understand anyone being jealous of a mother's love for her children. Also, he was sure there was nothing in the theory that a mother loves her children in proportion to the pain of their birth. So am I. He had his operation yesterday. I worked hard and was fairly unworried during the day, but I couldn't help getting rather agitated in the evening. I determined not to phone Margot till after the news, and I have rarely heard a longer news (due to Eden's report on the treaty with Russia). Then when I phoned at 9.00 Margot hadn't come back and K hadn't phoned the news. When I rang up at 10.55, Margot said she had phoned 10 minutes before and said he had come round at 6.00 and was all right. He had been unconscious from 12.0–6.00. I wrote to him today.

This evening in the rain I went to Purley after dinner to see Rosa's bust of Wyndham which Mac brought down yesterday. It is very good. I should like the opinion of someone who didn't know him as it is more difficult in one way and less in another for us to judge it. But it has vitality—it is alive. Rosa is very pleased with it.

The twins went out to tea today. Yesterday a completely strange woman offered to lend us a canopy to fit the pram. She turned out to be the new vicar's wife who has twins (boys), and another boy, Andrew. Her twins are not identical—one weighed 3lb and 4oz and the other 7lbs at birth and now this one is smaller.

Sunday 14th June 1942

It is nearly midnight. I have used my spare time this weekend to vet Ella's poems—hence the lateness of the hour.

Today I noticed for the first time that the twins were using finger and thumb only. Margaret was holding a small block with finger and thumb and Andrew a large one. Andrew now sits up quite firmly, almost as safely as Margaret. He suddenly achieved this on Friday. He tires more quickly than she does. She will sit up with nothing to support her indefinitely. His smaller skill at this is partly due to his dislike of sitting. He is always trying to stand. She can put her toe in her mouth when she is flat on her back. She did this, her leg pulled quite flat against her body, on my lap after her bath tonight. They both love the cushion

Margot embroidered for me in a Jacobean design. It entertains them for ages, looking at it and feeling it.

Wednesday 17th June 1942

It has been cold. Yesterday we had a fire, though the sun coming out in the afternoon made it warmer. I went to see E in hospital. He seems to be getting on well. He had only about an hour's pain at all and that was in the evening after the operation. The anaesthetic did not upset him. He had first a sleepy one and then ether and no sickness at all. The matron came in and was quite chatty.

Friday 19th June 1942

I got rather depressed at this point, partly due to having begun a period, partly because Hobday said Mrs S next door had remarked on Andrew's likeness to E and had discovered that I don't get any letters here from their 'father' in Libya. I don't mind coping with this kind of thing myself and I don't doubt Hobday's loyalty, though I do her wisdom, but I hate any suggestion of a shadow on the twins. I wrote to E yesterday suggesting that I write to K. I want to put the facts to her as I see them. I don't want her to have any chance to say in 10 years' time, "I didn't realise he felt like that or I would have done so and so."

Once more we are back on the Egyptian frontier. Equipment is said to be inferior but I am not sure it isn't Generalship. I get annoyed with people who invariably throw stones, but it is disappointing. The Russians seem to be standing firm.

Sunday 21st June 1942

Yesterday at midday the weather turned midsummer just in time. Today has been hot with a faint breeze and we have spent almost all day in the garden. The twins flourish in the open air and love it. They are happier and seem to find more to occupy them out of doors. Margaret will listen and look for a plane and follow it across the sky. She also watches a fly buzzing about. Andrew can stand in the playpen holding on to the bars with no other help and he can hoist himself to sitting position without help if he is in a convenient position. Margaret likes to sit up and sway backwards and forwards or sideways as if to demonstrate how secure she is. Margot noticed a lot of change in them both in a week. She thought they had both acquired a whole new range of expressions. Margaret screws up her nose and puts her head on one side to smile, just as Hobday does, and she lifts one eyebrow as I am told I do.

Saturday 27ᵗʰ June 1942

Hobday has been laid out by a neuralgia headache today and has stayed here tonight. She just managed to survive till I got home at 1.00, and then went to bed without eating the gooseberry tart and roast beef and peas she had cooked. Rosa and Margot came to dinner before going to a lecture on Buddhism in Croydon and Rosa came back to tea. She seemed better in spirit and health.

I went to see E on Tuesday. He had sat up for 30 minutes and was much better and going home on Thursday. I went to Purley on Thursday and to the library and got O'Casey's 'Pictures in the Hallway' yesterday.

The twins grow. Margaret can easily pick up a little chip of chocolate with finger and thumb. Andrew's passion is still to stand. He banged his head on his chair today but quite forgot it when I stood him up. He is growing to be a tyrant. He screeches for what he wants and has had to have a safety strap to keep him in the pram. He sits himself up and eats a biscuit quite neatly in spite of having no teeth. They both love to empty the wagon of blocks, turn it upside down and twiddle the wheels. I managed to get 2 more Puffins (Fables and Ships). One must snap them up because they are out of print in no time.

Sunday 5ᵗʰ July 1942

A catastrophe happened on Thursday while I was at Purley for the evening. Hobday slipped down in the hall. She had a cup of tea in her hand and was worried about the scald. This was really a small matter. Only in the morning when she got up with a bad head and was sick after a cup of tea did she realise that she had knocked herself seriously. All Friday she was in great pain and in the evening Mrs S next door got the doctor. She had concussion. He came yesterday and said she was better, but she had no food till bread and butter this morning. I was very worried yesterday but she seems much better this evening so perhaps we can manage. Mrs Bryant[33] comes tomorrow and Margot is having the last day of her Whitsun holiday on Wednesday, but it made me realise how dependent I am on Hobday while the babies are so small, and more reconciled to the speed with which they are developing.

---

[33] The cleaner

On Tuesday, there was a bad thunderstorm in the evening. The twins had gone to bed just before it developed and we hoped they would sleep as usual. Andrew did but Margaret cried. We left her for 5 minutes but she worked herself into a bad state of agitation so we took her downstairs and I held her on my lap for the one and a half hours that the storm lasted. When it thundered, she looked round wildly, clearly frightened by the noise. We brought Andrew down without waking him and even when he awoke in the light and talking he was quite undisturbed by the storm.

On Wednesday, I went with Margot to the Arts Theatre to see 'Awake and Sing' by Clifford Odets. We enjoyed it very much. I hadn't seen a play since early last September so it was a treat. It is a 'slice of life' type of play, the particular slice being a poor Jewish family in New York. It is serious and grim, its theme being how sordid or futile or competitive life is and how marvellous it could be and, as a final note, shall be in spite of circumstances. The merit is that the people are whole, the mother being the best. We see her good qualities, her courage and tenacity and enterprise that held the family together, but at the expense of her other qualities, so that she is now materialistic, hard and unsympathetic. Her father, who has kept his idealism and tolerance, is on the other hand merely futile and ineffective. The son and daughter look like carrying forward the mistakes of these two but in recognising the danger they hope and we hope they will succeed. A hopeful play in spite of everything.

Thursday 9th July 1942

This has been a hectic week. The Dr came on Monday and yesterday to see Hobday and was satisfied with her progress. She has, however, to go to Croydon hospital to have her head and spine x rayed tomorrow. She got up for a short time yesterday and for longer today and I found her up when I got back this evening. Somehow we have managed. I have got up early and caught a train at 9.00, fed the twins, dressed them, cut my sandwiches and made coffee for lunch, got Hobday's and my breakfasts, washed up, made the twins' bottles and given them and put them in their cot to play or to sleep. People have helped. Rosa came on Tuesday from 12.0–5.30 and Margot came yesterday from 11.30–8.30. Tonight, for instance, after dinner I bathed and fed the twins, washed up, washed a dozen nappies, 3 rompers, a bib,3 nighties and made a cup of tea just in time to hear the news.

Andrew has been rather fretful this week, cutting his teeth. He has the 2 bottom ones through. He rejoices to stand up and begins to pull himself up in his high chair. He is growing visibly and has an enormous appetite. Hobday says he has been spoilt this week! Margaret is very good, has a glorious smile and eats a biscuit or a rusk surprisingly quickly. Twice this week Andrew has awakened me at 5.30 am and I have quieted him. On Monday morning, he didn't sleep and I found his little fingers poking round my face, but this morning we both slept.

E phoned today and said he would try to come tomorrow afternoon. He is getting on well but the Dr has given a certificate for another fortnight.

Yesterday Atkinson called me into his room and I found WRJ there. He asked me if I would read the dictation at a proficiency test for typists (all Civil Service depts) on 8th August. It is a horrid job as it has to be exactly timed and one mustn't make a mistake. He selected me as having had acting experience, a clear voice and no obvious accent. Being asked to do this nasty job by 2 Pls[34] I couldn't refuse. WRJ is a coming man so I shall have to work hard and do it adequately. There are 2 passages, one commercial, one literary, of 480 words each and the last ones which he gave me to look at were very difficult to read and also to take down. The speed is 120 words a minute. WRJ has to invigilate and time me.

I am getting on very well—too well for my work output with RAH. We spend a lot of time talking. As I guessed, we talk the same language, are interested in the same subjects and from the strictest technical point we stray to other things and go on and on.

Sunday 12th July 1942

It has been sunny and fresh this week and in spite of continuous rain on Friday and heavy clouds now and then we were in the garden till 7.30 and the twins refused to sleep after dinner. Ella caught the 12.02 yesterday so we arrived before 1.00. It has been a pleasant weekend. I just left her to her own devices. She liked her birthday present (Herbert Read's 'The Innocent Eye') and read it yesterday. We found time to discuss most of her poems and she said she didn't know how she could have lived through the last 2 months without me. I have been very busy with domesticities—washing, ironing (10 rompers etc), cooking, washing up, though Hobday is much better. She was x-rayed on Friday and heard yesterday that the result was negative. She has been very lazy today and ought to be all right now if she takes care.

---

[34] Principal Inspectors

I worked at home on Friday afternoon to let her go to the hospital and E came over in the afternoon. Margaret is lovely. Her exuberant expression of pleasure is her joy. Her social reactions, her looking and listening and touching are all advanced. Andrew is more random in his handling of things—he has a very subtle and varied range of expression; he is more active than contemplative; his passion is still to stand up and it is difficult to make him sit. He can now hold on and stand in the pen for a long time, roaring like a lion with triumph. He also easily moves when he is sitting or lying—swivels round, half kneels, rolls over and round. His appetite is better than Margaret's and he seems to have grown a lot in the last 2 or 3 weeks.

Saturday 18th July 1942

In spite of a sunny dry St Swithuns, we have had rain ever since—gusty north wind and yet heavy as well as chilly. Just as I was leaving the office to go home (to Purley) yesterday the siren went. I didn't hear anything and as I was crossing London Bridge the All Clear went. Hobday said she heard gunfire and apparently one bomb fell, someone said, at Farnham. Milner is going to Workington for 3 weeks on relief and Westcott to Dorchester, so it looks as if I might have got there if I had asked. I have agreed to do the dictation for the proficiency test and now I probably have to give a test to a typist applying for a job at City 6.

Yesterday I had a letter from Ella to say thank you for last weekend. She sent me a poem which grew out of our sunny afternoon in the garden. Her letter made me very happy all day. I don't know any pleasanter feeling than that one has succeeded in some degree in doing such a difficult subtle job at the right moment. I shall value her poem always quite irrespective of its merits as a concrete record of an occasion when our paths converged to both our profit.

E came on Thursday for the evening to see the twins. After they went to bed, he told me about Compton Mackenzie's 'Aegean Memories' which he was reading. He is coming back to Finsbury 2 for a week on Monday. At lunchtime, yesterday I went with Miss Towers to the Royal Exchange to the lunchtime concert. I had never been there before and was surprised at the number of the audience and the splendour of the building. The programme was piano. Beethoven—6 bagatelles and a Rondo and piano and cello sonata—all late music and all new to me. It was lovely, especially the Adagio movement of the sonata and the Rondo, which was humorous. The readiness with which people flock to hear good music is one of the most encouraging things just now.

On the way home today, I went to the National Gallery to look at the Little Britain recorded watercolours and drawings. It was most enjoyable—London and surroundings; Suffolk, including 2 of Melford, 1 of Lavenham church and ones of Hampshire, Buckinghamshire including a series of Stowe by John Piper, Yorkshire, Wales, a fantastic and impressive series of Windsor by J Piper, Herefordshire and Amesbury. They made me itch to try to do likewise—how inadequate is the time at one's disposal for all there is to do.

The twins were weighed yesterday. Andrew was 18lb 2oz and Margaret 20lb 10oz. This means that Andrew is beginning to overtake. He looks bigger the last week or two and there appears to be much less difference between them. He can easily stand now in the playpen, holding on with one hand, and lifts his feet up and down alternately. Margaret can also stand, but firmly on 2 feet. They can both pull themselves up. She turns over in the pram and in the cot as she finds she can see more from a crawling position. They both shift about the playpen to reach toys, etc. much more easily. Margaret's range of notes is extending and she 'sings' more frequently—especially on the high notes. She talks more than Andrew now and has cut her 7th tooth. Andrew has been rather grumbly this week mainly because his teeth are worrying him, though he still has only 2 through.

Sunday 19th July 1942

This shall be a brief record of what I have done today—a typical Sunday of this period of my life—because it is so easy to forget the routine and the obvious once the pattern changes, and it must inevitably change. At 7.20, one of the twins woke me, not crying but just complaining and chattering. Perhaps 20 minutes later I got up and pulled back the blackout—another grey day. They both rejoiced to see someone up and greeted me with smiles and gurgles. I sat Margaret up and gave her 2 blocks to play with. I picked Andrew up and found his nightie sopping. Took off his soaked nappy and sat him on the pot while I fetched his yellow gingham romper and substituted it for his nightie. He sucked vigorously for 5 or 10 minutes and I put a clean nappy on him and put him back in the cot with a blue woolly toy to play with. Picked Margaret up and went through the same routine with her. She was much happier than Andrew and gurgled and sang and took my glasses off and said 'TTT' to me. Her romper was red and white check. I put them both back with a dry blanket and a page of last week's Sunday Times in which I had last night read, before going to sleep, a review of Rebecca

West of a book on Germany and an article on Hartley Coleridge by Desmond McCarthy. They liked this new toy and concentrated on tearing it up and chewing it up while I cooked my breakfast and sent Sally out in the garden. I cooked a slice of bacon and 2 pieces of fried bread in dripping, made some tea and spread 2 pieces of brown bread with margarine and lime marmalade and one with butter. Then with all this on a tray went back to bed. Welcome from the twins, which became warmer still when I gave them half each of the second piece of fried bread. I enjoyed my breakfast and tried to read the last chapter of Stephen Spender's 'Life and the Poet', but it was interrupted by my having to jump up and pick up the twins who kept pulling themselves into impossible positions, banging their heads on the cot or burying their faces in the pillow. I gave them half each of my bacon rind which they loved. About 9.15 I went down and made their porridge and gave it to them from bottles, played with them, put on their jerseys as it was chilly, though not wet, put out the pram and them in it. Gave them a rusk each and their rabbits and some blocks and came in to do some washing. But first the breakfast washing up and general tidying. Then washing about 10 nappies, 3 bibs, 5 table napkins and a tablecloth, a pair of stockings, a pair of green knickers, vest, nightie and hung them on the line. The wind was north still, but the sun began to gleam in the grey. I peeled potatoes—old for the twins, new for Margot and me, put them ready to cook, tidied my bedroom and the dining room. The twins went to sleep and I pushed the pram under the hawthorn so that Margaret should not have the sun in her eyes. I began to copy diary for Mass Observation[35] and at 12.20 I put on the twins soup and our potatoes. I intended to go to the bus stop to meet Margot but she came about 12.30 with Susan. She brought me 1 or 2 raspberries to eat and some rhubarb and a pasty each from Rosa for dinner. We put them to warm and also the rice pudding and what was left of yesterday's fruit tart and cabbage. We had dinner at 1.00 and then gave the twins their soup which was mainly vegetables. While I put it through the sieve, Margot warmed the Farola. They ate all the soup but Andrew didn't eat much milk pudding, though Margaret did. We took the playpen into the garden and sat the twins in it. Andrew grumbled a bit but they played with the blocks and the wagon and the wooden hammer. I made coffee and we sat in the sun, smoked a cigarette and looked at *The Sunday Times* and

[35] Doreen, as 'Diarist 5245', transcribed a slightly abridged version of part of the diary (from September 1940 until November 1944) for this project, now archived at the University of Sussex

Housewife. I knitted Andrew's green knickers and Margot read Dilys Powell and an article on education from *Time and Tide*. I gave the twins their orange juice and put them up to sleep at 3.45. I made the tea and we had a piece of cake and some bread and margarine and gooseberry jam. Margot went about 5.30 after helping to wash up. I gave her a rose and some honeysuckle. The sun was hot and peaceful. Susan and Sally were far from peaceful but enjoyed themselves and ran about so much that Sally slept all the evening. I brought the twins down about 5.15 and gave them bread and butter and syrup and a biscuit and we went into the garden again. At 6.30, I made them porridge and then gave them their bath, fed them and put them to bed, getting downstairs to tidy up at 7.30. I had supper and read T and T, smoked my last cigarette, listened to the news, the PS and a hash of Johann Strauss while I mended stockings and knitted, washed up, gave Sally her supper, drank some hot water, changed the twins and fed them and so to bed.

Sunday 26th July 1942

It is 12.35 and the first time I have sat down since breakfast at 8.00. Hobday is in bed again. She hadn't been at all strenuous but in Friday morning she got up with a headache and went back to bed where she stayed. She got up yesterday morning as Mr Saker called and she managed to put the dinner to cook, but returned to bed after dinner and is still there. It is I suppose a relapse, due again to her fall, but it is rather worrying. The neighbours are very good but it is rather hard. Apart from the headache she gets very depressed.

E came to dinner on Wednesday and from 4.45–8.00 yesterday and played with the twins nearly all the time. He sang 'Men of Harlech' to them. Margaret was enraptured but Andrew ignored it. They had tea with us and he gave Andrew his bread and butter and sugar. I had to rush back at midday so I only just saw him for 15 minutes and he came to London Bridge with me. He goes to City and London Valuations on Monday so we haven't arranged to lunch.

Margot came on Thursday evening as she began her holiday yesterday and didn't know if she could come today. She and Rosa intend to spend them apart and Hobday (before her relapse) suggested Margot and I should have this weekend. I actually wired to King's Head, Ivinghoe, but it was full, luckily as it turned out.

On Friday, I went to the Prom with Nancy. It was lovely to hear a concert again and we got a good view of the conductor without being overwhelmed by the double basses. I don't think I've been to a Prom since 1939. I missed the 'Queens Hall' but I must admit the immensity of the Albert Hall is impressive, and the huge crowd. And though I jeer at it, I couldn't shake off the associations—Hiawatha, Presentation Day with Beveridge standing about while Sir Henry stood slinging my 'russet' hood on; and Cecil speaking at a League of nations meeting while I suffered from the tummy ache caused by the organ voluntary. And one gets far, far more from a concert than I get from any radio I have heard. It is partly the atmosphere and the concentration. I cut the last item and hopped on a bus to catch the 9.07 from Charing Cross. I missed it and caught the 9.24 to East Croydon. But London was lovely in the glorious golden evening which lifted even slums to beauty. It recalled another such evening before 1939 when E and I walked over Hungerford Bridge and I felt an almost physical ache at the beauty and doom which I felt to be inevitable. I hadn't that sense of impending catastrophe this time, in spite of the bomb damage, the personal suffering, the immediate dangers personal and general, the appalling difficulties of winning the war and creating the new world afterwards. Is this new path nothing but a reflection of my personal happiness? I don't know. Lovely anyway. When I got home, I had to clear up the kitchen and deal with the babes and Hobday and prepare for the weekend.

Wednesday 29th July 1942

On Tuesday morning, Andrew woke me up at 6.00 and I got up to feed him at 6.05. Between then and 8.15 we had 2 short alerts in the rain. I heard nothing except a heavy plane, probably ours. At 3.20 am yesterday, the siren went. I had then been listening to gunfire for 20 minutes and wondering whether I ought to get up. Margaret woke up and cried, and that decided me. We got up, took pillows and eiderdowns to the Morrison, took the babies down and invited Sally in and tried to sleep. I heard several guns and planes but nothing very near except one burst of gunfire when Hobday put her hands over Margaret's ears. The babes were good and were quite thrilled when I made a cup of tea and gave them biscuits. The All Clear went at 4.45 and we returned to bed. This was our first disturbed night at Addiscombe and it would be when I had a cold. Carol next door was terrified at the guns. Her mother said she has been afraid of noise ever since the bombs fell on this road in April 1941.

Have listened to Brandenburg 3 from the Prom tonight. Margaret loved it though she loves singing even more. Andrew was quite cold and apparently heard not a note. Margaret is very good at investigating little things—a tiny fragment of newspaper, the screw on the adjustable side of the cot, the tiny label on the Harrington's squares. She manipulates these things with finger and thumb very skilfully. She is also more efficient at putting the last bit of rusk in her mouth. Andrew is improving at biting, though he still has only 2 teeth at the bottom. He practises raising and lowering himself and standing and walking and pawing the ground with endless assiduity and obvious enjoyment in spite of occasional bumps and Margaret turns on her tummy and crawls backwards very effectively.

Sunday 2nd August 1942

Rosa came over to lunch and is staying till Tuesday morning. I am enjoying having her and we were both thankful there was no alert last night.

Wednesday 5th August 1942

I never ever complete the short notes I begin! I had to stop last time because Margaret, demoralised by last week's warnings, when on 2 nights we took the twins downstairs to the shelter and they had tea and biscuits, awoke and wailed for a repetition. She wouldn't sleep till she had a biscuit again! We did hear gunfire and planes but there was nothing much. Rosa came on Saturday and stayed till Monday evening. She was rather nervous in a strange house and I was glad we had quiet nights. On Saturday night, I was awakened at 3.55 by an All Clear, but I didn't hear the distant warning which Rosa heard 15 minutes before. Saturday was very hot, Sunday was showery and Monday was fine apart from a downpour at 5.00. There was a fair in Ashburton Park with baby show, etc., part, I suppose, of Croydon's effort at Stay-at-Home holidays. Rosa and I took Susan and the twins out for 30 minutes in the morning. In the afternoon, we sat in the garden and I knitted while she kept her hand in by starting a mask of my face in clay. Andrew was fascinated and wanted to play with the wet clay.

I went to Purley to see Rosa last night as she is on her own this week. When I got back, Hobday said the twins had been crying a lot and she had had to put A to bed in the pram! Margaret wriggled to his end of the cot and disturbed him. Today she had arranged the 2 chairs as a bed for A and they are sleeping apart, Margaret in my room and A in hers. He slept quite well in the pram. On Monday morning, I gave M her bottle and then Rosa began to give A his. A third of the way down he stopped and cried and would not go on. At last, R said, "Perhaps he wants you to give it him as he saw you give Margaret hers." And that was it; he took it from me like a lamb. Similarly on Friday evening when E came down I was playing with Margaret and he grizzled and grumbled and it appears that he wanted me to pet him. He stopped at once when I caressed him. E thinks he already has a feeling for me. He is a queer little man—very ticklish, loves to stand up; both of them deliberately drop crusts and bits of fried bread over the side of their trays when they don't want to eat them. They lean over to see where they go. They also drop blocks or spoons in the same way. Yesterday Margaret stood for a second or 2 without support before sitting down with a bump. She varies her imitative 'TTT' now with 'PPP'/'BBB'. E gave them a golf ball today. Though they don't play together both of them like to trundle it and catch it when one bowls it back. We gave them a little chop bone each on Sunday and they liked them, especially Margaret who munched hers for 20 minutes.

Sunday 9th August 1942

Yesterday I had to do the dictation for the shorthand proficiency test. John took me out to lunch and then we came back to his room to open the envelope. The 2 passages seemed to me less difficult than the last 2. I took them away to practise with Hobday's alarm clock (as it has a second hand). I was anxious to give them a preliminary passage which I picked out of Time and Tide and timed like the other at 120 words a minute. I didn't do too badly, made only one small verbal slip which didn't affect the sense. It required great concentration to keep reading regularly and with meaning, and at the same time regulate the pace by the clock. J showed me the first girl's effort and I was relieved to find she had transcribed it correctly except for 2 mistakes. Last time only one girl passed so I am hoping that my lot got through much better. It rained in the afternoon. J asked me to stay and help invigilate so I sat and worked accounts. I did a lot of work; it makes such a difference being quiet and uninterrupted. The exam was done in the room where the war damage claims are examined. We were horrified to find that the papers were left lying about and we looked at one or two as a matter of intent. I felt quite light-headed afterwards; it had been more of an ordeal than I realised. J was very pleased—my exact time was 3 minutes 58 seconds for each.

Tuesday 11th August 1942

A wild day—west wind, brilliant sunshine, thunder and lightning, magnificent clouds and deep blue sky and terrific downpours of rain that temporarily turned the streets into rivers. I believe that there were 2 warnings last night but I remember hearing only one All Clear, and that faintly.

E came to dinner last night. The twins were very good. Today they had a tea party—the vicar's children and their nanny, Peter and John (twins of 5) and Andrew (18 months). Hobday loved it and managed a good tea for them and everyone seems to have enjoyed it. I phoned Rosa this morning and she said she finished A's head in clay and was pleased with it. I am to see it tomorrow as it may be used to demonstrate plaster casting next Sunday.

Sunday 16th August 1942

I am terribly tired, though less than on Friday. Andrew has been very difficult. On Wednesday night, he was restless; on Thursday he whimpered a lot; on Thursday night we had very little sleep—not more than an hour on end. Eventually I got him off in my arms and crept into bed and sat up against pillows. Friday Hobday took him to the clinic. We thought it was his teeth but Hobday said she had never had a child upset in such a way. He was quite frantic and worse if he was put down in his bed and left alone. The clinic rather pooh-poohed it—'nothing wrong with him; maybe he could do with more calcium', and he is having calcium tablets. On Friday night, he was worse still; he wouldn't have any milk or water but at last, in desperation, I put him to the breast. He fell on it, took about 3 sucks and fell asleep. So he remained all night. I sat up again, dozing against the pillows, and he slept quite well so long as he had his face against the breast or the nipple in or near his mouth. He awoke and cried whenever he shifted away. Yesterday morning we had Dr Elder who examined him all over—nothing wrong physically—heart, lungs good, no sign of rickets, head closing well etc. He diagnosed a fright—he had lost his sense of security. He couldn't suggest how. Might be any small thing that may have frightened him but the remedy was to 'spoil him'. He also prescribed a sleeping draught (with bromide). Last night he slept better till 5.00 this morning and later fell asleep at the breast. This morning he slept nearly 2 hours in the pram and this afternoon 45 minutes on my lap. Today he has clearly been much better. He has been standing in the pen and playing and more like his normal self so I hope he will recover. It is awful to be able to do so little—one feels helpless. It is lovely to feel him relax and quiet at the breast and then his slow regular breathing as he sleeps. We can't imagine what can have caused it—I suspect the party with the vicar's noisy twins, though he appeared to enjoy it. Margaret has been very good, not at all jealous of the spoiling process, though she has been turned out of the cot. She moves about quickly, crawling or 'hitching'. She can go forward but is faster going back. She consequently gets herself into some queer places—under tables and chairs etc. She practises all kinds of sounds—Ps and Bs, Gs and Ts, and makes complicated 'speeches'. She says 'Tata' for thank you, or in imitation. Hobday says she says 'Bic Bic' for biscuit. A has been saying 'Nan Nan'.

On Wednesday, I had the previous Saturday's half-day. I had an appointment at 11.30 with Parker (the Accountant) about Elliott Steam Tug. He was an enormous man, tall and broad, with eyes like topazes—not unpleasant. He was 15 minutes late and stayed till after 1.00 so I had to rush eating my sandwiches in the tube as I had arranged to meet Rosa at Kennington at 1.00 to look at her clay model of Andrew's head. She has done it from memory + a photograph taken on 15.4. It has A's look but is idealised. It is what I hope A will look like when he is 1 and a half or 2 years old! A kind of Platonic form of A or even of a baby boy. The most striking thing about it is its vitality. It positively sparks with life. It almost lights up the studio as she takes the cloth off it. It is a lovely thing.

On Thursday night, I went to the Prom with Nancy. We had just time for a cup of tea and the bus got us there just in time. I shouldn't have chosen that concert but in fact I enjoyed it very much: Brahm's 'Hungarian Dances', to get the latecomers in, Clifford Curzon playing Beethoven's Emperor, Tchaikovsky's Pathetic, a new French suite by Leighton Lucas and Roy Henderson singing the monk from Dyson's music to Chaucer's 'Canterbury pilgrims'.

Rosa came yesterday and Margot today. Rosa brought them a rag doll each. Margot took A out this afternoon and I slept in the sun in the garden.

Tuesday 18th August 1942

We are enjoying a minor heat wave, yesterday and today. This morning I caught the 7.42 am on a workman's ticket (11d) as my season ran out yesterday. The walk to Ibex House was lovely. It was a misty, luminous, sunny morning. The shell of Trinity House behind the trees of Tower Gardens was beautiful—I wanted to paint it. The houses in Coopers Row were just beginning their breakfast. I got to the office at 8.10. I intended to leave correspondingly early, but I had to rush for the 5.06. A Jew and a tobacco merchant came up from Yeovil and called at 3.00 to talk about his accounts. An interesting interview; he is a Jew of the best type—internationally minded idealist, still with a boundless faith in education; a deep admiration, tempered by impatience, with the English; the friend waiting for him was a Cossack in the last war, now a flying instructor in the RAF, who is even more impatient!

Andrew is better. E came to dinner yesterday. We got back at 6.00. At 6.30, I nursed him as he hadn't slept much in the day. I took him upstairs and he went to sleep quickly. I had given him his sleeping draught and he went to sleep still dressed and without his supper. He slept right on till 4.15 am. He whimpered then, and I nursed him. He slept for perhaps 45 minutes before Margaret woke at 6.00 and the day had begun. This evening he was better still and sat up to dinner, had his bath and bottle and has gone to sleep without medicine. He slept 2 hours today and finished his meals, so I hope he is getting back to normal. Margaret was lovely last night, playing with blocks and crawling about on the floor. She is almost putting one block on another and wants to hold 3, though she doesn't succeed.

Saturday 22nd August 1942

Ever since Tuesday I have caught the 7.32am, getting to the office at 8.00. Yet I have rarely had so much to do. Work has poured in in an increasing crescendo and I have just had to have it accumulate. Moreover, I have had a bunch of interviews, interesting and varied. On Thursday, a solicitor (the Clerk of the Tallow Chandlers Company); their hall almost escaped the blitz and they are letting it at a rent to cover their overhead expenses for odd days to other less fortunate City companies. The interview was a success, though both callers were exceedingly pompous. I learnt inadvertently that the hall was first built in the 15th century. The freehold cost £20, to be paid in instalments, £1 at a time at the company's convenience, and it was spread over 20 years! It was burnt down in the Great Fire and immediately rebuilt and still survives.

Tuesday 25th August 1942

Soft warm drizzle today so that the twins are asleep in their pram in the hall with the front door open. I can begin this while waiting for Rosa to come.

Today rain makes me feel all the luckier. Yesterday E had a day's leave. Mrs Bryant arrived at 9.00 and Hobday came over at 10.00 to look after the twins. I got up at 6.30 and gave them their breakfast, cut cheese and lettuce sandwiches and 2 pieces of cake, seized the map and met E at East Croydon. We went by train to Gatwick and walked along country roads to Burstow. The country, typical of the weald, is dull and flat, but the green of the hedges and fields was pleasant and the gold of ripe corn or stubble beneath the stooks was welcome and less rare than usual. Though only 3 or 4 miles from Horley, Burstow is a dream village which I had never seen before. It is not easy to encounter by chance since it is not on a main road, or even a side road. It is still small with a sprinkle of small cottages and a large house, the Old Hall. The church is fascinating.

{*Rosa came at this point and I resume at 8.30, after dinner, coffee and a cigarette*}. Inside it was lovely and reminded me of the Stave church at Oslo— enormous beams and transverse arches. We were just going when the vicar's wife walked in and asked us if we wanted to know anything. She in fact knew less than E did but she was an interesting person. Burstow had a surprisingly bad time in the blitz because, she said, a tank corp was near there. At 10.00 at night, a bomb fell in the vicarage garden between the vicarage (a fine big old house) and the church. It was nearer them than any bomb has so far been to me. She invited us to look round the garden and, learning we had a picnic lunch, suggested we had it in the boat house by the lake and gave us water and 2 glasses. It was pleasant, so remote and sleepy and peaceful (goldfish plopped and bubbled), moor hens stalked about and lifted their green feet or swam with little pokes of their red necks, wagtails and thrushes splashed in the shallow water. After lunch, we looked at the garden. Round the lake there was a vegetable garden which had a lovely row of sweet peas. A look at the orchard and the hens and a bridge to the island laid out with 2 flower beds like a bedspread; a walnut; a sweet chestnut, a rose bed and a bright green lawn. E said, "What a temptation to swallow the 39 articles! Andrew had better be a parson." There is certainly much to be said for such a lovely background. We walked from there to Salford's and caught the 4.16 back to Croydon. E came to see the twins. He saw much improvement in Andrew. Margaret fell off the sofa and banged her head. We gave them their bath and bottle and they went to sleep and we had coffee and talked till 9.00, when he went home.

Margaret deliberately waved goodbye to Rosa today—the first time I have definitely observed this. She crawls very fast and quite economically, pulling her legs after her most efficiently. R got on with clay modelling this afternoon and A was very keen to help.

Saturday 29th August 1942

Tuesday and Wednesday were wet but on Thursday we began a heat wave suddenly. It has been dazzling sunshine with a breeze for 3 days. This evening the heat became oppressive and we have had downpours of rain with thunder muttering. Now, at 10.30, after twice getting Andrew off to sleep again, I have heard what I think must be guns, though I haven't heard a siren. There is little to be seen at the front or back except a searchlight trying to pierce the low cloud and occasional flashes which might be gun flashes or lightning.

The twins have so far been very good. The only snag is that Andrew isn't sleeping too well. Yet, last night he slept right round till 4.00 this morning. Tonight I got him off easily but he has awakened twice already. Thursday night he awoke at 10.00 and at 12.10, when I took him into my bed till 3.15 and finally at 5.30 am. This means that I get tired and don't have much deep sleep. Margaret is rushing ahead. She crawls quickly now. She picks herself up to stand against chairs or the table edge or the stool; is fairly safe holding with one hand, objects strongly if A touches her; cries for the pot; has a particular voice for addressing you; yesterday put the trolley through the bars of the playpen twice; this requires quite exact manipulation as the angle must be just right; will play with blocks for a long time; intrigued with one's speaking, poking a finger in one's mouth as if to feel for the source of words!

Listened to the radio performance of 'Village Wooing' last night and enjoyed it. K spent Thursday with Rosa. I want to see her. It is most mysterious how inconsistent accounts of her are.

Wednesday 2nd September 1942

The weather has been good on the whole, less sultry and with some showers but lovely sunny patches.

On Sunday, Rosa and Margot came for the day and we had Sunday dinner at midday for the first time for ages. On Monday morning, I went shopping in Croydon while Mrs Bryant was here and bought some yellow wool for the twins. I have a good many old coupons to use before 10th October, but unluckily not enough money to use them. I also went to the library and got Havelock Ellis' 'Autobiography'. I have found the first 60 pages—(all I have managed so far) most interesting. E came in the evening to see the twins and to dinner. He is rather concerned about Andrew's psychological bother—so am I! Tonight I tried to get him off to sleep without the breast. I thought I had managed it twice but after trying for over 2 hours I eventually let him suck and he went off quite quickly. He worked himself into a frantic state whenever I left him—even downstairs—which must be worse than any regressive tendency revealed by the sucking fixation during the day. He is better; he doesn't mind being left either alone or with Margaret and he fell asleep in the pram this morning and this afternoon. That is why I tried to persuade him to sleep tonight. Margaret was sweet with E—kissed him and loved him quite spontaneously. It was quite touching.

I have been asked to talk on Income Tax to a professional women's club on 14th September. It is awkward as I am not supposed to do it without authority from the BIR. There isn't time for this and it is such an obviously useful thing that I said I would. E suggested my phoning Griff but he is away all this week. I shake in my shoes at the thought and they want to know about allowances! I always seem to have some ordeal ahead to disturb my peace!

Saturday 5th September 1942

11 months old today are the twins. Margaret and Jock Robertson[36] have been out to lunch and tea and to see them. They brought them a teddy bear each. They are not so ready to accept strangers now; Margaret approached very gradually and Andrew grizzled a bit and did not settle till we were having lunch and he could stand up to Jock's chair and look at us all through the back. He is much better. E came last night and saw considerable improvement. He has developed a lot and is more independent. He is getting quite efficient at crawling and can also pull himself up and move round the furniture holding on. They both love tearing up paper and also playing with rings. Andrew managed by chance, probably, to spin one yesterday. Margaret has decidedly reached the anal stage. She looks with interest at what she produces and plays with it if she gets the chance. She also tries to put her fingers in her milk and orange juice and crawls out to the kitchen to play with Sallie's water dish. They begin to take more notice of each other. Andrew turned round to face Margaret in the bath last night and they both go for the same toys which pass from hand to hand with little rancour, Margaret is more violent in getting what she wants but A is more persistent. They had a new toy—the nail brush—in the bath last night. For 2 nights, I have got him off to sleep without sucking. Last night he slept till 3.40 but then I had to take him into my bed and he awoke Margaret (who was not quite up to her usual form—she was sick after her groats). For a minute, I had them both crying.

Rosa came over early this morning to enable me to go to the office. I caught the 12.12 back. Just as I was going to the station (at 12.0) the alert went. When I

---

[36] Jock was a friend and colleague of Margot's

got home at 1.00, Rosa said she had been with Sallie and the twins in Ashburton Park. With no warning, guns went and planes sounded. Everybody rushed home. She felt worried because of the twins and even forgot Sallie at first.

It seemed queer to be back in the office after a fortnight as a suburban housewife and mother! Though I am of course very amateurish and unplanned I must say I have found it quite interesting and not nearly so strenuous and difficult as I anticipated. I have probably washed 150 nappies as well as nighties, rompers, vests, woolly coats, blankets, pillowcases and towels for the twins; ironed many of these things as well as my own frocks etc; cooked the twins' meals which now consist of oatmeal +half a pint of milk for breakfast (after titbits and fried bread, bacon rind and bread and jam), meat soup with potato, carrot and turnip and spinach or cabbage, and milk pudding for dinner; groats or oatmeal after their bath. They also have brown bread and butter and jam or honey for tea and a mug of one third milk and one third water and a biscuit for tea and orange juice or apple in the morning.

I have had visitors practically every day. I have done the shopping and been twice to the library and had my hair cut. I have done a minimum of housework but nearly every night has been disturbed by Andrew. Rosa, Margot and E have been over several times and helped me with baths or giving the twins their meals or playing with them. I can see what an advantage it is to be near the shops in these days. Yesterday it took me an hour and a quarter to buy the weekly groceries—butter, margarine/lard, tinned ham, biscuits, tea, sugar, bacon, matches, cheese, meat for the twins' stewing steak and for me (half a shoulder of lamb), potatoes, tomatoes, watercress, beetroot, cabbage, carrots, plums, whiting for the twins and for fish pie for E and me (this took 20 minutes as I had to queue). And I slipped out alone while Mrs B was there.

Of course, I do less cooking than Hobday but I get things into less mess and I clear up each crumb as it falls and, in spite of the heat wave, I have wasted very little (the end of last week's joint on Wednesday, a little milk which turned, though I had boiled it,—I gave it to Sallie, the end of the cheese, which went mouldy and a small piece of cabbage). It is less strenuous in summer with no fires but I don't think I should do too badly with Mrs B 2 mornings a week. Moreover, I have spent quite a lot of time playing with the babies. I should have been better still if A hadn't disturbed me. As it was I started often feeling tired in the morning. There is a lot to do and it is strenuous but I think it is healthy.

The exercise is not bad (even wringing nappies). It is a question of planning and at the same time being flexible.

The greatest difficulty is to be doing many little things at the same time— putting the twins on the pots and watching them for results, boiling milk for bottles, washing the trays and their chairs and collecting things after them; keeping Sallie in her place. It is a kind of physical and mental quicksilver as against the purely mental quicksilver of the office. The office produces a less healthy kind of fatigue, though both jobs would be burdensome if one were not basically fit and I should, I think, find it extremely wearisome to run the twins and the home if I were pregnant. Moving quickly and deftly is half the art. The office, with its regular hours and accepted routine, is more obviously a discipline but the other job imposes its own discipline with wide limits.

What I did enjoy was the freedom and peace of the afternoon, sitting reading in the garden in the sun with a cigarette or talking to R while the twins were asleep. Yes, 12 days leave is much too short but it has been a holiday unique in my experience and I have enjoyed it and learnt many things. Incidentally, I found the tie less irksome since the war has this year made holidays away almost impossible for anyone.

Tuesday 15th September 1942

A long gap, due partly to the fact that Margot came for the weekend Saturday till Monday morning and she made me sleep for 1 and a half hours on Sunday afternoon and in the evening we listened to 'Distant Point'. The result was that all I did on Sunday was washing, 3 and a half pounds of blackberry jelly and wrote one letter. I had Saturday afternoon 'off'.

Last night I took the risk and went to the Thames Club to answer questions on income tax. I rang Griff on Monday last week to ask him whether I could accept their invitation to speak on it and he said he would pop round and see Bradford. I thought B had heard enough of me for a lifetime last year so I was quite relieved when he phoned back to say B was on leave. He said I had better not, but whenever I said anything I must make it a condition that no report was made or record published. I couldn't completely withdraw and on Tuesday Miss Hamlyn, a chartered accountant, phoned me and we arranged to lunch on Thursday. She turned out to be a charming woman, perhaps 45, very ladylike and brown, rather like a wren only darker. She gave me a good lunch (for now) and an acquaintance of hers sat at our table halfway through. She was a gutsy, breezy soul who has been very successfully running a tea estate in Ceylon.

Yesterday I unfortunately forgot to take my watch, had no idea of the time of day. I was 25 minutes late meeting Miss Hamlyn, thinking it was 12.05 instead of 12.15. The club met at 6 Belgrave Sq., one of the huge aristocratic houses with no lift and wide, shallow stairs and lots of wrought iron and marble. A grace and spaciousness pervaded it still, though now it is the Belgrave Institute. I was introduced to the chairman, secretary and various other people and given a cheese sandwich, a very pre-war fruit tart, a cup of coffee and a cigarette. Then we went upstairs for the meeting. Miss H made a little speech and then the chairman introduced me and invited a bombardment of questions. Curiously enough, I didn't feel at all nervous, not nearly so nervous as if I had a prepared speech, though to have to answer any questions on the spur of the moment is rather frightening, but I felt an element of fun in it—a kind of game or competition and I think I did quite adequately.

Of course, knowing one is an expert compared with anyone else there helped. The questions were almost all sensible and the members were intelligent and took in the answers fairly easily. The woman who proposed the vote of thanks had asked more questions than anyone and in her speech she said I had been clear and instructive and surprisingly entertaining and amusing. On the whole, I felt I had added to the goodwill of the department even against its regulations. The next meeting, to which I was invited as a guest, is 29th September. Andrew McClaren, MP for Stoke on Trent, is speaking on coal. The secretary buttonholed me after and asked me to join the club. She would like to propose me and was always anxious for 'Quality'.

I had tea with Griff at his suggestion last week and he told me about his new job as PRO[37] to the department. His appointment was made in a hurry and he insisted on a proper status and title. He would not hear of being CI (Publicity) or anything similar. I heard of several interviews with newspaper people—of how he has to go to the House and had cut the stuff to the Lobby journalists; of how he spends any 'spare' time recasting forms, and rewriting notes for guidance; he wrote the Quiz and is doing one for Schedule E. He likes the job and likes working with the BIR, but has to work very hard—[till] 11.00 pm each night the week before when he was in Llandudno on a committee. He couldn't be more suited to his job—for once the BIR had a stroke of genius in selecting the man for the post.

---

[37] Public Relations Officer

Saturday 19th September 1942

I brought home my EPT instructions to do the 3 and a half hours' to get them up-to-date and didn't go up to town this morning. I did the work mainly last night and phoned Rosa to suggest going blackberrying this morning. I called for Susan on the way and reached Purley just before 10.00. We picked a good load. Rosa had a few and I have begun to make jelly of the rest. E came to dinner and played with the twins and did some odd jobs for us. He noticed a lot of difference in 8 days and rejoices to see A so much better. They are developing very fast. Margaret is improving her articulation, and her, "Oh dear!" is very clear. Hobday said she was sitting on the pot and fell over, bumping her head. She picked herself up and said, "Oh dear!" On Thursday she held the mug upside down and said, "Empty!" Her understanding of words is increasing—she knows 'gee-gee', 'Sallie', 'Aunty', 'Andrew', 'pot', 'choc', 'bickie', 'dinner', 'up'. They both help with dressing and undressing, poking their arms in and out (if they approve) and pulling nighties, etc. over their heads.

I was knitting in the chair today and A played with the ball of wool, ending by dropping it over the arm. He tried to pull it up so we tied a tape to a ring and he at once hauled it up and played a new game of dropping it and pulling it in. He would pull it with one hand till he could reach the ring with the other. He walks quite quickly round the furniture holding with one or both hands. They both have more confidence standing and can stand for a second without holding. E has put a new plug for the wireless because they both knew how to pull the other one out and there was a possibility of them getting a shock. Margaret goes for the tap of the gas fire with appalling concentration.

We had a letter from Plymouth. Auntie Paul[38] had heard from Don[39] from Gibraltar. He was in the Malta convoy and saw the Eagle go down. Rosa heard that his ship, the cruiser Phoebe, had been hit twice but not seriously. He sent us a snap of the King and Queen on her when she took them to Belfast. Rosa looked very brown and liked Fowey very much. She heard one siren while she was there and none in Plymouth where she stayed 2 days with Auntie Paul. She said both the aunts had aged a lot. They had a worse time in the blitz than we realised. They had to be dug out of their cupboard under the stairs 3 times and many nights did not expect to be alive next day. She said Plymouth had been tidied up. The

---

[38] Rosa's sister

[39] Doreen's cousin

shells of the buildings are standing and have a certain beauty. She felt it was a marvellous opportunity to build a lovely new city.

Sunday 27th September 1942

All last week the weather was unsettled—brilliant sunshine with cloudless sky quickly covered with grey, fluffy storm clouds, blustery north or NW wind, driving rain, thunder and a harvest moon of soft brilliance—so bright that one could read on Thursday night. Friday and yesterday were cold, so cold that we burnt twigs and enjoyed a grateful blaze on Friday and a proper coal fire, though a tiny one, yesterday. Today, however, has been a throwback to summer—a misty warm sun, a lazy day, so warm that Margot (who was suffering from a cold) and I sat in the garden and basked in the sun and we took 2 photographs of the twins (in case next weekend, when they are 1, it is too dark for a snap).

I have worked very hard all the week and just begun to reap results—nearly all my assessing done and on Friday I worked Chandrapore Tea. On Monday, I had a tummy upset, the worst I have had since the Chloroform upset me nearly a year ago. I couldn't eat anything till evening and then only a little bread and milk. I went to the office but shocked everyone by looking like a corpse.

The twins are lovely. Margaret put one block on a box and another block on the first on Friday and today I saw her hold 3, 2 in one hand end to end and the third in the left hand to hang against the first 2. She is eating much more maturely and more rarely throws bits of bread, etc. over the edge of her tray. Andrew today put one block on another but he still prefers to flip them along with one finger or drop one from a height or throw them over arm. He is virtually recovered from his nerves and has been in marvellous spirits the last few days. He roars with laughter or chuckles in the pen. This afternoon he was playing with Margaret. He treated it as a joke but her expression was stern and she took the thing seriously. They were playing with her Bakelite bowl. He watches things in the street now from the pram as much as she does and likes a horse more than anything. He laughs as soon as he hears it and watches for it to come up. Margaret can pat-a-cake (since Tuesday), though she will do it only when she feels like it. Andrew just began to do it today. They are both practically standing without support. A was very friendly to E on Friday. He seems to regard him almost entirely as a piece of jumping apparatus, and Margaret is friendly but won't let him pick her up.

We were horrified in the office yesterday at the possibility of no heating till Nov 1st. If it is enforced, it will be most short sighted. Sedentary work must suffer if one's fingers are cold and there is no way of keeping warm. It isn't like housework, for instance, where one can do some ironing or cooking if it is really bitter. There would be a fall in efficiency and a crop of sick leave.

Wednesday 30th September 1942

On Monday at lunchtime, E and I went to the Royal Exchange concert—the Glyndebourne Singers in songs from Mozart's Operas—3 songs from Figaro, 3 from Don Giovanni, 1 from Magic Flute and 2 from Cosi Fan Tutte. I have never heard them better sung, especially Ernest Urbach in Figaro. It was lovely but too short. E paid for both tickets as he firewatched at the office on Sunday night and got 4/6d for meals. Last night I called for Miss Hamlyn at Whinney Smith and Whinney and went to the Thames Club as a guest. Andrew McClaren MP was speaking about coal. He was 20 minutes late so I missed the discussion but I enjoyed him—most vehement and extremely pro-miner, anti-mines Dept, anti-government, of course. I sympathised with his attitude, largely with his indignant championing of the miners. He gave an able sketch of the history of the mines. His speech was clearly one-sided. He denied any problem and blamed the incompetence of the government and the exploitation by the land owner for everything. I caught the 8.48. The Secretary of the Club was most complimentary and begged me to join but I said I hadn't time. Hamlin, however, promised to phone me when anything interesting was on and I can go as a visitor.

The twins continue lovely. Andrew has awakened about 3.0—3.30 the last few nights but has slept quietly when I got up and held his hands in the dark. It is chilly getting up for him these nights. K has failed her exam again. I feel impatient with her mainly because she wants to go to the opera on Saturday and Rosa can't come over so it would have been lovely for E to come and see the twins. Maddening!

Monday 5th October 1942

The last half of last week was lovely—sunny and warm; misty in the morning with starry nights, but today has been stormy with gusts of rain. Still, the twins have had a few gleams of sun for their first birthday. They have had 11 cards; Margot has given them a lovely wooden horse in red and green, which rocks; Hobday made them a chocolate iced cake with candles each (2 inches of a taper) and gave them 6 hankies each. Rosa gave them a baby plate each; E gave them a little chair each and a table painted blue; I gave them a wooden donkey on wheels and 8 wooden animals on a little gangway on wheels; ES sent Margot a cheque for £1 to buy them a present. I was most touched at this—it was sweet of him.

E came on Friday to dinner and was fascinated by them. Their chairs and table had come and they liked the colour and were quite content to sit in the chairs. A imitated a cough out of pure mischief at tea—"Ahem! Ahem" and roared with mirth. Margaret plays bears with great enjoyment and waves a hand. The photographs were better than the last lot but disappointing. If one gets the photograph placed well, i.e., by attending to the camera one gets the wrong expression; if one gets a good expression (by watching the babes) one cuts bits out and gets the snap in the corner of the film. Still, not too bad perhaps.

Monday 12th October 1942

Two lovely golden misty days but cold in the mornings. Yesterday I developed my usual October cold and it has been made worse today by the frigidity of the office. I find it impossible to concentrate in the cold and wearing a lot of clothes doesn't make much difference. I have done very little work today and grumbled a lot.

Wednesday 14th October 1942

My cold is better but still unpleasant and it is uncomfortably cold at the office. Yesterday was lovely—a warm golden afternoon. I had my appointment in Harley St at 2.30 and set off in good time; walked to the bank, tube-ed to Bond St and walked slowly up past the shops to 66 Harley St. The street looked seedier and there were numbers of gaps where bombs had fallen and one lovely big water reservoir reflecting the neighbouring houses and the sky. After 5 minutes waiting, I saw Dr Sharp. He asked me how old I was—"Not the dangerous age, but some women are dangerous at any age." I thought: facetious! But he was more skilful than that. He said I had waited too long to be examined and so had developed a mendonian cyst. It might be treated medically instead of surgically—would I like to try? It might not work for sure but if it did a recurrence was less likely. He would give me a prescription to take to a homeopathic chemist. I did, and got a little bottle of minute pills to be taken 3 times a day. Dr Sharp examined my eyes and prescribed new glasses (£2). I asked the cause of the cyst and he explained that it was due to blocking of the ducts

70

that carry the lubricant to the eye and the piling up of the material. He added, "I like intelligent questions and I don't often get them." I said I like intelligent answers and I don't often get them from doctors. So he said, "No—explain in Latin and then in Greek—anything to make a mystery and not reveal how little we know." Has no illusions about Harley St. He said there was a man called Inman of Southampton—very clever but had queer ideas. He thought cysts were due to sex repressions. I gave him enlightenment, he said.

Saturday 18th October 1942

The twins both have colds but quite loose and snivelly, which is unpleasant but not so dangerous as chest colds. On Wednesday, they had their baths. Andrew was tired and seemed quite languid till I offered him his milky chocolate (instead of milk and water). He loved it and for the first time held the mug on his own, drinking it all by himself in spite of his weariness. It showed that to a large degree what he (and Margaret for that matter) do and when they do it depends on incentive and interest. He drank as efficiently as if he had been practising for weeks, but he can't be bothered to hold his mug of milk. Margaret has developed a queer trick of scratching the carpet with one hand. We think she must be imitating Sally 'making a bed'. She will imitate many tricks now—'TTT', Hobday waving a hand, clapping, offering things, a biscuit, a block, etc., coughing, peep-bo as well as her old responsive smiling. Andrew is great at climbing; he will climb on a case or on a stool to get higher. They both go to their toy cupboard to take things out, though not to put them away. Margaret particularly likes to put blocks into a box one by one, empty them out and start again. Andrew prefers to do it with the pot.

Saturday 24th October 1942

A busy, interesting and entertaining week. Hobday came back at 7.50 on Monday morning and I nearly caught my early train. Margot was on holiday all the week and I had suggested going to the Greek Art Exhibition with her and Rosa at lunchtime. The exhibition was small and most of the large things were casts but on the whole it was surprisingly interesting. It stressed the continuity of Greek Art, beginning with little figurines from the Cyclades and so to the marvellous embroidery of the last 4 centuries. We just revelled in the embroidery, the most fascinating I have seen since the Chinese. Of the original pieces the terra cottas and bronzes were best—some lovely little figures and the

Cottenham marble, just a fragment on low relief of a man reining in a horse. I had taken far too long but it was not enough and I couldn't see the London Planning Exhibition at all. I left Rosa and Margot to see this and went back to the office by bus.

I had planned to have a day's leave with E. We were lucky to have the best day of the week—brilliant sunshine all the morning, though there was a sharp breeze. I met E at East Croydon at 10.00 and we went by bus to Reigate. We struck south of Reigate across the heath to Leigh and then to Letchworth and got the bus back to Croydon reaching Addiscombe at 5.20, in time for E to play with the twins for 1 and a half hours and see them bathed.

The twins remembered E, though he hadn't seen them for 15 days. He said afterwards that he felt very proud when Andrew smiled at him. He played bears with them on the floor and Margaret was not at all shy. She loves playing this; she crawls away while the other person says I'm coming after you—then she hides her face in someone else's lap and looks up every second or two and laughs with excitement. She stood without holding several times. She rarely falls, but when she realises she has nothing to hold she gracefully and deliberately subsides, like curtseying. Margot brought Andrew a piece of elastic and a button and he loved it. She hung it on the little horse and he pulled it. It naturally jumped up in the air when he released the elastic. He was quite staggered at first, but after doing it twice he liked this new game and watched to see where the button fell, each time crawling off to retrieve it and trying to hang it on the horse on his return. The twins both like the knock-it now. They pull out the sticks and put their fingers in the round holes. They see the relation of the sticks to the holes but can't yet fit the sticks into them. Andrew is more efficient at walking from one piece of furniture to another and has almost abandoned his sideways walk. E saw a lot of progress in Margaret's walking too. In addition to standing without support, she knows how to put one foot before the other.

Sunday 25th October 1942

To continue—(I was too tired last night to finish and went to bed instead) Andrew woke me up at 2.50 but went to sleep after I had covered him up and no one awoke again till 7.10. Hence, I am less tired tonight. On Friday night, he was very wakeful and I had to take him into my bed at 3.00. This pleased him and for a long time he laughed and played instead of grumbling and crying, but this was not less disturbing to my sleep!

Saturday 31ˢᵗ October 1942

A wet week. I think it has rained heavily every day. On Monday, it was both wet and cold. If I hadn't had 2 long interviews, I should have done almost no work. With no heating at all, it was unbearable in the office. It was so bad that before the afternoon was over the ban on central heating was removed and since then it has been a little better. I had been asked to give a blood transfusion at 5.30 on Monday, but owing to my prolonged interview I did not get to UCH till 6.00. I had hesitated and thought of just going home but I was glad I hadn't when the nurse thanked me for coming on such a night and the doctor said the blood would be used in the next day or so. He looked very young but was the most skilful of the 3 doctors I have encountered in this way. The blood flowed quite well and he must have taken nearly 1 and a half pints altogether. I swallowed my cup of tea and caught the 7.13 to Woodside. It was one of the worst nights I have experienced—blowing a gale with driving icy rain and so dark that I couldn't put up my umbrella. All I could do was to walk along behind a man with a torch till he turned off and then go as quickly as I could.

E came out to see the twins on Tuesday. At lunchtime, he said he wanted to get a toy in a city shop—a spindle with 7 round blocks on it and he would like me to come. I went. It was a lovely shop. We had a look round and found a second hand rag book for 6d and then E made a find—a bell instrument beautifully made—with an octave of bells in tune, with a hammer, soft and loud and a damper. It was £3/9/6 and I was appalled at the price. But of course it was an unrepeatable find. He said, "It is just what I have been looking for, for Margaret. It is irresistible. I will give it to them for Christmas"—and bought it, called for it and brought it down at teatime. They were most intrigued by it, though Margaret will not try to play it. She listens to anyone else playing it but seems nervous of doing it herself. But Andrew is getting on well and can manipulate the hammer quite effectively.

Thursday 5ᵗʰ November 1942

A continuously wet day again. It has been generally wet and cold all this week so far and I have been more than once reduced to working in my big coat. On Sunday, Margot came for the day and E came to tea and stayed till 8.45. We bathed the twins and when he turned on the light downstairs the bulb went and the lights fused. I had to borrow some fuse wire from next door. Our nights are still not quite quiet. Last night, e.g., Margaret awoke at 1.00 and had to have a clean nappy and Andrew awoke at 5.30 and had to come into my bed. Still, it is better on the whole, though yesterday morning we overslept. In the evening, I went to Purley and learnt that Don had been killed in action when his ship was damaged—where we don't know. Kathleen has had 2 letters from him and a parcel (of a silk embroidered nightie and 2 silk frocks for the babies) since the wire announcing his death.

Sunday 8th November 1942

Yesterday morning it was pouring with rain but by noon it was abating and since then it has been fine—perfect autumn weather—soft blue sky and sun warm to the face—misty with vivid gold and bronze of the falling leaves. Rosa came to dinner yesterday and we went to Ashburton Park afterwards. Margot came today and I took the twins and Sallie to meet her and this afternoon we went to see the trees again. E came on Friday and the twins wore their cream silk rompers and new blue cardigans. They seemed to have developed a lot suddenly. They are both almost walking. They stand alone with no difficulty. Andrew likes to get himself in tight corners—crawling under chairs all mixed up with the bars. He hates to be helped. He dislikes anyone else playing the bells and is most efficient with the little hammer which we have put away as it is too good just to rag out. They both seem bigger and much heavier and their appetites are as good as ever. Last night was the first time for ages they didn't wake at all till 7.20. I picked them up at 10.00 and gave them dry nappies. They can both put one block on another with ease and Margaret has suddenly quite taken to her red rag doll that Rosa made her some time ago. They remember Rosa and Margot and E quite well. They both showed some jealousy—especially Andrew, when E played with Margaret.

It is queer how startling news comes at 9.00 am on a Sunday. Today it was US landings in French North Africa following our success in Egypt.

I have just finished 'Midnight Hour'—a penetrating and profound account of spiritual experience which I found difficult but very interesting. I am inclined to attach significance to the age (late middle) of the author. Concentration on religion when the secular duties have been more or less completed seems to me normal and right. He stresses the inadequacy of 'religion after the flesh', but he has experienced the stresses and satisfactions of a normal career and the responsibilities and rewards of being a husband and father. But of the significance of his spiritual experience I have no doubt—the necessity to lose his life to save it—to die in the self in order to permit rebirth into something higher—

all this is convincing and told more skilfully than I have ever read it. I am not wholly convinced by his conclusion that through the Church of England came his fulfilment—even a regenerated C of E, though I too was reared in the beauty of the liturgy and am still moved by its beauty.

Tuesday 10th November 1942

At lunch today, I suggested writing to K to put the issue squarely before her. E was sweet but doubted whether she would ever comprehend 'the harmony of the spirit'. He agreed that the twins are lovelier than he expected was possible— and that the time he has with them is 'rich' for him. He said that now we could comprehend to some extent the idea of the fatherhood of God—"this is my beloved Son in whom I am well pleased." He thought the relation of parents to children was a reflection of their relation to each other—so true, but my heart rejoiced to hear him say it.

People crowd to buy papers—the Americans are racing ahead in North Africa and Churchill's speech at the Mansion House to which I have just listened was triumphant if sober and it had his usual good touches—We might believe it was the end of the beginning.

Sunday 29th November 1942

Rather tired and there is only 30 minutes till 9.00 when Churchill is due to speak on the radio. There is a lot to note as often in these crises so it will have to be short.

The Milners[40] have been to tea here today. Margot came 10 minutes after Hobday went to Kennington and E came about 4.00 and stayed till nearly 8.00. I have just had supper—celery cheese and watery coffee. Mrs M is a nice little thing in a red frock, brown coat and smart little hat, but less pretty than I expected. Margaret screamed for 10 minutes at first but slowly made friends. Andrew was quite friendly all the time. He is usually ready to welcome anyone who will jump him. She has developed a lot during the last week. I saw her walk a few steps yesterday and Hobday said she took 3 unsupported last Monday afternoon (23rd November, just over 13 and a half months). She is quite confident on her own on the rocking horse—stays on indefinitely and knows just how to rock him, sometimes very violently. She gets off carefully and efficiently, like someone getting off a bicycle. She smiles and talks and looks round for

---

[40] The husband was a colleague of Doreen's

admiration and likes a song to go with her riding—"Gee up Neddy to the fair—What shall we buy when we get there? A halfpenny bun and a farthing ice! Gee up Neddy, Won't that be nice?"

Her vocabulary is growing, though her words come and go. On Monday, when E came to dinner, she kept saying 'Dada', which we discovered to be 'down'—to Sallie. She begins to notice dressing and undressing and has undone buttons at bedtime. Yesterday I saw her eating her porridge very well, dipping her spoon in, holding it up the right way and putting it direct into her mouth. She was less efficient when her right hand got tired and she changed to the left, but not bad on the pot and we usually have a paddy. She screams and goes stiff and bangs her head sometimes and goes purple in the face. She watches Andrew and they play together and quarrel and give and take much more now. They do not wear nappies in the daytime and we pick them up at 10.00 and dry them or sit them on the pots if, as sometimes, they are dry and we usually have a quiet night till 6.30 or 7.00.

Andrew got off my bed this morning quite deliberately and carefully, dropping off, landing with a thud on his bottom. He can get off the rocking chair on to a stool in the same way, as well as off his own blue chair. He is annoyed if he is lifted off, yet he can't get up off the pot very conveniently. Margaret just gets up, looks in and crawls away on toes and fingers. This morning she was watching the patterned side of Margot's cushion in my bed, evidently most intrigued when it was turned over, trying to fathom where the pattern went to. Also she looks in the wardrobe for the little girl in the looking glass.

I was more moved about the French fleet scuttling itself at Toulon rather than let the Germans in than anything else in the war, I think, except Greece. The dilemma for each individual Frenchman must have been appalling all these months. It was a magnificent if tardy defiance.

Sunday 6th December 1942

Mr Hobday has been on leave since last Sunday and goes back on Wednesday. I worked at home yesterday morning to let them go off for a long weekend. So this is the third evening I have put the twins to bed. Margot was fire watching at Brixton last night so Rosa came to dinner yesterday and stayed till this morning. She liked it and the twins were very good except that Margaret woke up and screamed this morning at 6.55. I think she must have had a bad dream as she was still nearly asleep when I went to her. Apart from this they were sweet and continued so today when Margot came direct here. Rosa bought them a green coat each for Christmas from her and Margot and they look very nice in them and 'admire' themselves in the mirror. Andrew walked last Monday 30th November without help and has been continuing with great excitement and squeaks of ecstasy ever since. He is better now than Margaret, who waddles and takes very small steps. E came on Thursday and thought Andrew had developed a lot. He can easily build a tower of 3 blocks, nearly 4, and can add a fourth to one of mine. Margaret makes a good attempt to brush her hair and can pull off her socks at night. She also enjoys my ceremony of the buttons, "One button; two buttons, 3 buttons etc." Margot said that K is coming here to see the twins a fortnight today—having made sure that Margot would be alone with them.

Saturday 12th December 1942

E came on Tuesday and the Hobdays went out. During the Brains Trust we loved a little. Andrew was in bed when we arrived at 5.35. He had refused tea and been tired and querulous so Hobday had got him to sleep. Margaret was sitting eating her tea alone. We played with her till 7.00. She was surprisingly different by herself, less assertive and aggressive—no competition, and she much enjoyed 2 people's concentrated attention. Rosa came today and was much struck by both their improved walking. They are both fairly secure now and can safely walk right across a room with no assistance and holding a small thing in one or both hands. They have both—Margaret more so—grown more demonstrative. They put their arms round one's neck, like to be cuddled, lay their faces against mine, enjoy being kissed and kiss back. Margaret asks to be lifted to one's lap to 'love'. She, and sometimes Andrew too, bite in 'love'. Margaret understands many words—sock, shoe, button, hot, hankie, hand, ball, upstairs (which she says very clearly), tea, drink, biscuit, soon, Sallie, glove, gee-gee, sing (to give a short immediate list). She takes off her shoes and socks when the button is undone; she rubs her nose with her hankie having taken it from her sleeve when told. They have had slight coughs and Hobday got them some cough mixture. Andrew loves it but Margaret will only take it from me. When Hobday gives it to her, she lets it all run out of the corners of her mouth! For a long time she has insisted on playing a game when she goes to bed—"Upstairs 1234567 All good children go to Heaven." Then she is put down in the cot but immediately jumps up roaring with laughter and would repeat this part of the game as long as one is willing. They went to the clinic yesterday for their second dose of immunisation against diphtheria.

A letter from Marjorie Rogers today asking me to help her to do something about the failure to promote women. It is awkward. It is mean to refuse, being one of the only 2 who have been promoted and after I received so much help. Yet I must be rather a black listed character.

Sunday 27ᵗʰ December 1942

Over a fortnight and I have been very busy. Last weekend was crammed full.

I worked at home for Saturday morning (on Saturday evening) and Rosa, Margot and I walked over Riddlesdown and picked 2 great bunches of holly. December has been very mild (so far) and the grass was green. I came back to Addiscombe for late lunch as Hobday wanted to go to Kennington. E had come over on Friday evening so I was on my own. Last Sunday K came to see the twins and Margot looked after them. Hobday came back to make sure they were looking nice! Margaret was sweet but Andrew a bit grumpy. I gather that it went off without incident.

I met Ella and we went to the Arts Theatre to see Bridie's new play 'Holy Isle'. We both enjoyed it; stimulating, witty, provocative, quite inconclusive. It is a fantasy on the theme of whether one needs government and if so what kind, with a smack at the kind imposed or influenced by business men, missionaries, hereditary monarchs etc. Margaretta Scott and Vivienne Bennett kept it going. A pleasant change and refreshment.

Margot and Rosa came about noon on Christmas Day. Hobday cooked a fine wartime dinner of roast pork, apple sauce, sage and onion stuffing, Christmas pudding (bought for the first time in our lives, but good), tea and biscuit. Margot put almond icing on the cake, made of soya bean flour and flavouring. Mince pies, sausage rolls (pork sausage meat from a tin), cheese straws, a few carefully kept Cox apples, dates, sweets and a bottle of lemon squash completed our Christmas fare, so we didn't do badly. Hobday went to Morden after dinner. Margot had to fire watch last night and left at 4.30 so we had tea early. We went for a walk to get warm in the morning. In the afternoon, we knitted and in the evening Rosa and I listened to 'The Case of the Frightened Lady' till we felt quite creepy, especially when Susan suddenly began to growl.

I lunched with Marjorie Rogers on Wednesday and do so again on Friday before a meeting at Le Huquet's flat on Saturday.

The twins develop so fast that one is bewildered. Andrew now enjoys riding on the rocking horse and can get off by himself. He easily builds a tower of 4 bricks—can add a 5th and a 6th, is trying to put the posts in their holes on the knock-it, plays peep-bo with Margaret round the big arm chair. She knows 'hat' (a scarlet beret I have given her). They have a great game pulling things off their heads—their berets, a block, a newspaper etc. Margaret likes to empty the trolley full of bricks over her head! She is interested in her clothes and likes her new green dressing gown and her yellow woolly frock with flowers on it. Andrew showed a little interest in the pocket of his dressing gown when I put a hankie in it but otherwise is not interested in clothes. He likes to see how things work—plays with the screws on the pram, my suspender belt and the electric light switch, the latches on my case.

1943

Margaret at Addiscombe, aged 18 months   *Andrew at Addiscombe, aged 18 months*

Andrew and Margaret at Addiscombe, aged 19 months

Saturday 2nd January 1943

A rather good week, though I haven't managed to do much work.

I had a day's leave on Thursday. It was a lovely day—brilliant sunshine and quite warm out of the wind. The snow made it too muddy to get off the roads. We had tea in Horley at the Green Lantern (we saw a drunk Canadian there making more of a mess with baked beans than Margaret does of her porridge) and got back to Purley about 4.45. Rosa went home for a rest and to cook the dinner, leaving Margot and me to go to the Regal to see 'Bambi'. I enjoyed it and thought it better than 'Dumbo'. Some of the dawn and dark scenery; the indication of the seasons; the thunderstorm; the forest fire, have startling beauty; the animals are caricatures of humans or completely anthropomorphised—Bambi's mother, the perky rabbit, Feline, who grows up to be Bambi's mate; grey owl are all highly individualised and attractive or entertaining. The pleasantest sequences are perhaps Bambi's mother showing him how to enter the meadow with caution; rabbit teaching how to skate; his approach as a baby and as a grown deer to Feline. But I would not take a child because of the nightmare hunt when Bambi saves Feline by driving off the dogs, and the forest fire. These would be too terrifying. And of course it is sentimental, but real cinema art, and how much it achieves. One gets really interested in the fate of these drawings—in fact Margot wept twice!

Yesterday I lunched with Marjorie Rogers to talk about the failure to promote women and today I stayed up in town to go to a meeting at Le Huquet's flat to discuss what should be done. Goldner, Reid, Rochford, Kelly, Le Huquet, Rogers and I were there. E stayed up till 2.30 so we had over 2 hours together. We went to look at the exhibition of 19th century French pictures.

Sunday January 3rd 1943

There was quite a good collection of Cezanne, Renoir, Manet, Pissarro, Sisley, 2 Van Goghs (including an impressive self-portrait), Degas (I especially liked a woman ironing and a half nude washing in a small bowl), but Delacroix I liked no better. 3 Corots, one of which E liked better than any other picture there. E went from Charing Cross and I had a coffee and then walked to Le Huquet's flat in Queen's Rd. I was the last but one to arrive and left first, only just catching the 6.25. Margot and Rosa had put the twins to bed.

They are developing. Margaret adds new words understood every day and can take off her shoes and socks. She knows buttons in any context—"dut! Dut!"—on her own or anyone else's clothes. She insists on feeding herself and gets on very well. She can carry milk from her plate to her mouth in a spoon without spilling. One has to be tactful in persuading her to take a spoonful. Andrew gets off the armchair by himself. His appetite is smaller than hers and Hobday will take him to Dr Elder to make sure he is not anaemic. I should like him to have a blood test—he gets very tired. On the other hand, he has a lot of energy and uses it, so there can't be much wrong. Still, we want him to reach his optimum.

Wednesday 6th January 1943

E came at 3.00 on Sunday and stayed till 8.0—4 hours of the twins. He said they went by very quickly. Margaret sits quietly on his lap for a long time when he comes. Andrew wants always to do things. E brought him another old pipe which he took and went straight to try banging it on the bells.

Saturday 9th January 1943

I have been rather slack at the office lately. Yesterday I had to lunch with M Rogers again and had from 12.00 to 2.15 Today I have been working at home as E was fire watching and so was able to come and see them again. I brought an

EPT case but it has not taken me long to do. I haven't got much on hand but I must work harder.

We had a lovely time with the twins, playing. Margaret grasped the idea of scribbling when we gave her a pencil but Andrew appeared to scorn it—with the air of 'I shall have enough of that later; I could do it but I don't intend to do so now'. He built a tower of 6 blocks one evening this week while waiting to go to bed. We think Margaret has learnt to say and understand 'gone'. E loved me last night for a minute or two while Hobday was cooking the apple fritters and again this morning. It was just the same as it used to be—first in the office, in trains, in Elsie's flat, at Purley, in the country under trees or on hills or cliffs—so many odd, varied places. He went at 12.30 after seeing the twins have their dinner, as Rosa was coming for the afternoon.

Sunday 16th January 1943

It is 8.15 pm. The twins are asleep. I have just been up to cover them up. I had my supper at 7.20 and since then I have been reading Time and Tide and smoking a cigarette. And the alert has just gone! It is slightly misty moonlight and Hobday said she would be back before 9.30 (when the second bit of 'War and Peace' is being broadcast). I heard some of the first this afternoon.

Wednesday 20th January 1943

At this point on Sunday, the guns began. I brought the twins down to the dining room. I put Margaret on cushions on the floor and got Andrew off to sleep in my arms. Then I heard planes and decided they ought to be in the shelter. I put Andrew in without waking him, and I was just trying to soothe Margaret's crying when Hobday arrived. She was at West Croydon when the guns began and got carried by the crowd on to a bus and just ran home. We stayed in the shelter listening to the barrage which was very noisy and contained queer swishy noises. It was difficult to tell whether the stuff was going up or coming down. The planes were flying very low, diving and zooming—it seemed—in and out of the chimneys. In a lull, I made tea and Mr Allan, the warden, knocked to ask if we were all right. He said, "It had been a bit dirty." At 9.40, I turned on the wireless and we listened to 'War and Peace' from the shelter. It contained the battles of Ulm and Austerlitz and it was sometimes difficult to tell whether the gunfire was radio or outside. We went to bed and Andrew was disturbed and I had to let him sleep with me. At 5.00, we heard the siren again. I waited till the guns began, which they did within 5 minutes. We took the twins down and Hobday lay with Margaret and I lay with Andrew. We had an almost continuous racket for 30 minutes and then off and on. At 6.00, the All Clear went. I had made some more tea and as I was cold I went back to bed. Hobday stayed in the shelter till 7.30 with the twins as they were asleep. Andrew slept all through both raids. Margaret was awake but quiet through most of the first and asleep most of the second. Sallie came in the shelter and was quiet but trembled at the noise. In the second, we hadn't time to get her till a lull and she cried and scratched to come to us.

Several bombs fell at Norbury and Thornton Heath. As Rosa said, "We are unaccustomed to blitz." I was worried about the twins and alternately afraid for them and blazing with fury! On Monday night Mary came to stay. We had an alert at 8.15 which lasted only 30 minutes. We had Mary downstairs and Hobday had just fetched Andrew (who was unwell) without disturbing him when the All Clear went. We heard some planes and guns, but not near. Last night was quiet. Today at 12.30, with no warning, there was a terrific gunfire. Wilson had come in for a chat and he and I and Johnson and Milner looked out of the window south and saw a great red sheet of flame from a bomb exploding. The balloons were just going up and when all was quiet the warning went. There was not even a watcher signalling danger. At 12.40, I set out for lunch as usual. I had not got to Leadenhall St when the guns began again and the bursts were high up, NE, not quite overhead. I saw a balloon burn; not more than 5 minutes' noise; E was 4 minutes late. He said we ought not to come out during Anti-aircraft fire. I suffered from a nagging worry all the afternoon while I was working out the EPT position of Hindley and Co. I rushed off at 5.00, got a Star which only made me feel worse as it reported that an LCC school was hit and several suburbs bombed and machine-gunned. The train was normal and I was relieved to find everything whole. Hobday had rushed out to get Andrew from the pram as a plane swooped very low. There was a lot of noise and machine-gunning at Addiscombe. She said Rosa had been over to see Margaret and Andrew this afternoon and seemed all right. She was working at the hospital during the raid.

E came to breakfast last Sunday week after fire watching and when he had had tea and bread and marmalade and I had put the twins out in their pram he came upstairs and we had a lovely fuck. I felt he had been working up for a few days—the first time since last April.

Sunday 24th January 1943

At 3.00 on Friday, ES phoned. He was in town on leave (belated summer) for a week and suggested tea. I met him at 4.15. The meeting made me feel depressed and guilty. He is like someone with a broken main spring. I don't know how he felt but he seemed completely out of reach. This after I had warmed a little to HDJ[41] who needs help in a different way. He is completely submerged in the work and so hopeless that he talked about resigning and getting a light job in the country. He bought a house in Chipping Campden last year with the idea of letting it now and retiring to it eventually. He takes refuge from the cold world in his art but he is not quite oblivious of the herd. An interesting encounter.

E came on Friday, Rosa yesterday, bringing Margaret a fine rag doll— 'Topsy' and Andrew a rattle. Margot came today and helped me cope with them and my cold. Andrew is better—spirits very good. He screams with joy when they play peep-bo round the big chair. Margaret undid 2 very long screws on the pram this morning while he was asleep. She now says 'bad' and 'good' and 'look', and they are learning the meaning of 'bird'.

Saturday 30th January 1943

Margaret is now interested in pulling toys on wheels along with string. She walks backwards very efficiently so as to watch them. She also loves to play with a feather, blowing it, and gets cross because she holds it too firmly for it to fly away. Andrew can get on the rocking horse now. They both co-operate well in dressing and Margaret tries to put her shoes on, but can't, and to undo her buttons. Now she won't go out without her red pixie hood. They both walk down the path to the gate to see me off. They had milk chocolate this week and quickly grew to love it. They go and stand by the drawer asking for more.

McCreath phoned me on Thursday and said that the GP subcommittee discussed our letter on Monday. It was decided to consider another one to be sent to Loach. He thought we had grounds for asking for information. The centre appointed Mitchell (Shepherds Bush) and Bentley (whom I regard as a fascist in method) as a subcentre. They are to co-opt Rogers (if available) and me! I was dismayed as I know how much time can be spent but I couldn't refuse as Rogers is so often out of London.

---

[41] A colleague

Saturday 6th February 1943

HDJ is finding Holden's work heavy going. He works hard and is too conscientious—a neurasthenic. He is afraid of a breakdown and talks of resigning. EA[42] talked to me about him this morning and was more sympathetic than I expected, but I doubt whether J will survive.

I talked to E about the twins and put my suggested compromise to him. He discussed it quite seriously and wants me to refrain from writing to K for a while. Meanwhile the twins develop. Margaret can say 'thank you' and 'ball', and can climb upstairs in 2 or 3 minutes but can't get down. Andrew can climb 4 or 5 steps and has some idea of getting down. They both pull the trolley along by a string. Margaret showed E where the bibs were (hanging on the drier) yesterday when he was looking for them. Andrew now insists on feeding himself and is much more messy then Margaret. He lifts the spoon more quickly and jerkily and soon tires, but won't be fed. The result is that he gets less, though now and then his appetite is good. This morning, for instance, he clamoured for milk when he got up, ate up his fried bread and potato, had some bread and butter and marmalade and a bacon rind and then came on my lap and ate up all the crusts, finishing with about 2 tablespoonsful of porridge. Rosa came early and cooked the dinner, making a potato cake which was a great success.

On Thursday (after a preliminary lunch on Wednesday), Rogers and I went to the sub-centre meeting to confer with Bentley and Mitchell. We found them more sympathetic and reasonable than we expected. The AIT is to ask for information. Why the discrepancy in proportions of men and women promoted?

Monday 15th February 1943

E came down to see the twins on Saturday afternoon and stayed till 6.45. Margot got there at 6.00 and looked after them for the weekend. They were very good and I went over on Sunday to lunch. I stayed at Purley and was lazy—had breakfast in bed and got up about 11.00. It was a treat and I found Purley very lovely—the birds and the air and the hills and the garden. There was a cherry nearly out, Margot's almond tree covered with buds, aconite, candytuft, primroses, Arabis, primula, yellow crocuses, forsythia all in flower.

Saturday 20th February 1943

This week has been lovely till today when it was dull with a kind of overhead

---

[42] Head of her department

fog. Yesterday was the loveliest day's leave I've had for the year, as a fitting last day. The sun was so warm that we basked for 45 minutes and my skin felt slightly burnt. It still glowed when I went to bed. I had spent Thursday night at Purley since Mr Hobday was on leave and I wanted to leave them free, and Margot was fire watching, so the first concern was the weather. Rosa reported it a lovely morning and it was. I went by bus to Croydon, dropped my books at the library, looked up the buses and went to East Croydon to meet E. He was late as it was foggy further in, so we had a quick coffee and caught a bus to Chelsham. The sun was brilliant and we were surprised to see cherry blossom full out. It was marvellous. We walked over Worms Heath and on an up and down and roundabout road to Beddlestead and so back to the main Sanderstead-Westerham road. Just off the road we kissed. The day was so lovely that he remarked, "I suppose Andrew inherits his ecstatic squeaks from you!" Just before the crossroads where last February we turned off back to Addington we saw and heard a fold full of sheep and very small black lambs, the first I have seen. We picnicked by Beddlestead farm, in a place full of birds (mostly chaffinches, blackbirds and buntings). The Westerham Rd had celandine in flower. We saw 2 swans flying and banking. We walked down from the ridge of hills and it seemed hot. At a crossroads, an inviting pile of flint splinters lured me to lie and bask and listen to the larks singing over the corn just springing. We loved for 45 minutes and would have fucked if it had not been such a public spot. Then we had to hurry the last 2 miles or so into Westerham to catch the bus and E had no time to see the town at all. He just saw two inns, Wolfe's statue, the church spire in the mist as we approached, the Westminster Bank and some comparatively cheap tea pots in a shop. A lovely, lovely day. We came back to tea, played with the twins, the Hobdays were out at the cinema so I put them to bed and we had a peaceful sleepy dinner with coffee and cigarettes by the fire and so he went at 9.00. I was sleepy and went to bed at 10.15, but sat up reading the Beveridge debate.

Johnson is settling down and thinks he can manage. He went to a doctor who knew Freud and treated Einstein's son and he seems to have done J good. I gathered he was suffering from a mild mother fixation. He went off yesterday to Bournemouth for his leave.

Saturday 27th February 1943

The main preoccupation this week has been Andrew's illness. The Dr has seen him 4 times. The temperature went up on Sunday and his breathing was difficult. He seemed in pain during the day. When the Dr saw him on Monday, he found he had a sore throat. He suspected measles because his eyes could not stand the light but they haven't materialised. I think he had a kind of flu rather like mine last month. He had M and B tablets which brought his temperature down but when he stopped taking them he relapsed and on Wednesday night at 10.00 he had a temperature of 104.6. Hobday phoned the Dr who gave her some more M and B. Since then we have been very careful, keeping him in bed, letting him come down only for a short time. He tires quickly and has little appetite but he seems to have turned the corner now. He must not go out before Tuesday at least.

Margaret has continued to develop for another week and has now been promoted to a hair ribbon. The Dr pronounced her 'pretty as a picture'. Her understanding of words and requests is increasing daily. She walks about the back garden now. Yesterday a very pretty tabby kitten invited itself for 24 hours. Both the twins were interested. Margaret kept calling it, "Cat Cat," holding out 2 fingers to it. She likes the daffodils and forsythia in the dining room and goes from one to the other and back, apparently comparing.

Saturday 6th March 1943

Andrew is better, except that he does not go out in the cold wind. He is normal, with a good appetite, a colour, very lively, though he tires easily. He insists on feeding himself now with a spoon, though he does let one fill the spoon ready for him after the first few spoonfuls. He tends to pick up very little or too large an amount. He loves custard, likes egg and bacon and fried potato and Yorkshire pudding and Rosa's biscuits. Margaret has a very good appetite and insists now not only on feeding herself entirely but also in drinking her milk and Ovaltine independently and incidentally drinks far more milk. Andrew has developed a passion for lids—the lid of the bread bin, the casserole, the coal box, the porridge saucepan, the emulsion bottle, the biscuit barrel as well as those of his own toys. He is fond of Topsy, the doll Rosa made Margaret, the 2 teddies and Aunt Sallie. They both like the horses and Margaret sits on them, and she can now get on the rocking horse, though still not so efficiently as does Andrew. She can climb better—on to chairs and once on to her chair and so to the window ledge. Her star performance in understanding was when Hobday, cutting bread and butter for tea in the kitchen, said, "What shall we have on it?" and Margaret appeared a minute or two later with the marmalade pot which she had been to fetch from the sideboard cupboard.

We had an air raid on Wednesday night (2 nights after a heavy one on Berlin). Everyone expected it. Siren at 8.30. Guns were heavy and near. We took the twins into the Morrison. Andrew slept through it but Margaret didn't. She cried at the siren and I held her hand and stroked her head when the gunfire was loud. We heard several planes fairly low or diving and what may have been some bombs. It was worse at Addiscombe than at Purley and they apparently came up the estuary. I heard there were bombs at Penge. At 4.30, we had another alert— a smaller affair but the gunfire was loud enough to make us get up and take the twins down. Neither slept this time and Andrew quite enjoyed himself and ate his biscuit and drank his milk with gusto. The worst thing was the shelter fiasco at Bethnal Green tube station when a great crowd fell on the entrance stairs and 178 were suffocated or crushed to death. A detailed account was given on Thursday 9pm news. I heard that there was a panic due to someone seeing a flare fall near Liverpool St and shouting, "Landmine!" Nearly everyone I have seen has been impressed and horrified by such a disaster. A good piece of news this week (though what an appalling state when such news is good!): a convoy of 22 Jap ships was attacked and completely destroyed.

Sunday 7th March 1943

After a chilly grey morning, the sun shone brilliantly by this afternoon and I took the twins into the garden and sat on the seat knitting for 2 and a quarter hours while they played and climbed up and down. They would not sleep this morning so when I put them to bed at 6.00 they were very tired and took a long time to go to sleep. Andrew suddenly today began climbing all the way upstairs and did it at least 3 times with great ease, as efficiently as Margaret. He is lovely. Rosa remarked yesterday that his expression varies much more than hers. When he is cross or frightened or scolded, it is the picture of misery, like an old man, his face wrinkled and hideous, but when he smiles his big, wide smile with shining eyes his whole face seems illumined—a transfiguration, literally. He built 5 block towers easily today and also an engine and pushed it along. Rosa played, "Can you keep a secret?" yesterday and I tried it in bed this morning, just saying the words. They at once tickled one palm with the forefinger of the other hand. Margaret spent most of the afternoon sitting on a seat beside me, taking my hankie out of my pocket, brushing her mouth or nose with it and putting it back and repeating the process! Sallie jumped out of the bedroom window on Friday and Hobday could not collect her for 45 minutes. I suppose she will have puppies—unless there was safety in numbers. She was leading a procession of about 10 dogs!

Saturday 13th March 1943

A bright, sunny week with cold, frosty mornings and east wind. E has not seen the twins for a fortnight. He hopes to come tomorrow, but it is doubtful. K retired to bed with flu 8 days ago and has been there ever since. I have been more dismal than at any time since the twins were born. I know what she is like. She is quite likely to be ill more or less for 6 or even 12 months. Indeed, what incentive (except her work) has she to recover? Being ill gives her all she wants—it completely destroys E's freedom, cuts him off from the twins and prevents any discussion. I have been sorely tempted to write to her—doing evil in the hope that good may come. I suppose I shan't. Or to accept the inevitable—cut E off, concentrating on my family relationships for the twins. I always do find it difficult to wait, inactive, and the recollection of 1937 and 1938 depresses me.

The Russians look like losing Kharkov again, though they are still advancing in the north. It is a slow job in Tunisia, and still we bomb Germany.

Sunday 14th March 1943

A lovely day—we did not light the fire till 4.30 and spent the greater part of the day in the garden. E came at 3.0—his first sight of the twins for over a fortnight. Margaret thawed slowly but Andrew was radiant. He noticed considerable development especially in Andrew. The twins love being in the garden. I put a rug for them to sit on. Andrew sat on it for ages playing with smooth round stones which he chose with care and put in patterns. Margaret came in 3 times to have her hand washed, having got it earthy! Andrew went upstairs 3 times today. Hobday said he didn't do it during the week.

Saturday 20th March 1943

Today and yesterday were dully bleak. We need rain but it has only been damp with a little drizzle. Earlier in the week the brilliant sunshine made the days warm, though we had had frosty mornings.

The twins have had 2 inoculations against whooping cough. Andrew likes Dr James better than Dr Ross. He greeted them with, "So here are the famous twins!" and on the second visit brought his wife down to see them. Andrew has been very lively all the week. He has begun to dig in the garden soil with his hands and Hobday said he was most interested in 2 or 3 worms he encountered, particularly in the way they disappeared into holes. Margaret has been off colour for 2 days (cutting her last 2 teeth, we suspect), so she went to bed early last night. Andrew was full of play, first with the rocking horse and the 2 push horses. I gave him rides till I was tired, though he wasn't. Then I gave him the 2 smallest of the nest of boxes. He liked them and at once saw the point of fitting one in the other, putting the square block in the smallest box quite easily. Playing with 3 gave him more to think about but he grasped the idea quickly and showed some delicate manipulation in fitting square in square. He was cross when bedtime came. He likes to climb upstairs carrying the 2 potties. Margaret usually throws them down again, to his annoyance. He has a better idea of coming down than she has. He can go up or down the bottom 4 or 5, but she waits to be lifted, even from the 3rd. They both climb nimbly on to their chairs to look out of the window. Margaret has been attached to a book (Zane Gray in red Nelson edition!) for the last 3 or 4 days, even taking it to bed with her. She is careful with it, just turning over the pages and playing with covers. I think it is in imitation of reading in bed, as I usually put the book on the bed beside me. They can both scribble with a pencil, Margaret more strongly than Andrew, but they get very little practice owing to the scarcity of pencils and paper.

E hopes to come tomorrow. K gets up today for the first time after 15 days in bed. She is better but still very feeble. The war makes little headway. Our bombing seems to have eased off. The Russians have lost Kharkov again and are falling back in the Donetz; nothing happens in Tunisia; we go on losing ships.

Saturday 27th March 1943

The twins have got whooping cough. Hobday took them for their 3rd injection on Monday and Margaret was not well then. The Dr thought she had merely a heavy cold but on Tuesday afternoon her temperature was 104 and Hobday gave her the last M and B tablet. This brought it down to 99 in an hour and she hasn't been feverish since 3 or 4 days. However, she ate almost nothing, though she drank a lot of orange juice and milk. She has improved (except in temper), and but for coughing and a runny nose and pale face seemed nearly normal today.

Andrew has a runny nose and more violent coughing than Margaret. The paroxysms exhaust him but in a few minutes he gets over them and is then full of spirits. Rosa came to lunch and stayed till 6.30 and he was sweet with her, playing Ring a Ring of Roses, Can you keep a secret? And Pat-a-cake with her and giving her Topsy and Mr and Mrs Baby Bear (a delightful family of small bears presented to them last Sunday by Jock Robertson.) She was completely vanquished by him. The Dr came on Thursday and today but has not heard them whoop so he will not diagnose definitely. Margaret said 2 new words today— 'Doctor' and 'Rosa' and shakes her head and says 'no' and nods and says 'yes' with complete understanding. All this week 'no' has been commoner than 'yes'. No doubt they are merely at the beginning but so far not too bad. E is most concerned.

I went to the London Centre meeting on Thursday before going to Purley for the evening. EA and Milner went. It was a dull meeting and the only other woman was Jenkin. I feel rather disappointed with the women. They expect me and Rogers and the Association to fight their battles for them, but they can't even be bothered to go to the most important centre meeting of the year. McCreath spoke very well but looked very ill. King was very effective and put Dale neatly in his place. The level of speaking was poor.

Saturday 10th April 1943

A wearisome, harassing week. Every night has been more or less disturbed by the twins coughing. I have had to get up about 6 times. This, or the accumulated effect of little leave and no holiday, and winter, has made me feel terribly tired, and without having anything specific wrong I have felt feeble and shaky. Yesterday at lunch I suddenly felt faint and giddy and had to come out into the air. Also, on the 6th April I had a letter from Saker terminating the tenancy unless I would pay the original rent of £117. Of course, they could get more but they regard me as a good tenant. I first asked for a fortnight, thinking I would see what the budget held before committing myself, but he replied that he couldn't wait so I had no alternative but to accept the offer. His attitude has hardened considerably in the last 12 months. Anyway, if I can go elsewhere I can break the tenancy; but I wanted to get the position of E settled before moving. I am rather weary of the long argument and striving and inclined to work towards joining Rosa at Purley and virtually cutting him and the twins apart. And yet when he came on Wednesday it was so lovely to see them together. All 3 so enjoyed it. He gave Andrew a train in 5 pieces and Margaret 9 skittles and a ball and the twins loved these new toys. I don't know; he is writing an essay to get the issues clear to himself and wants me to wait till he finishes before writing to K.

EA gave me Paterson Simons, which was one of Holden's worst cases. J is a broken reed. Milner and I between us have taken hours of work from him.

Wednesday 14th April 1943

Two lovely days, and the twins have been in the garden in the warm sun all day. Their coughs are better and they are in fine spirits. I had to get up for them only twice last night. On Monday evening, Hobday put on the gramophone—it was the first time I had seen the twins with it. Andrew is interested in the mechanism—winding it up, changing the needle, putting on the brake and taking it off, but showed interest in one record only—a flute piece. Margaret was not very interested in the machine but eager to hear the records—2 soprano songs from Madam Butterfly excited her. She swayed and danced in rhythm, holding out her hand and pointing, joining in the singing! She listened quietly and attentively, just swaying slightly in time to Myra Hess playing Bach's 'Jesus Joy of Man's Desiring'. The contrast between them was most striking and I was much impressed with Margaret's obvious enjoyment. She had 'One Fine Day' 3 times and wanted it again! Finally, we had a display of temper when she had to go to bed! They have both got used to the big bath again and enjoy it. They have a beaker and pour water over themselves and clean their teeth.

The budget is no worse (except for cigarettes) and judging from *the Times* report I look like getting the HK[43] Allowance—£25 in hard cash, which would just comfortably pay my additional rent.

Saturday 17th April 1943

Each day from Tuesday onwards it has been sunny. Yesterday was summer heat so that I was glad to put on a cotton frock when I got home. Today the heat has been tempered and lightened by a breeze so that it has been ideal—not too hot and not too cold.

The twins have been in the garden all the week except when they slept or for some meals. They hardly cough at all in the air and at night very little. Margaret is perhaps worse than Andrew. She tends to vomit owing to the violence of her

---

[43] Housekeeper

cough. He whoops instead, though he looks a different boy after the sunny weather. His eyes look clear and bright; his colour has returned; he is full of energy and fun and he is improving a great deal in cleanliness. He asks to sit on the pot, which is more than Margaret does. They like to sit up to the big table for meals. Margaret manages her small fork very efficiently and Andrew is not bad, though he falls back on fingers sometimes. Their appetites are much better. E came yesterday to dinner and was not in this morning as he is fire watching tonight. I went to Croydon and to the library and got Massingham's 'Remembrance' which is lovely.

Wednesday 21st April 1943

Yesterday was lovely—a succession of small felicities. At lunchtime, I collected the snaps I had left to be developed and printed and found they were the best batch yet—certainly the best of Margaret. Immediately I got 2 blocks of chocolate for the twins (the first for two and a half weeks). I had 2 successful, if tiring, interviews.

The twins were in the bath when I got home at 6.00 and were particularly attractive, though they insisted on sampling the chocolate at once and Andrew tried the effect of submerging it and hastily put it all in his mouth when he found it was disintegrating.

On Monday evening, E and I went to hear St John Passion (Bach) at St Michael's, Cornhill. We were in the front row, just by the double bass but it was lovely. Margot and I took the twins to the birch wood on Sunday afternoon and let them walk about. Margaret is more enterprising and independent and went off a long way. She was very pleased with a dandelion. E came to breakfast after fire watching.

Sunday 25th April 1943

My birthday and Easter Sunday—the first and last time they coincide. It has been brilliant sunshine, cooled and marred by a blustery wind which has blown down the fence again. We had rain nearly all Good Friday so it was little hardship to be working. Yesterday was sunny with lovely galleons of clouds—sailing the blue sky.

I caught a bus to Caterham and met Margot. We walked up the hill to Tillingdown and along the crest to the ruin in Marden Park. The trees were looking beautiful, at their freshest, especially the beeches. The more I do that walk the more

I love it, for each occasion adds a memory. The distinctive feature this time was the flowers—first bluebells and ragged robin in a wild little copse with fluttering showers of cherry petals, then cowslips on the higher slopes of the downs. I stayed at Purley and Margot came to spend the night with Hobday and the twins.

Today Rosa and I got to Addiscombe at 12.00. She and Margot gave me a three quarter length coat for the summer. We had chicken for dinner as a treat, which Hobday had ordered weeks ago from her Devon farm. It was delicious, the first I have had since leaving the nursing home in 1941. The twins were delighted to see Rosa. She had made Margaret a rag book and gave them a tiny book each. Margaret is a regular book worm—nothing pleases her more. She looks attentively at the pictures, demanding what they are. Her other passion is flowers which she loves, whether growing or in a vase, or to hold. I pick her a dandelion or a piece of cow parsley or a buttercup—she likes yellow best, and she holds them and smells them till they wither. Andrew is not so keen—he prefers tins and stones. Margaret can point now to most of her limbs and features—hand, foot, toes, knees, bottom, eyes, hair and curls, ear, nose, tongue and can point to the same features on Andrew or anyone else. She seems to find difficulty only with her tummy. They usually sit up to the table now, eating on their mats, unless they are having a social meal like tea, which no one else is having. Both drink out of their mugs very neatly and can use a fork and spoon. Margaret is better than Andrew, but he is quite efficient. His left foot turns in still and Hobday is a little concerned about it. He had new shoes last week. Margot and Rosa went about 5.30, but are coming over tomorrow.

Saturday 1st May 1943

All the week it has been cold and grey and often raining and blowing. We have had no heating in the office since 17th April and it has been bitter. It is impossible to keep warm. I have been wearing woollies, tweed skirt and winter coat but yesterday I woke up with a cold. It is difficult to concentrate and my output this week has been poor.

I went to Purley on Thursday. The twins are fairly well in themselves but their noses run a lot and they still cough. Andrew is making great efforts to articulate words. He tries difficult ones like 'sneeze'. He gets more variety into his sounds and he will 'sing' when requested. He is much more appreciative of music and begins to dance and sway in rhythm as Margaret has been doing for ages. We had the gramophone on Monday and he sat on the table watching and listening with evident enjoyment. They are both learning to walk downstairs forwards, holding the banister and one's hand. They go up just to come down and get very cross if I haven't time to guide them down in the morning. In addition to playing with the twins, bathing them and giving them their tea, I have done some washing, washed my hair, made a hat out of a velvet pattern Rosa brought me, begun another baby's cardigan, read some of 'Return to the River'— the life of a salmon, which is lovely. Had supper and listened to two thirds of a concert, news and 'Gram Swing' and a thriller play. So now to bed. Rosa was very nice. It is odd that apart from her fundamental refusal to accept my view of E I get on with her better than I have for years. It is probably due mainly to my being more content and satisfied—in having something worth doing and big enough to fill my life.

Sunday 2nd May 1943

A cold, wet Sunday which just cleared up enough to allow Margot and me to take the twins and the dogs out for an hour before tea. This morning I gave the twins a pencil each. They both scribbled more vigorously than I have ever seen them, Margaret with prolonged concentration. She made one or two good attempts to imitate me doing a vertical line and watched me draw cats. She begins to look at pictures in the paper and will pick out 'a lady'. I was most impressed, however, with her efforts to fit her 12 blocks into the trolley. She knew they fitted, selected all big blocks (rejected the small ones), and fitted them all in 2 or 3 times, finishing with great satisfaction. The task was an effort and she panted and cried with vexation when the blocks wouldn't fit in. This requires skill as each has to be exactly in place. E said she had mastered the 5 Chinese boxes on Wednesday and could do the nest of boxes easily. She got a big bump on her forehead this evening. Margot brought her a few buttercups and daisies and she was thrilled—sat on the floor and played with them beautifully for a long time, holding them very carefully by the stalk.

Sunday 9th May 1943

A wild weekend—rocking gale, squalls of hail and rain and sunshine, brilliant in the afternoon so that when Margot came about 3.00 Ella and she and I took the twins for a walk to the birch wood. They came out of the pram when we got there and Margaret picked dandelions and collected acorns. Margaret's speech increases—she calls 'clock' when she sees one, or a watch. She says 'dead' when I kill a bluebottle and goes on saying it, rather liking the sound! This morning she said, "Get up!" which surprised me so much that I got up! One morning at breakfast she said, "More bread." Andrew improves slightly, but says almost nothing quite clearly. They had tea at the Rectory on Friday and enjoyed themselves playing in the sandpit there. Andrew collected the clippings when Hobday clipped the hedge and worked so hard that he was quite worn out by tea time. Their scribbling improves and is now most vigorous. Andrew made his mark in the book he gave Margot for her birthday. Margaret can walk downstairs by herself the last 4 steps holding the bannisters. Andrew can come down backwards. He is much cleaner and drier than Margaret at present. Ella came for the weekend. Andrew was most friendly and let her wash him without a protest in the bath last night, but Margaret wouldn't go near her except for a short time this afternoon when she gave her some blocks. Otherwise she cried at sight and even refused to sit down in the bath because she was there last night and wouldn't sit at the tea table. It is most noticeable but quite inexplicable.

Yesterday E came for the afternoon as Rosa had come on Thursday. I was very happy when he came up and loved me for 2 minutes before dinner.

Milner has a week of his summer leave next week and is going farming at Reigate.

Tunis and Bizerta are in our hands—much quicker than we hoped. I heard church bells this morning. The air quivers with expectancy.

Saturday 15th May 1943

The weather this week has been extraordinary. Monday was so cold that Ibex House actually started central heating. It poured with rain and blew a gale all day so that I had to move my table a yard to get out of the rain pouring in, which made puddles all along that side of the room. On Thursday night, we were disturbed by a great din; first, bombers going out, then thunder (with lightning); the roar of rain just pouring down, then an air raid, so that gunfire and thunder were mixed up. Yesterday was a heat wave with butter turning to oil. Today has been brilliant with cool breeze; a perfect day.

Mary came for Tuesday night. Margaret was much more friendly than to Ella. She would allow no intimacies but obviously liked her better—it was partly Mary's scarlet cardigan. Andrew was less friendly. E came out last night and Rosa today.

E and I spent Wednesday lunchtime looking at St Helen's, Bishopsgate. It was much bigger than it looks outside and exceptionally wide. Half belonged to the monastery and half to the parish with a 15th century arcade between.

We listened to Eugene Onegin which I knew nothing about. It was lovelier than I expected with beautiful flowing music, though the story is melodramatic. After the news, we heard Gielgud in Linklater's 'The Great Ship'—a play patriotic and propagandist in theme which for me succeeded because it had truth and passion and was finely written and acted. I found it exceedingly moving. E thought it had almost Shakespearean breadth, an experience too rare on the radio.

Sunday 16th May 1943

I love these busy full weekends with Rosa on Saturday afternoon and Margot from 12.30 to 6.00 on Sunday. Washing, ironing, cooking, sewing or knitting, and today cutting grass, playing with the twins, taking them out in the pram. One sits each end and they sit like king and queen surveying such sights as appear— a bus, a lorry, a baby, a couple of dogs, a trio of pigeons. Or pushing each other in a puppyish romp, gurgling with laughter. We reach the park, fresh green with sunlight glinting through the trees and Margaret holds out her hands to be lifted out. We sit on a bank in the sun while Margaret walks around—so far away that she looks like a buttercup, in her yellow gingham frock, but she walks like Churchill. Andrew, in blue suit and new pudding basin hat, potters, "Sh-Sh!" Bath time, when they pour water over themselves with a beaker. Margaret, who strongly objects to being washed, washes herself with gusto and surprising efficiency. Andrew loves to have water poured down his back and they love me to pour water, from high up, on to their toes. Then the long quiet evening which is always too short for all I have to do—coffee for supper and a cigarette while I read Time and Tide—lovely.

There is just a glimmer of a possibility that E might ask to go on farm relief for 2 weeks at Yeovil, when I ask for Exeter, and stay with me at Seaton. The bare idea thrills me—with or without the twins. He loved me in the train on Friday between Woodside and Bingham Rd and when we got in before tea. Very fierce! I love him just as much.

Both the twins can come downstairs on their own. They are busy exploring. Andrew can point to his (2 more) nose, teeth, tongue, hair, eyes as readily as Margaret. She looked at my finger nails tonight and compared them with her own.

Saturday 22nd May 1943

A week of almost perfect summer weather—sunny, yet fresh with moonlit nights of soft brilliance. Only on Friday the evening was clouded and heavy and this afternoon was overcast with a few heavy drops of rain. The roses have rarely seemed so richly lovely or so numerous; clematis is out, lupins almost past their peak, delphiniums out, hawthorn, lilac, most laburnum finished. Unfortunately the beauty of the weather has been slightly marred by 6 consecutive nights of alerts—mainly nuisance raids. Most nights we have lost at least 1 and a half—2 hours sleep and have had to descend once or twice to the shelter. Gunfire has been heavy at times. The planes, usually single, have droned low over the roofs. Milner was shaken up on Monday by a 1000 lb bomb in Christchurch Rd which fell 200 yards from him on a doctor's house, killing 6, including the Dr. We lost a few tiles last night through shrapnel and the milk girl was disturbed by a bomb near her, Nothing compared with the 1940–1941 blitz, of course, or still less with our blitz on Italy and Germany but we have grown unaccustomed to disturbed nights.

Milner came back on Monday with his arms still sore from sunburn. The first 3 days of his week's leave were very bad and they couldn't do any farm work. As the weather improved they did 2 days sorting potatoes (a filthy and stinky job) and planting them at Gatton; 2 days hoeing cabbages and manuring them with ammonia sulphate at Belmont. He found the food scanty but otherwise the camp was well run and he seems to have liked the work. He earned 20 shillings and 6d towards his keep of 28 shillings.

The twins are fine except that Margaret cries at the alert and heavy gunfire and last night clamoured to go down to the 'funny bed'—the shelter. Andrew went to the clinic on Tuesday. They said his leg seemed all right. I was pleased to learn that he had gained 14oz in 2 weeks after standing still for 3 months. His vocalising is improved. He is almost successful with 'double Dutch', says 'Bow Wow' and 'Bo'. They both understand nearly all that is said to them and a lot that isn't. Andrew enjoys pulling the stopper out of the bath; his reluctance to come out to be dried has caused him to catch a slight cold. Margaret is queer; she hates sitting down in the bath but loves it when she is settled in the water. Their appetites continue good. Andrew's thirst is enormous; he is getting intelligent in looking at pictures and they both produce more scribble and much stronger; they can make red pencil write; previously they could only make a mark with a soft BB pencil. They take more notice of each other—will give the other a biscuit, a toy, etc. if asked. Margaret brushes his hair, but they quarrel over toys, push each other etc. They love to see the trains. E and I took them to the park today. Andrew watches a train with a worried look as if the responsibility for war transport rested on him. He hears an aeroplane before anyone else and will watch for it to appear, pointing it out. He is interested in buses, likes to play ball with anyone who will play. Today he walked off by himself half across the park. E was fascinated.

Tuesday 25th May 1943

Work has flared up—3 interviews yesterday, the general inspection next week. EA has checked some of my cases. A thunderstorm at 5.00 this afternoon and yet it is chilly so that Hobday lit a fire yesterday. She and Mr Hobday went to the cinema last night and to a show tonight. He had an interview today with the solicitor about the divorce.

The twins have slight colds but are vigorous and lively. A long, nice letter from Ella, asking me to go for the weekend but I can't ask Margot to come.

Margot came early on Sunday to let me go to a Progressive League lecture by Curry of Dartington Hall on the Independent School. He is quick and intelligent, hates corporal punishment and teaching 'nationalism'—"I would rather burglary—it's less dangerous." He was giving pros and cons of one comprehensive state system of education and rather inconclusively concluded against it. Stimulating and interesting. I caught the 12.38 back and got home in the middle of dinner, just after a short alert. In the afternoon, we went to the park and basked and then back to give Rosa tea. They stayed to dinner. I was lucky on Saturday and Sunday night on my own; no alert—the first quiet night for a week.

Saturday 29th May 1943

Today the twins have had a new experience which E and I have shared with them—their first picnic. It was a perfect summer day—cool and fresh in a light frock at 9.00 (equivalent to 7.0), but hot at midday in spite of a light breeze. After dinner, we set off up to Upper Addiscombe Rd to get a bus to the Shirley hills. He carried Margaret and I carried Andrew, a bag with thermos of milk, cake, apple and 2 spare pairs of knickers. Andrew was thrilled with the buses and was tense with interest when we got in. He watched trees and houses rushing by, listened to the roar of the engine climbing and was disturbed when the bus stopped. We went to the top and walked under the pines. Andrew was interested in dandelion clocks and pine cones, Margaret in buttercups. I have never smelled the pines so strongly—even E noticed them. We sat down and the twins at once began playing with pine needles, twigs and earth, picking up handfuls of them to throw over each other and me and E. Margaret buried her foot in them with glee. She dirtied her knickers but I was able to wash them. Andrew went off by himself. He loves a steep little slope like a ditch and goes up and down precariously. We moved over to a more open place and the twins had their milk. The pint proved inadequate but they enjoyed their apple. E and Margaret went off to the tea house and he said she met a baby and tickled its toes with great pleasure. We caught a bus back early and they walked part of the way back. Andrew was dry when we got back but wouldn't sit on the pot. Margaret made a pool in the road coming back from the bus. We had been three and a half hours, so they were good. They were tired but I think they enjoyed the outing. They were thirsty when we got home so I gave them orange juice while I boiled milk. Andrew drank his but Margaret cried because she wanted milk and then because I gave it to her in the kitchen. I had to sit her up to the tea table, then she was content. They had their bath and were in bed by 6.45. Andrew went to sleep quickly but it was after 8.00 before Margaret was quiet.

Saturday 5th June 1943

The twins are 20 months old today. Both have been well this week. They have been full of spirit. They are just at the stage for sand and have found substitutes in the crumbled asphalt of 2 tennis courts in the park and in coal dust which they played with in the newly cleaned dining room on Thursday. Margaret will now echo, or try to copy, words said to her, whether or not she understands their meaning. Andrew at last begins to use words—'Bow-wow-wow', 'Peep-bo', 'More up down'. He still clings, however, to mere noises, expressive as they are, for bus, aeroplane, 'Teddy' or 'Sally' or 'Nanny'. Margaret loves to have the cake mixture bowl which she scrapes out with a spoon. On Thursday when E was here she tried showing off and attempted to put it on her head. It was too heavy and she dropped it and broke it. She looked quite subdued—there was none of a triumphant 'look what I've done' attitude. It is charming to see them offer each other things, a biscuit, a lump of sugar etc. Andrew builds 6 block towers easily, carefully putting each one square on the one below and finishing with a bigger one. He can also couple the train E gave him. Margaret's scribble has developed; she holds a pencil correctly and controls it well. She draws lovely curves, sometimes complete circles, and tries to copy me when I draw a cat or a chicken. She clearly uses words with meaning; last Sunday, when a dog she had listened to stopped barking—"Gone Bow Wow!"

A rather hectic week. On Monday, Reen Hosier[44] phoned and said she and Charles were in town for a day to see their solicitors and could we lunch? E and I met them. She was looking well and we resumed just where we stopped talking over 3 years ago. Charles was looking older but fitter, though his deafness was worse. They like living at Pewsey and she invited me to bring the twins to stay and, if possible, go on farm relief to Newbury. Next morning I phoned Robertson and asked him if he could send me there. He said he would remember if there were any changes but the scheme was finished in general. Still, I could go to Reen for my leave. On Monday afternoon, Raper-called, over from Belfast for the AGM. He said Northern Ireland is still lucky because the Americans are generous with their supplies of fruit, chocolate, butter etc. He told a good tale of the Stranraer boat just missing a mine by a quick swerve to one side. When they machine-gunned it to blow it up, it turned out to be an empty beer barrel! I had tea with him and Mrs Raper on Wednesday.

On Tuesday, Margot took Rosa and me to see 'This Happy Breed' for her birthday treat. Coward was good. In fact, the best acting came from him. The play was on the plan of 'Cavalcade', but it wasn't bad. The most interesting thing was how hideous the fashions from 1919, 1926, 1931 and 1938 looked. We had very good coffee in the interval.

Saturday 12th June 1943

The men came to mend the fence on Thursday and Mr Hobday has been in his element supervising them. It was difficult to get him away for meals. Andrew says 'more' now. Margaret has been trying it on this week, crying when she was left at night and throwing all the bedclothes on the floor—3 nights running. She is very self-willed, but is better on the pot. Andrew is rather obstinate at present. They are both very imitative now—copy the way one sits or stands or lies, what one does with clothes etc.

I have at last got a cost of living bonus—£20 per annum (against the men's £25), which is £11 after Income Tax. Still, it is something! I am to go to Newbury for 3 weeks in August.

---

[44] A friend and former colleague

Saturday 19th June 1943

A week of chilly grey skies, heavy downpours of rain, brilliant, deceptive mornings. I had the best day of the Whitsun holiday for going out last Saturday. Sunday was chilly with showers. Monday was chillier with more showers and a thunderstorm in the evening. The noise woke Margaret and I picked her up to comfort her and she did a pool on my lap—sheer fright. E came on Sunday morning and Margot to breakfast after fire watching. Rosa and Margot came on Monday for the day. We had alerts Saturday, Sunday and Monday nights—2 each night. I put a hand over Margaret's ear and the twins did not awake, but I wondered what to do when the guns grew loud. I just stood, like some echo of Richard 3rd and the little princes, a pillow in each hand to protect them from glass. One can't leave Margaret even for a second and I can't carry the two together.

The twins seem to have lost their colds. Margaret can now say 'pull frock wool', 'bump dead' (of flies). Andrew, not able to reach some scones on the shelter, fetched the stool from the dining room to stand on, so got one today. On Monday, he was trying to get on the garden ledge by climbing on the fire bucket and fell in. With his head and feet sticking out and his middle well submerged, he looked funny. When I had dried him and given him clean clothes, he returned to find the reason for the mishap.

E has gone to Worcester for his uncle's funeral today. I don't know what he will do—Marjorie[45] has nowhere after 20 July, when her husband goes back to Sheffield, and wants to stay at Kingston. This is awkward as she doesn't know of the twins. It will be difficult for him to get away and also to discuss the position with K. I was dismal but was cheered when he said, "I can't desert the twins!" I have offered to lend Marjorie my house while I am at Newbury.

Saturday 26th June 1943

Today I have been to RHC[46] old students' meeting—the first time I have been back since 1937 at least. It was a lovely day, sunny but fresh. I lunched with E (who came down to Addiscombe for the afternoon) and met Mary, Dorothy and Isabel at Waterloo after queuing for my ticket (4 shillings against 2/3d pre-war). We walked up the hill and entered the grounds by the lower gate. The grounds were intensely cultivated with fruit and vegetables, though Jane Austin

---

[45] E's sister

[46] Royal Holloway College where Doreen was a student from 1924–7

Walk and the terraces were as of old except that the lawns were shaggy. East side is occupied by the ATS Staff College so we walked round to West. I knew and remembered every inch perfectly, though I felt rather as though I were walking in a dream. To the annual meeting, which was as futile as usual, with only 2 or 3 people audible. I was struck by the fact that the staff had aged very much, far more than any contemporary students. At 3.45, we had tea, almost pre-war, with home-made cake, raspberries and cream and thin fine china cups. Misery[47] had tea with us and I told her about the twins. She talked of post war plans. She is keen to have students from abroad, especially the Dominions and USA.

Travelling down was good but it took me from 5.15—7.30 to get back. E had gone and Hobday was waiting. Yesterday I rushed to Piccadilly to meet Margot and Rosa and spend an hour at the Academy—tiring but pleasant and interesting as Alan Howes and David McFall had sculpture showing. At 5.00, I had to go to Somerset House to meet Bentley, Mitchell and Le Huquet on the women's question. Bentley took us down to the cafeteria and divulged some interesting points on service politics. I must admit I like him not too badly out of meetings. He is a real crusader with disinterested passion, but he is too much of a partisan—anti-Head Office, whatever it does. So now I am so tired.

The twins grow. Margaret's appetite is very good, Andrew's fairly good. The chimney sweep came yesterday and they saw him. Andrew was intrigued when he heard the brushes in the wall of the bedroom! They begin to play pretend games—"I've got a little baby," lying down and pretending to be one. This morning Margaret on her own went and squatted down by the pot. They almost put on their shoes and socks, making great efforts with the button.

Saturday 3rd July 1943

A week of sunshine after cool grey mornings. The grass is noticeably browner than a week ago, willow herb and buddleia are flowering—it is high summer.

This morning the twins' sand (given by E) arrived and they love it. I saw Andrew carefully putting it inside his knickers! Unfortunately his left hand (which he prefers on the whole) was scalded with tea today. He asked for some and then moved his mug nearer him just as I was pouring a little in. It pained him a lot but I hope will not blister. He is unlucky with burns. I put Vaseline on it and a bandage after cleaning it. He enjoyed himself yesterday helping Hobday

---

[47] Nickname for one of her lecturers when a student

put the fence for the sand, trying to hammer nails in. Finally he pushed a row under the bottom plank. He can now kiss with a proper smack and is very proud of it. Rosa and I took them to the park. Andrew wouldn't keep his hat on after Rosa took her red linen one off. Margaret would do nothing but sit on our laps. She was very taken with Rosa's hat—wanted to try it on and look at herself. Andrew loves to clear the table, putting napkins away, mats, salt, spoons, etc. and knows just what there is to do and objects strongly if anything is omitted. Margaret has tried hitting me on the head with a wooden ball, saying, "Dead!"—sadism.

There have been many rumours that our invasion starts this weekend—we shall see! The drills are making the office impossible. I was nearly driven crazy this morning. It is a pleasure having interviews in the morgue for the quiet.

E intends to discuss the twins with K this weekend. Rosa's sculpture of St Francis is to be exhibited in the studio and will probably be finished by the end of July.

Saturday 10th July 1943

A stormy, chilly week, with growls of thunder in the distance and sudden rain squalls. The week has flown; on Tuesday E and Mary came for the evening. E wanted to see her. He suggests making a codicil to his will leaving £1000 in trust for the twins, as an interim measure. Also, he wants her to take over Uncle Worcester's estate.

Andrew has had his hair cut yesterday, just over his ears and round his neck and looks adorable. They still love the sand and were surprised at the difference being wet makes. E played with them on Tuesday and made a cutting and tunnel for Andrew's train, much to his delight.

Tuesday 13th July 1943

Yesterday E treated Mary and me to lunch so that he could hand over Uncle Worcester's estate to her. He came down in the afternoon and played in the sand with them, making a tunnel for Andrew's train and sand pies with a flower pot. When they came in for their bath, he made 4 or 5 more for them to find in the morning. It touched me to see him out there alone, foreseeing their pleasure. How can I stop him from seeing them? Deprive him of this delight? In face of such enjoyment? He dried Andrew and played with him after his bath and Andrew was more demonstrative than I have ever seen him before, caressing his face, as if he felt and knew their kinship.

Sunday 18th July 1943

Another blustery Sunday after what promised on Friday to be a heat wave. It turned close and hot just in time for E and me to go to the Prom; yesterday was sunny with a breeze, a perfect day. Today has been grey and windy but not cold.

I have been to Ella for the weekend while Margot came to look after the twins. E came yesterday afternoon till 8.00 and Margot said Margaret let him bath her and wipe her—a great favour. They behaved beautifully and ate large meals, even Andrew, whose appetite has not been good for the last week or two. He drinks a lot of milk so we don't worry much. Also, he is full of energy, so he can't be suffering from under nourishment. Sheila, Kath and Richard[48] came to tea yesterday and I was interested to see him. He is very big and tall, but looked pale—almost ethereal. He has light curly hair and blue eyes with dark lashes and a most winning smile. He had not been well but he certainly looked very fragile compared with the twins. He talks well, though he stutters a little, and is very friendly. I had a comfortable, lazy morning with breakfast in bed and *The Sunday Times*. We had dinner at 1.15 and went for a walk before I left at 4.00 and got home at 6.00.

The Prom was lovely in spite of the heat. We had dinner at the Venice first and got there at 6.40 so as to get a good seat in the balcony. The Violin Concerto (Kersey) and the 4th Symphony were the main things and I enjoyed them completely. It is odd that the music itself seems lovelier with Rosa then with Nancy. I hadn't been to anything in the evening with her for ages, I think since war began, certainly since the blitz began. It was just as nice as it used to be.

When I went to Purley on Wednesday, Rosa said she had been asked to present the prizes at the kindergarten and was quite overcome. It was yesterday and she had learnt a small speech by heart. Margot said she ought to have a feather boa.

Everyone it too optimistic about the war. We got on well in Sicily and the Russians look like doing well again at Orel. Someone told me the Italians would be out of the war in a week or two! How I do long for some leave. Ella said the teachers have had their holidays restored. Most of the new SI and HG[49]

---

[48] Ella's sisters and nephew
[49] Senior Inspector and Higher Grade Inspector of Taxes

promotions were in this week's WDN. Salmon is now an SI—without a special. I am glad, though he will despise it.

Saturday 24ᵗʰ July 1943

A rushed week at the office. I begin to get the rush inevitable before going away—trying to fit in appointments and get cases settled. Also, Hobday and I are having a rush of dressmaking, etc. before taking the twins away for the first time; new frocks for Margaret and new suits for Andrew; mending and knitting. On Monday, the Milners came to dinner so we had our 'Sunday' dinner. Tuesday E came. On Wednesday, I had a day's leave and went walking with Margot. It was one of the worst days for the summer. It was grey and spotting with rain all the morning. We managed to eat our lunch more or less dry but from 1.00 onwards it rained harder and harder and we got wet to the knickers. I went to Purley for the evening.

Sunday 1ˢᵗ August 1943

A heat wave all the week finishing with a blazing day and a thunderstorm last night. Today has been fresher with cleansing wind, sharp edged clouds, sun and rain together. I have been busy at the office getting straight (I left only 2 EPT computations, one letter, which came in the last day, and I should have done those if I hadn't had an appointment on Friday afternoon). At home sewing for the twins, washing, getting haircut and washed, packing and collecting to pack. I have got my ticket to Newbury—1ˢᵗ class!

E came on Friday but not yesterday or today. Margaret has felt the heat but Andrew seems to flourish in it. They have lived in sun suits and had a bath of water in the garden. Andrew trickles water down his tummy and Margaret loves to be showered from the watering can. They had a marvellous time watering the garden and pouring water from the bath to the can with a tin. Unfortunately they did the same when they had their bath and almost drowned the bathroom the first day. I have caught the 7.32 every day this week and so saw less of them than usual. Andrew has been dry all day and Margaret is improving. I had her up till 10.00 last night as the thunder frightened her too much to have her upstairs. With care, I got her to the point of 'replying' to the thunder with 'Bang'. She was cross this morning. This afternoon in the recreation ground she loved the wind in the willows and looked at and smelled the roses charmingly. She has had to have 2 new pairs of shoes. The difficulty is play shoes—she has to rag out good shoes because of the glass splinters in the garden when normally she would wear rubber and canvas sandals. The better pair was 9/11d and the utility pair 4/6d. They are just like cardboard.

Sunday 8th August 1943

A full week which I must try to begin, though it is 11.20 pm. On Monday, Margot and Rosa came over for the day and we had a peaceful day simply going to the recreation ground in the afternoon. Hobday came back at 8.00 and I spent a rather hectic evening packing for me and planning for her and the twins. On Tuesday, I set off in a rush. I met E at Paddington for an hour where we had a coffee. Margot was seeing a child off there at 11.05 so she came and talked for 10 minutes before my train went. I watched the queue and thought complacently of my first class ticket. I was disappointed to find when I finally said goodbye to him at 11.00 that there was no first class! I did get a seat but we were 6 a side and 2 standing. Change and a wait at Reading and I reached Newbury at 1.07.

I found I could get a weekly season to Pewsey for 13/4d which worked out cheaper than a monthly, or separate tickets. I had lunch and found the office situated over the Westminster Bank, overlooking the market place. McGhee is youngish, a Scot with 3 children, 2 girls at boarding school in Reading and one child with grandmother at Bristol, wife in full time job; a little man, Oades, the IA[50], was passed over for HG, a year junior to me. Mathematics from a Southampton school and St John's Cambridge. His wife is in a part time job. A grumbler against Head Office, but none the less conscientious. Both are bitter over moving to Newbury. They were 2 years in digs looking for houses and this May took a large country mansion between them 3 miles south.

They greeted me cordially and Oades said, "Put at the bottom of your works report 'cheering IA'." He talks and talks. They had saved some 90 accounts for me—a good few farm accounts. I was given a few tips and yesterday an original long letter on one. On Thursday, it was market day. I got an indifferent lunch with difficulty. The noise in the office is deafening—convoys of lorries, etc., shouting stall holders and planes flying low, but the swallows swoop and skim the roofs all day. I can see green hills above the red roofs. The people have open air skins and half-way-to-the-west accents. The town has character and some distinction; a lovely bridge, a cloth hall, timbered houses.

---

[50] Inspector's Assistant

Saturday 14th August 1943

No opportunity to continue—I have not come in till between 8 and 9, then supper, wash up and bed.

Hobday and E brought the twins down on the 6th and I joined the train at Newbury. Margaret looked staggered to see me suddenly and sat on my lap at once. Andrew was sitting on a soldier's knee looking at a book and took no notice of me at all, though after a while he gave me a kiss. They behaved well and had done all the way. They looked out of the window and Andrew, particularly, was very quick at seeing a bus, a lorry, ducks, etc. going under bridges. They said, "Peep-bo!" they had a good tea of milk and bread and butter and went to bed. The strange cot took some getting used to, and the bath was worse. Andrew won't sit down; Margaret was unexpectedly easy, was not frightened and seemed quite unperturbed. Andrew was more excited and tense but they stood the journey well and settled down fairly quickly. They love the animals—horses, cows, Bimbo, Tigger, the chickens. They trot round the garden, look at the trees and birds, let the hens out, feed the horses with grass and are quite fearless. Margaret's appetite is colossal and Andrew's is better. He is not good with dinners but does well at breakfast and tea and drinks his usual large amount of milk—and very rich milk. They have got used to Charles and Reen and can both say Uncle and Auntie—in fact Andrew's language has developed in a day with a jump. He has also said, "Have tea, hair, eyes, Rosa, hectic, cow, chicken and Bimbo" this week for the first time.

His articulation of old words is improved and he imitates other peoples'. He also copies Reen's finger language to Charles[51]. He is very good with them (in the same way as he is with animals) and is quite conquered by Margaret—wants to 'guy' her. Verity, the vicar's daughter, loves them and comes in nearly every day to play with them. Reen likes them and they have been very good except that Margaret will not use the potty.

It was lovely to have a weekend with E after so long—2 whole nights. It was just as marvellous as ever. He quoted, "omne post coitum triste"—and I said no—not for me. He said, "No, for me—but it is only 1 in a 100 who don't feel so." I said, "It is because we don't often." He said, "Partly, but it is more than that"—and it is. It was so sweet. I was surprised to find my excitement mounting all Friday—the afternoon seemed interminable. Then the thrill of seeing him lean out of the window. In the morning, the twins looked staggered to see him in bed

---

[51] Charles was deaf

with me. Andrew soon smiled but Margaret looked glum for some time. On Sunday morning, they smiled more quickly.

I went to the office on Saturday but caught the 10.32 back! We had wanted to go to Avebury but we couldn't start till after lunch and there wasn't time, so we walked up the canal—an old kind of walk for us. We saw several herons, a kingfisher, moorhens and coots. Lovely flowers—pink and blue cranesbill, water forget-me-nots, a beautiful bog asphodel, comfrey. E climbed a gate to sit in a field for a rest—so did I. We began to love; after a while I felt something touch my face. It was a red ant. We had disturbed a whole colony. We got lots of bites and they were in my hair. We walked back to Woodborough by road and came by train from there. We had done 12 and a half miles. On Sunday morning, Charles took the twins and us up to feed the horses and cows. They were terrified by the car till it moved and then they quietened and they loved the horses. E and I walked up on to Pewsey Hill before lunch. It was lovely but too short. We took Bimbo and saw rabbits and a hare. It was chalk and rich with the familiar flowers—bedstraw, campanula, scabious, harebell, moon daisies, milfoil, birds' trefoil, knapweed. In the afternoon, Charles took Reen, Hobday and the twins out in the pony trap. E and I explored Pewsey church. We had just time to look at the village before tea and it was time for him to catch his train. It was lovely but too short.

Sunday 15th August 1943

A perfect day, sunny with a breeze. This morning I did the beans sitting in the garden with help from the twins. After dinner, Hobday cut sandwiches and filled one thermos with milk and one with tea and we took the twins and Verity by bus through Oare village to the top of the hill and walked along the rim of the chalk ridge. We found a good spot for tea and I left the others there and walked right round the end of the hill—Martinsell Hill—with a Neolithic camp. It is 975 feet, the highest point in Wilts, with a lovely view and a top-of-the-world feeling. We found wild raspberries and I saw magpies and a woodpecker. The sun and the wind were glorious and we all wanted another tea when we got back. Yesterday I went in the opposite direction to have tea with the McGhees at their big country house (shared with the Oades) on Greenham Common—lovely country nearly in Hants; a complete contrast to Wilts—all pines and heather (at its most vivid just now), gorse and blackberries. The only common flower is harebell. Their garden is a dream, though it needs far more work done to it—2 conservatories full of tomatoes, red and yellow, an old brick wall with fruit trees—figs, nectarines, pears, Victoria plums—2 lily ponds, a big semicircular lawn in front of the house, a pine avenue, a big vegetable garden. Mrs McGhee is working full time and runs her half of the house, yet she looks like a sweet pea! Their 2 daughters are at boarding school and 1 son with his grandmother.

Sunday 22nd August 1943

Margot called at Newbury office on Friday morning after walking from Theale on Thursday. She had difficulty in finding a bed and had to come to Newbury. I hadn't been able to get her one in Newbury so she was lucky to get anywhere. She came on to Pewsey with me in the evening. The twins were surprised to find her yesterday morning but very pleased. Nim[52] has been better behaved since. She felt the heat and had an obstinate phase; would not sit on the pot.

I intended to catch the 10.32 back yesterday, having almost cleared up the day before, but McGhee asked me what I thought of Oades—his depression, etc. and how I thought he should treat him. I talked a bit of psychology to him. He said he thought Mr and Mrs O were unsuited and Mrs O was interested in another man (married with 3 children). I was rather concerned because O is nice and has ability but it is going to waste. He is just pouring it away in bitterness, pessimism and hate, projected on to the BIR, Loach, the war etc. I took him out to coffee for a final lecture and told him they should have a baby. He said she wanted one but nothing happened. I gave him Dr Malleson's address. He admitted the truth of my diagnosis and perhaps he will do something. I told him about the twins to prove that everyone has difficulty. I caught the 2.35 and felt quite worn out—the hardest day's work of many hard days since I got to Newbury. A letter from Milner saying Marjorie was having a baby and there is a pile waiting for me at City 6. I am taking one week only mainly because of Hobday.

Saturday 28th August 1943

Back at Addiscombe after an eventful week. The holiday was marred by my carelessness in leaving my handbag containing approx. £14, identity card, my ration book, 2 sweet cards, POSB book, cheque book, numerous snaps, very sharp pencil, purse, cigarette case, etc. in the train, loaded as I was with rucksack, reins and Margaret. Have reported the loss and I searched in the wrong train!

---

[52] Nickname for Margaret, sometimes Nimmy

Have little hope of seeing it again. Luckily 2 ration books, my watch and best flapjack were not in the bag. Well, it can't be helped, though I could kick myself. E met us at Paddington and came all the way. Reen came to Newbury. The twins were good and had nothing to eat or drink except a little milk at Charing Cross when we had tea. They were dry until Lewisham and clean all the way. Margaret was rather frightened of the trains and crowds and Andrew got tired. They had lots of milk and bread and butter when they got back. Though they were good and we got corner seats I feel very tired. We had rather a rush for the train.

We had a pleasant week. The twins were good and Reen thinks I am better managing the twins than Hobday. At least, I discovered a way of getting Margaret to sit on the pot—asking whether she would sit on a little or big potty! She always chose big and did a stream! She continued to do 'bigs' in her knickers except once. Andrew continued very good and with increased appetite. On Monday, Charles took us for a drive in the trap up Pewsey Hill. It was lovely but rained before we got back. The twins liked the rain—Margaret opened her mouth to taste it! On Tuesday we all went for a drive in the trap up Huish Hill and had a picnic at the top. It was a perfect day and the view was superb. Joey, the cob, was fine too. We met a convoy of US Tanks and the hill was steep. On Wednesday, Margot looked after the twins and Reen and Charles took me in the car to Ramsden (Oxon). It was a fine day till the evening when we had 45 minutes' downpour. We went via Marlboro, Swindon, Farmington (where we lunched), Bampton (where we stopped to look at the annual horse fair and Charles nearly bought another), Witney.

Saturday 4th September 1943

When I phoned Paddington last Monday, I was told my handbag had been found! I fetched it in the evening and was impressed with the railway's efficiency. There was nothing missing. I sent the man who found it £1. It was more than I deserved for my carelessness. There was a lot of work waiting. Assessing has been put forward 2 weeks so EA was glad I got back a week early. Hobday came back on Monday morning, quite pleasant after a rather hectic week's holiday. Mr Hobday has gone to Yorkshire for 5 weeks' training before a few more days at home before going abroad. I shan't believe he is going till he has gone. I went to Purley on Wednesday as it was Hobday's birthday on Thursday. E came out last night and was impressed with the twins. Andrew's appetite has fallen off a little but he is lively, talks a lot and is good. Margaret is charming at times, is most anxious to do things to help—washing, washing up, dressing, putting away—but she has a terrific temper and shrieks with rage if she is crossed at all. I believe ignoring her is the best cure and she soon gets over it, but she goes blue in the face and yells instantaneously at the slightest thing. She is getting most interested in drawing and will concentrate on it for 45 minutes Producing small marks with great labour instead of her old free scribble. E and I estimated that Andrew's vocabulary is approximate 100 words now, though he rarely uses 2 together. Margaret loves to hold Sallie's lead, though often gets pulled over. Sallie was on heat and got out while I was away so presumably she will have puppies. I got Oades the new Pelican 'Mathematicians Delight' today.

Saturday 11th September 1943

The great news this week is the surrender of Italy. Hobday and I discovered it at dinner when the 8.00 programme on Mendelssohn was changed to victory music (Beethoven's 5th). Next day we were not keen on work and the flags were out in the city. The immediate profits so far seem to be Taranto, a landing near Naples—a small Italian naval ship has got away without being bombed by the Germans—and the bamboozlement of Germany. We have still a tough job. Still, it brings the end nearer and we have repercussions in the Balkans. I do hope we can get to Greece before the cold weather.

Rosa had visitors today so E came. I think he enjoyed himself. We tried to take the twins to Shirley, but the buses were full so we went to the birch wood and collected acorns. Margaret was dry all day. Andrew not, though he dutifully performed at each opportunity. He has had his hair cut again and has been in good spirits. His vocabulary grows every day and he commonly talks in 2 word sentences and has a few idioms: 'that's all', 'quite sure'. Margaret still says less but articulates better.

A thunderstorm last night included terrific claps. It first woke Margaret, who was frightened. I was standing by the cot to comfort her when I felt a tingling down the back of my right leg; a flash of lightning was followed by the second crash. Margaret was so afraid that I had to keep her in my bed. One evening we went to see baby rabbits and the girl took one out for her to stroke. She showed slight signs of fear and wouldn't touch it, though she smiled when I did. This is the first sign of fear in a furry animal I have seen. Andrew is learning a new building—a castle and a courtyard and is mad on it. He built the bricks into a town—8 wooden blocks on top and nearly as high as himself.

Sunday 12th September 1943

A warmish day. Margot came at 12.30 after dinner. We took the twins and dog to the park. Rosa came to tea on the way back from the studio and then stayed till the twins were out of the bath. Sallie has been off-colour—possibly she is going to have puppies. Margaret was quite concerned and brought her drinking bowl into the dining room and tried to persuade her to eat a bacon rind. They were drawing with Rosa. Andrew liked to watch Rosa draw but Margaret insists on drawing herself. Margot and Rosa noticed a great development in his talking. Also, he has twice asked for the pot. Margaret made a 'bed' from the stool this evening with cushions and chair backs and hankies.

Saturday 18th September 1943

Today has been perfect, but autumn; golden sun, no wind, mist and a chill in the air, though the sun was warm on our backs in the park. On Wednesday night, we had an alert. When Hobday and I heard a bomb drop, we took the twins down to the shelter. It lasted an hour and they were very good—went back to their cots like angels and were not frightened except that Margaret was afraid of the All Clear siren!

The twins are becoming more complex. Margaret imitated my exact posture, drinking my last cup of tea before going for the train, hand on chair, one foot back! She fetches my shoes for me, helps me take off my coat, gets out my powder puff almost before I have finished washing, wants to brush her own, my and Andrew's hair. They ask for particular songs while they drink their cocoa in bed, especially Andrew, who seems to know them better. He is also getting interested in letters—can pick o and a and b etc—as well as numbers (though he doesn't distinguish these). His vocabulary continues to grow—2 or 3 words a day. We had an appeal envelope delivered which Margaret fetched. We discussed it and I said, "Yes, a shilling." She went straight to my case, agitated to have it opened, then took out my bag and handed it to me to take the money out. I gave it to her to put in the envelope. She then put the bag back and shut the case.

A worrying week in Italy; the German propaganda did have an effective comeback on Salerno and Mussolini, but with the joining of the 5th and 6th armies the worst seems over. The capture of Split by the Jugoslavs has not been underlined but seems very significant to me. The Russians continue to advance. Have begun Heard's 'Man the Master'.

Saturday 25th September 1943

Ever since Tuesday morning we have had unclouded sunshine—4 days of perfect sun. The first 2 were cold with keen north wind and frost at night, the last 2 warmer. Last night it poured with rain but today it has been sunny but colder and it has clouded over at times. I felt the sunshine could not hold till today, when Margot and Rosa and I went blackberrying. We picked as many as last time after a disappointing start. Just off the road to Bletchingly we found more than we could stay to pick. Tea in Redhill and I got home at 4.35 to find Hobday gone and E with the twins. They welcomed me uproariously and we had tea; looked at the new ABC book; played Mulberry Bush and Ring o' Ring of Roses; had bath, cocoa and songs. After they were in bed, we had an hour and fucked. It was lovely.

The Russians have retaken Smolensk—reached the Dnieper and are nearly at Kiev—marvellous.

The twins are lovely. They both like the new ABC book, but Andrew more. He is fascinated with the letters. He will go on over and over again pointing to them and saying, "Yes?" Though he knows quite a lot he is as interested in them as in the pictures, if not more. Margaret knows the difference between right way up and upside down. Humpty, upside down, puzzles her among the others. After about 4 perusals, they know all the pictures. They are both getting good at colours. They name red, green, blue, brown, black, but I have never heard them try to say 'yellow'. Margaret is having a spell of passion for Topsy—carries her about saying 'Baby'. She stood with her looking at a picture of an ivory Madonna and child, evidently comparing it with herself and Topsy! She makes most elaborate beds for her—wraps her in a shawl, sits her up to the table, gives her plates and bread etc. E has got Andrew a box of 51 bricks and is giving him a blue dressing gown as well for his birthday.

On Wednesday, I went with Margot and Joan (E)[53] to a lecture at County Hall by EM Forster on English prose between the wars. He was as sensitive and civilised as I expected but livelier, with more vigour and humour than I thought. He talked of atmosphere; the issue of peace and war; the underlying movements—industrialism; the immigration from country to town and the growth of deliberate psychology knowledge. He illustrated mainly from 'Tolerance' and 'Lytton Strachey' and was most suggestive about both: things only Strachey took seriously, truth and human affection. A most enjoyable hour.

---

[53] Friend of Margot's

Saturday 2nd October 1943

Had a day's sick leave yesterday. On Thursday night, for no very clear reason I was sick over and over again till I felt as if someone had left the stopper in and my tummy was just overflowing. About every half hour all night till 5.00 am. I wondered what I had got. There has been a diphtheria case at Ibex House. Yesterday I was very tired and feeble, but steadier, and today I returned to the office, though I couldn't look at wartime lunches. It is at such times that one gets most impatient and fed up with the war.

The twins have had colds in the head but seem to be getting better. All the trouble was probably due to the bitter cold early in the week. It was impossible to work in the office. I lunched with Marjorie Rogers and 5 of the other women on Monday. She was representing us at the women's meeting at the Albert Hall on Wednesday.

E is giving Margaret a doll's bed for her birthday and Hobday has made the bedclothes for it. Andrew knows practically all the letters. Margaret knows those she likes—D and R, for example, but loves to 'read' a book, finding letters and looks at the paper for 'clocks' and shoes and people etc. They still love what Andrew calls the ABC book. He can say the last word of the line of nearly all the nursery rhymes; sometime she sings it in tune and his pronunciation improves. Margaret is still keen on dolls.

This afternoon I met Margot and Rosa, and Rosa took us to see the Bridie play at the Playhouse 'Mr Belfry'—stimulating and inconclusive and moral—A debate on religion and life between the narrow Scots minister, the modern intellectual and the devil, with the devil really having the last word. Most enjoyable. Elsie came at 10.30 last Saturday for the weekend. The twins liked her—even Margaret kissed her good night. It was pleasant to talk at leisure again and she and Rosa enjoyed a talk when Rosa came to tea on Sunday. Heard from ES yesterday. He sent the twins £1 each for their birthday; so sweet of him.

It is 10.00 and our bombers are going out again. Naples fell yesterday and the Russians still go on. I must go to bed with a hottie (although it is mild).

Saturday 9th October 1943

The twins were 2 last Tuesday and they had lots of cards and presents, a party and an iced cake with 2 pink candles for Margaret and 2 white for Andrew. E gave Andrew bricks and Margaret a bed and they each took their presents with complete concentration. A clear sex differentiation: Andrew is skilful at buildings, makes bridges and walls and castles in some variety. He works so hard that he forgets to ask for the pot and is with difficulty persuaded to eat his meals. Rosa made Margaret a new doll, Judy, and she now has a large family, which goes to bed, has meals, goes for walks etc. They had several new books and are both most interested. Yesterday Margaret, having wetted her knickers, took them off and hung them on the guard to dry!

Last Saturday night we had a nasty raid. I was awakened by what I took to be our bombers coming back to Croydon; at 2.00 I heard an explosion and 5 minutes later a longer and louder one; 5 minutes later the warning went. I put Margaret's dressing gown and slippers on and she followed me as I carried Andrew down to the shelter. We were there an hour. It was worse at Purley and we heard that 2 German planes followed our planes in, dropped a bomb on the aerodrome, were chased off and one came down just behind the house in Purley Close. On Wednesday, I went to Purley and we had a short uneventful alert but on Thursday the alert went at 8.45 and didn't finish till 11.00. We had heavy gunfire and planes low and heard several explosions and shrapnel pattering on the roof. It seems to have been noisy nearly everywhere and I heard that bombs fell at Bromley, Beckenham, Sydenham, Highgate and Woodford and Wood Green.

Margot and I took the twins to Streatham to tea last Sunday with Mary Roney and her aunt. We went by bus and tram and Margaret walked all the way up and back from the tram. They were very good. Andrew adored Tinker, the black cat with brown eyes, and Margaret liked a toy Airedale.

Tuesday 12th October 1943

E has tackled K at last and she is considering. It is something. He is so pulled in 2 directions. It is hard for me to be firm. He is on leave next week so I have let him come tomorrow. He said as he was going he felt a fool to get himself into such a position till he remembered that it was alive and the other would have been death and it is better to be 'Alive'.

Saturday 16th October 1943

Milder this week and we have had sunshine the last day or two after dull, damp Novemberish days. Andrew doesn't shake off his cold. Margaret has lost hers. They had both lost weight on Tuesday. Andrew's appetite ought to be bigger. He looks small and fragile still, though he has terrific concentration and mental energy. E invented a game with a marble—a 'run' made of bricks with bridges, and one trickles the marble down to the other. It has caught on finely; they play every night—the first definitely cooperative game. They squeak with laughter. Mrs Bryant brought Andrew a butterfly that flaps its wings and this is popular. He can count up to 6. E was most impressed with this. It seems to be a mental test for 4 years! Mary Roney came on Wednesday and was impressed with him, especially his letters. He asks for the bricks every night. He needs to be more robust, though Margaret is magnificent physically; she has a strong will and it needs ingenuity to avoid tantrums. Hobday hasn't sufficient. I worry rather over her. It would be a pity to spoil her temperament. Andrew's is extraordinarily sweet.

Very busy at the office. With Milner away, the phone is my job and most calls are for him. It is most distracting. HDJ is very friendly and invited me to walk to London Bridge with him yesterday but I was meeting E at Cannon St to take the *Times*. I met him this morning after fire watch too, at 12.05. I have been depressed about K, though she hadn't made up her mind about anything. The twins need him so much. I would do almost anything to give him to them. She is a hopeless case, though, I fear adhesive and clinging and he will not be completely honest with her for fear of hurting her feelings. She has no imagination and no comprehension of what he is losing. And I am quite helpless.

Sunday 17th October 1943

Sallie has had 12 puppies with little apparent discomfort, all alive and squirming, but surprisingly varied in size: 9 black, one cream with black markings, one brown and one dark fawn. So far as one can judge the black Labrador was the father. But it is early—I found her this morning at 8.15 with one and the rest were born during the morning. I gave her warm milk for breakfast, more milk for dinner, bread and milk this afternoon. She cleared it all. The puppies were suckling by midday, squeaking all the time. She licked them incessantly. We let the twins see this afternoon and they were charmed—"baby bow-wows"! Margaret looked puzzled and very careful before her expression indicated approval.

Friday 22nd October 1943

We have had alerts every night this week. Hobday wasn't back on Sunday, so I had to carry both twins down together. They have lasted about an hour and activity begins at the same time or within 5 minutes of the siren. Seem to be very fast fighter bombers; last night only one burst of gunfire but the fighters went up. We heard one bomb which shook the house. I just missed the 8.24 and the 8.43 reached London Bridge at 10.20. I understand that an engine was derailed at Catford—nothing to do with the raid, though the interminable waits and their uncertainty were reminiscent of the blitz. This evening I saw that at Clapham Junction there was a lion on the line, so if it isn't one thing it's another. At lunchtime, HDJ came with me to the studio to see Rosa and her work. He liked the atmosphere and his tea and is contemplating joining for painting. He liked Rosa— "A most attractive woman—magnificent eyes—lovely skin—such vitality." The twins get tired—the disturbed nights are telling on them. Two of the puppies have succumbed but the other 10 are flourishing and seem well nourished.

Saturday 30th October 1943

8.00, and the alert has just gone. Margaret had a bad bilious attack on Thursday night (the first either has had) and ate nothing yesterday except thin bread and butter and no more today. They are both sound asleep and Hobday is away so I hope I shall hear nothing more but the All Clear.

Last Saturday afternoon I went with Rosa and Margot and Auntie Katie to see 'A Month in the Country'. Except for the difficult part of the tutor it seemed to me better acted and produced than as I remember it at the Westminster. A subtle play—we all liked it. Elsie came on Sunday for the day and in the afternoon Hip and Peta[54] came out of the blue. We were just going out and Hip had a cold so I suggested going to the park. It was a lovely day and I wanted Andrew to have all the sun and air available. Margot said I was rude but I wish she would let me know beforehand. Rosa came to tea to see the twins. E came back on Wednesday and has been much concerned about the situation ever since. He hasn't seen the twins for two and a half weeks. I weakened yesterday and said come on Monday but he said he would think it over. Today he said the embargo (not seeing them) is not without its effect on K. I thought I can be strong now if it makes things easier in the future and so he is not coming. It makes me unhappy. They want him, he wants them, I feel a pig and cannot myself enjoy them as I should. They develop. Andrew loves his new bricks, and fits a green triangle against another triangle to make a square. His finger manipulated well. He does this on a bridge without upsetting it. It is much more delicate than Margaret's. "I

---

[54] Former college friend and her small daughter

build a house" and they put the animals, etc. inside and around. She has complicated dolls' play—they have breakfast, are ill, sit on the pot, go to bed and are kissed and sung to. She herself won't settle for the night without Topsy, Daisybell and Teddy. She likes to manage Andrew and will feed him with a spoon. Last Sunday she scraped up the sugar round his dish and gave it to him. Elsie was impressed with this. Andrew was clinging to Hobday on Thursday night after being disturbed and she told him she was cold and tired and he released her at once and lay down.

The All Clear went at 8.35. A short alert, but for 10 minutes we had heavy gunfire and planes. I ran upstairs and heard a bomb whistle before I could get the twins down. I was terrified for them. When I did get them in the shelter, I was shaking all over. It is alarming being single handed.

Monday 8th November 1943

Ella came for the weekend and Hobday got back early last night. Fortunately, as we had an alert at 8.40. We took the twins in the shelter and they slept so we left them undisturbed all night. On Friday, we had an unpleasant 20 minutes. A bomb whistled and swished interminably till it thumped, shook the house, blew the blackout down and caused a cascade of what I thought were bits of ceiling but we didn't identify it. It was a direct hit on a nursing home in Upper Addiscombe Rd, a quarter—half a mile away. Margaret was afraid and cried, "Nanna," but Andrew merely remarked at the end "Bang!" We have had alerts nearly every night. E was late this morning—a time bomb on the line at Malden! Quite like 3 years ago. On Friday, I lunched with Oades who was up to see Dr Seigham about his depression. He had a 2 hours sitting and is to come again with his wife in a month. He told me on the phone that it was maddening to have to pay for advice precisely like the advice I had given him! E came on Saturday after three and a half weeks away from the twins. Andrew was quite ecstatic and Margaret just sat on his knee at every opportunity. He was very much moved by their joy.

Saturday 13th November 1943

4 years ago today Wyndham died.

It has been fine most of the week and not too cold, with bright moonlit nights. We have not had an alert since last Sunday night, but the twins are still sleeping in the lounge to be handy for the shelter, and they can give lifelike imitations of both sirens. I had a day's leave on Tuesday, the last day of Margot's holiday and we took the twins up to St James Park in the morning. We caught the 10.02 from Bingham Rd. They loved the train and Andrew impressed the carriage by reading out the letters of the station names. Margaret was afraid of the traffic at Charing Cross. The noise confused her, I think, but we paused to look at the pigeons in Trafalgar Square and Nelson's lions. Margaret noticed the equestrian Statue of George Washington outside the National Gallery, saying, "Gee-Gee! Man!" When we got into the park it was quieter and both enjoyed walking in the leaves. They loved feeding the ducks and geese and seagulls and sparrows and pigeons with bread, and showed no fear, even when a greedy goose nearly gobbled Margaret's glove off. E joined us at 11.30 and we walked over the bridge around the other side. Andrew did not like the swan, saying, "Go away!" We saw 2 pelicans like rocks by the island but not nearly enough for the twins. We had coffee at a Lyons and E had lunch. The twins had more than half his roll and butter. Margaret liked her lemon juice but Andrew expected milk and wouldn't drink it. We caught the 1.07 back and E came to London Bridge. Andrew went to sleep and didn't awaken till I was carrying him along Bingham Rd, when he opened his eyes and said, "Bill gone!" They rushed excitedly to Hobday to tell her about the expedition, which was most successful.

I was worried about Margot last weekend, but after seeing her on Thursday at Purley I was more hopeful. She went to see Dr Malleson about her periods and got on to general discussion. Dr M was concerned about her 'morbid anxiety', which she thought was motivated unconsciously. I have worried about her. She is a buffer between Rosa and me. She is also much too anxious about the twins and E's relationship with them. She ought to have more freedom and opportunity to meet people, especially men. I wonder whether she spends too much time with me and the twins. But it is difficult to break the attachment with Rosa, now that she is alone. To change her job might help. I got an application form for the register for relief work abroad. Better still would be a Fellowship tenable in the US for a year or two. I was glad to find Rosa not averse from her changing her job. The problem is tied up with the question of E. He had a good deal of discussion with K and said he thought she would 'tacitly' agree to a compromise, and apparently adopted my suggestion of weekends with me and the twins and Monday—Friday with her. It will need a lot of working out—where to live, what name to use, what name for me, who to tell, what furniture to get and so on, and I feel the decision should be implemented as soon as possible. If Rosa would agree, the house at Purley would be ideal and healthy for Andrew, but I fear she wouldn't unless we could marry (if then). I considered all possible alternatives. ES has been transferred to London HO. I wonder about him. But when I saw E and the twins last Saturday and on Tuesday I felt that every possibility of creating a good, full, and honest relationship between them must be tried. They are so clearly bound together. Well, things are slow but not standing still and I feel they are moving in the direction I want.

The Russians are getting near Poland—perhaps the spring will finish Germany. The 5 puppies we have kept are lovely—have cut their teeth and can run about. Their eyes are open. Three are taken—one goes to Mrs Bryant's sister, one to Plymouth, one to Brixton. Andrew is very fond of them and will pick them up very carefully and put them back in the box. They can lap. Margaret knows them all by name. The twins are practising with tea knives, putting butter on bread.

Sunday 21st November 1943

Bitterly cold all the week, with fog to make the weekend worse. Unlucky, as Mr Hobday has been on leave and I fear a hole in the coal has resulted. I find him rather trying, as doubtless he finds me, though he is good hearted. I have left them together as much as possible here or at Kennington. I worked at home yesterday morning and let them go off at 1.00. On Tuesday, E came and they went to the cinema. On Wednesday, I went to a lecture with Margot by Sir Richard Lambton on education. We liked him for his enthusiasm. He made me want to rush off and start an adult education college. His desire to share the good things he has enjoyed with everyone is most attractive. On Thursday, I went to Purley for the night but didn't get here till 9.20 because HDJ had 2 dress circle tickets for 'Lottie Dundas' and couldn't get anyone else so took me. We both enjoyed it—an unusual play of psychological interest. The plot is no more important than the plot in Forster novels. Sybil Thorndike played the mother in low key, with restraint—more impressive. Ann Todd had the difficult part of the young girl—a near genius, near maniac. Enid Bagnold is always interesting and never repeats herself. Yesterday Rosa came for the day, in the fog, and today E came at 10.00 till 4.00 and Margot at 12.45 till 5.00. E had been fire watching. We played with the twins till they went to bed at 11.45 and he said then, "I suppose we've just got time to go to bed too." I was quite surprised. We fucked happily for 20 minutes and then there was a knock—next door! The twins continue to develop. Andrew speaks easily in 3 word sentences and calls himself 'Andrew' and 'Man'. He carefully builds 'floors' of his bricks and rows of 'houses' and plays with Margaret's bed quite a lot. She is distinctly contra-suggestible—uses 'no' and 'not' more than any other words and yet is very imitative. Puts her hands in her pockets (like me), insists on using a knife (like me), turns over the pages of her books, looks at newspapers. She had her first 'writing lesson' last night. I helped her to draw whatever letters she chose. We want them to go to nursery school soon. Croydon has none! ES phoned on Wednesday. He is at City 20 and is coming to dinner on Thursday.

Saturday 27th November 1943

Cold and foggy with sun and north wind this week.

On Thursday, Margot and ES came to dinner. He was sweet with the twins, especially Andrew, who liked him and regarded him as a potential playmate. Margaret was shy for a little but quickly thawed from the vantage of my lap and glowed with excitement when Margot came. The alert went at 7.00 and, though Margaret abandoned the immediate retreat to shelter on being promised 'when the bangs begin' she insisted on going to bed in it until 10 minutes later the All Clear went. It is clear that she feels more secure in it.

ES is relieving at City 20 and is most pessimistic about Pay As You Earn—thinks the whole machine may break down etc. The code will be the size of the London phone book. He said it appeared that the twins were famous throughout the city. A woman TO had heard of them and followed my example with good results! I thought the 8 days' wonder would have died away in 2 years! Last night I took Squeaker to Purley, en route for Brixton today. Eva went off yesterday and Bimbo on Wednesday. We still have Leo and Martin Chuzzlewit as they have long journeys to South Wales and Plymouth. Susan mothered Squeaker charmingly last night and rejoiced to see him. Rosa phoned this morning to say she couldn't come over owing to a cold so E came and had a consecutive period of 6 and a quarter hours with the twins. We played with new bricks, building 2 kinds of marble house, a floor, bridges, towers, looked at picture postcard reproductions of paintings, at books—the big apple book, the little apple book, the big Guidebook and the ABC book—'drew' and 'wrote', played ball. They both had good dinners, ate their Virol, drank milk but ate little with tea. By 7.00, when he went and they were in bed, they were a bit too tired. They are getting subtle; I had looked at a book with Margaret to distract her from upsetting

Andrew's building and then invited her to look at the cards. He wanted to look too and the way she told him to play with Andrew's new bricks made it clear that she had completely grasped why I had shown her the books! Andrew handed a sweet to E when he had one taking his Virol and wanted to give us one. I was taking Margaret upstairs so E said, "When she comes down." I was some time, but Andrew was waiting to give me the sweet. A lovely afternoon, if rather wearing.

Saturday December 4th 1943

Sunny, but a cold wind. I went to the library at 9.00, then to the office, coffee with E, back to dinner with Rosa and the twins. Elsie came at 3.20 and we took the twins to the park and played 'football' so that they ate a good tea. Elsie went at 6.50 and I put them to bed, had supper and a cigarette and now it is quiet and comfy by the fire with Sallie and Chuzzlewit asleep. How swiftly the weeks fly— a sign, I suppose, that I am busy and happy and satisfied. I enjoyed going to Purley on Thursday, playing the piano and seeing Rosa and Margot. I enjoyed having E here last night playing with the twins; and Rosa and Elsie today, and always the short times I have with the twins. Andrew has developed in music. He can play a scale on the bells and finishes with tremendous excitement saying, "Nice!" and he loves the nursery rhyme records. Margaret is relatively unmoved and prefers a book. She is still mainly interested in pictures and letters and can 'read' books. On Wednesday, E and I went to a lecture by Seebohm Rountree on 'Freedom from Want'. We liked him and he was interesting but too short. He had to cut down as he went, but I was rather despondent. Democratic freedom from want requires such a standard of behaviour from everyone—can I rise to it? Can each one of the taxpayers in City 6? Lunched yesterday with ES. He talked more and was concerned about Margot. I wondered whether he had a solution for her. She might do worse.

Saturday 11th December 1943

A too crowded week, so that a peaceful evening is heaven. All sorts of small excitements and rushes, nothing in themselves but cumulative. E came on Tuesday. On Thursday, I lunched with Oades, who was up trying to get a job with the Chamber of Shipping as a research assistant to a man he knew at Cambridge. I had tea with E at Cannon St. Yesterday I lunched with ES and had tea with E again. Margot and Rosa and I intended to go to the Westminster to see

'Ideal Husband' but couldn't get seats so Rosa came to dinner here and then to the cinema with Margot. E came after lunch and stayed till 6.40. It has snowed today and has been both cold and wet so we didn't take the twins out. We all played vigorously and Andrew got too excited, but he is a dear child, most sweet tempered with Margaret who is a tyrant. He is learning the look of numbers now and is puzzled by the 2 in 12. He ate a fine, big dinner, though not much tea this morning. I took Chuzzlewit to East Croydon to send him to Plymouth, but they refused to take him at the weekend. I took him to Paddington and there the difficulties ended, as they took him for the 10.30 and I just sent a wire to say so. I didn't get to the office till 10.30 but haven't much to do at the moment after wrestling with New Sylhet Tea and a pneumatic drill for 2 days.

Sunday 19th December 1943

I worked at home yesterday morning, but it was too wet to walk over the downs to get holly. I met Rosa in Croydon and we bought Margaret some shoes from Rosa and Margot and I went to the library. Today I woke at 8.30 and we had a rush to get through breakfast before Margot came. We dressed in a hurry and caught a train from East Croydon to Charing Cross and took the twins by tube to Oval to spend the morning with Hobday while Margot and I went to the 'do' at the Art School with Rosa and Johnson and Elsie. It was an interesting party for me with criticisms of work by Frank Dobson, Charles Wheeler and Philip Connsard. Beer and sandwiches and cake. Rosa and Margot and I went back to Hobday and at 3.20 we set off home. The twins were thrilled and switched her radio off and on, played with her big doll, looked at herb books etc. They enjoyed the journeys too. Luckily, we stopped on Charing Cross bridge with a fine view of the river, Westminster bridge and its trams, barges and sea gulls. Hobday came back last Sunday with flu and I had to stay at home on Monday. She picked up well after the initial nursing but I got up and got the breakfast each morning till yesterday. On Friday, I lunched with ES. Oades was waiting for me on Wednesday. He has got the job with the Chamber of Shipping if the BIR release him. He is much too hopeful and will come a crash if they don't. Even if he gets the job he will have to leave Mrs O behind till he finds a house. And I doubt the wisdom of this. E came on Friday evening. He had been to Hamleys at lunchtime and had bought 10 Little N***** Boys book (3 and 6d). We spent the whole evening looking at things. They should have a marvellous Christmas. We had a short alert last night. The siren didn't wake the twins, but 'our gun' did. We had to go to the shelter, and to get them to sleep afterwards I had to leave the light on.

1944

From left, Andrew, Margot, Margaret and Rosa at Collingbourne

Andrew at Collingbourne, aged nearly 3 years

Margaret at Collingbourne, aged nearly 3 years

Andrew and Margaret at Collingbourne, aged just 3 years

Andrew and Margaret at Collingbourne, aged 3 years

Saturday 1ˢᵗ January 1944

New Year's Day—first to catch up with the fortnight I have missed. On the Wednesday before Christmas, Margot and I went to the Westminster Theatre to see Wilde's 'Ideal Husband'. Good seats, chocolate, coffee and cigarette in the interval and 3 hours' wit and spectacle. An almost pre-war entertainment except for the rush to get there by 6.00.

E came on Thursday and we both worked hard fitting up the tree. Hobday took the twins into the kitchen to eat oranges while we turned on the lights so that they came in and saw it glimmering in the firelit room. Andrew just danced with pleasure and Margaret climbed on the chair and stared at it. Then E brought in his presents, first the doll's pram. She unwrapped it and Andrew was sweet—almost as thrilled as she, saying, "Nimmy's dolls' pram!" Then his wheelbarrow. "Paper off!" he said at once, and then E gave him rides in it. She has some bricks like his 'new bricks' (so as to leave him in peace with his!) and he had rubber letters and numbers. She at once said, "New Bricks!" They took them all to bed that night. It was sweet—as lovely for us as for them.

I finished Margaret's new yellow frock and knickers for Christmas and Andrew wore his Noah's Ark blue jersey and navy knickers and looked a real boy in them. Margot and Rosa came about 11.30 am on Christmas Day and I took the twins to meet them. When I left the duck had not arrived, though it was sent off on the Tuesday before Christmas, but it came by late parcel post, arriving at 11.40. We had already begun to roast the pork which we had had for the meat ration, but everyone chose duck. Andrew liked it and also liked Christmas pudding. He had a pain in the afternoon! Hobday retired to bed with one of her now rare headaches and had no dinner, though she just finished cooking it. The twins went to bed in the afternoon and slept 2 hours each day so that they stayed up later than usual. Margaret quite enjoyed handing out presents but Andrew preferred to concentrate on what he was doing. Margot and Rosa went home at 6.30 by train but came over again on Sunday at noon.

Margot and I brought the twins by train to Riddlesdown—their first visit to Purley since they were born; also the first time they had been out in the dark. "'Tis dark now," said Andrew, but was quite calm and interested. He found 4 clocks on East Croydon station. Margaret was more agitated and didn't like being put down but she liked the steam train and she noticed the railway bridge we went under. They both loved Rosa's house and were at once quite at home. They liked looking at the trains[55] and also at the chimneys and smoke. Rosa gave them Christmas cards and a basket to play with. When I played the piano on Monday morning, Andrew stayed in the kitchen where Rosa was cooking and sang to himself, but Margaret came in and listened, gradually approaching and finishing by sitting on my lap banging on notes! They slept well and didn't cry once. Margaret didn't awaken but Andrew's feet kept falling off the box ottoman. "Andrew out again," he said quite pleasantly. I hopped out of bed and put them in and he fell asleep at once. We were surprised that they slept so happily in a strange bed. Hobday came to tea and we had nursery rhyme records afterwards before bringing them back by bus.

They made Christmas a festival of joy for us. E came on Tuesday and thought they were looking fine. Andrew can sing the whole of 'Ding Dong Bell' with a fair approximation to the tune and exact reproduction of the words. He jumps well and is physically active, running in circles, swarming on tables, chairs. He can do his 'wees' by himself, pulling his knickers aside and aiming his stream accurately and taking his pot upstairs and emptying it. Margaret tries to do the same but doesn't pull her knickers down! If she does she has to sit down. She begins to appreciate the inconvenience of being a woman!

Lunched with E yesterday before he goes to Nottingham on Monday. The great Christmas news was the sinking of the Scharnhorst—apparently only 36 out of 1400 were saved. Fairly slack at the office for the last 2 weeks. We have had 3 out of 7 clerks away ill this week.

---

[55] The railway to London, and its trains were visible from the Riddlesdown house

Saturday 8th January 1944

It has been a week of unusually fine weather for this period—bright sun, dry, not too cold and not too mild.

The twins have both been lively and full of energy, exploiting their new toys. Margaret loves the blackboard and uses chalk at a great rate. She draws pussycats one on top of another! Adds, deliberately, 2 sets of whiskers, an eye and a tail (and once 2 tails). She can make Q as well as O and I quite independently. Their language develops. These were spontaneous remarks I happen to remember this week: Margaret (in the shelter during raid) "lots of bangs!" repeated 4 or 5 times; "Andrew in funny bed!"; "Nannie shut front door" (this after it had rattled in blast and sounded as if it had been blown open); Andrew, when E arrived and was in the hall, "Bill come in dining room?"; "Andrew have cup of tea in kitchen." He also plays with the 2 meanings of too and two. It seems incredible that they should have learnt so much in 6 months.

Saturday 15th January 1944

E came to dinner last night. It had been a sunny day and the twins had been out all day and so were in good form. Margaret was demonstrating to him and performed finely on the blackboard. She wrote M and m, N, T and S with no help, in addition to I, O and Q. She put, in approximately the right place, a cat's eyes and whiskers, tummy, tail and feet when I had drawn the head and body. She drew the wheels and windows of a train in the right spots. Andrew was engrossed with a tunnel which E brought him. They were in bed by 7.30. Our bombers had been droning for over an hour going to and from Berlin. As we had dinner I noticed the jerky note of a single engine and said, "Sounds like a German"! There was silence and a minute later 2 bombs exploded. The twins cried and had to be picked up. No siren, but they wanted to go in the shelter. I heard this morning that one hit the Davis Cinema in Croydon killing 8 people and one hit Alders, breaking all the glass on North End. This morning there was a thick fog and after going to the library I didn't get to the office till 10.20. I met E at Mansion House and we went to the Leicester Galleries to look at the collection of Sir Michael Sadler. An interesting mixture, mostly French and English. We had macaroni cheese and mince tart and cheese. It was like old times before the twins and I enjoyed it. Then he went home and I went to RHCA meeting, mainly out of consideration for HJ[56] to whom a retiring cheque was

---

[56] History lecturer when Doreen was an undergraduate

given. She seemed the same, but a bit thinner, a bit shrivelled mentally and physically after 17 years. I saw Mary to chat with. I didn't stay to tea. Margot and Rosa were looking after the twins and I got back at 5.20 just before they returned from the birch wood. The twins went to tea at the Vicarage on Wednesday and Hobday said they were very good—did her credit. Andrew is getting more possessive with his toys (i.e. more like Margaret). Her speech is gaining inflexions. She saw me in bed this morning and watched me get up, then announced (like the Shell ads), "Mummy's in bed, was I?" She uses participles often and many prepositions but not A and The.

Saturday 22nd January 1944

Last night's 2 raids (8.15—10.05 and 4.30—6.0) were the heaviest I have experienced since Belfast on 1/5/41. The racket was terrific. The guns were so noisy that it was difficult to be sure of anything else. Here were clearly more Germans than for any raid in the last 2 years—90 according to the Standard. Everyone I saw (from Dulwich, Streatham, City, Purley, Essex) said the same— a racket, but they didn't know of any damage. E was fire watching from the roof and said there were flares and he saw several sporadic fires. We put the twins in the shelter. Margaret was awake but quiet. Andrew slept through the first and enjoyed the noise in the second. "Lot of Bangs!"; "More noise!" he shouted gleefully and demanded that I should sing, "Oh dear, what can the matter be?" It was blowing hard and Hobday didn't sleep much all night. I developed a heavy head cold on Wednesday and, though it is better, getting up in the middle of even a mild night is not good treatment! Drawing with chalk on the blackboard is still the main interest and it has developed Andrew's control specially. They draw the windows, wheels and smoke of an outline train. He draws the sun and she draws chairs and cats. E came on Tuesday. He went off today till Tuesday night to clear Uncle Worcester's estate.

Saturday 29th January 1944

Another evening wasted by a raid. I even missed the news, 8.25—9.50. Being alone I put the twins in the shelter at an early stage. Andrew slept throughout. Margaret cried when I moved her and again when the near guns banged, but she fell asleep quickly. I kept my hand over her ear. The barrage was noisy and nearly continuous so that I couldn't hear anything else clearly except planes now and then. E came back on Wednesday after a very busy weekend in which he sold the Worcester property for £1,800 including furniture. It cost Uncle W £800 exclusive of furniture about 10 years ago. The prospect of my getting a house reasonably seems remote. I went to Purley on Monday as Rosa had a chicken as a birthday treat. Rosa came over today early and cooked the dinner, letting Hobday go off before 11.00 because she is coming back tomorrow to let me go to Purley to see Roy and Marjorie and Peter[57]. I am interested to see him as he is 7 weeks younger than the twins. E came out on Wednesday.

The twins play with letters. I made BED for A, but he preferred SED as fitting together better! His drawing is much improved by the blackboard. Mary came on Thursday. She thinks my weekend compromise might work. I don't know. I could work it, but if E has no confidence in himself I doubt whether it would work, but Mary agrees that a compromise with the twins, e.g., appearing as their uncle, is wrong.

We are to have a beggarly 2 more days this year—making 18 days leave in all. Still, one must be glad of tiny things.

Sunday 6th February 1944

A lovely mild, sunny week until it turned cold in the middle of Thursday night, between 2 air raids. The air had the soft freshness of spring; the tree buds began to swell; crocuses, snowdrops, primroses, scylla, wallflowers are out, but today was bitter cold, tempered by sun.

E came to breakfast and we all went to the park to play 'football'. He went off at noon and the twins slept for an hour before Margot came for the afternoon till 6.00. Yesterday Rosa came to dinner—so did Elsie.

Thursday night's raids were more than a nuisance. I was at Purley for the first, which lasted 40 minutes. Margot phoned when the guns were at their noisiest to say she was at Purley station. I got back easily afterwards. The second alert was from 4.50—6.25 and was noisier and did more damage. My train was off, so I had to queue for a bus to East Croydon in a snowstorm. The line was normal by midday when E came down for the afternoon (since he was fire watching last night). Margot told me 80 people in Paddington were homeless and at least 8 were killed; 3 bombs and a phosphorus time bomb.

Hobday took Margaret to Croydon to have her face sketched last Monday and also to get her a gas mask. "Not likely to need it before March," they said. Andrew continues to be contrary, but it is a necessary stage. Last Sunday I went

---

[57] Roy was Doreen's first cousin, Margery his wife and Peter their son

to Purley in the afternoon and met Roy, Marjorie and their Peter. He is taller than either of them and has very big hands and feet. A fine boy with fair hair, dark eyes and pink colour. He is observant, clean and neat; looks at books but with no comments or clear recognition; he enjoyed the nursery rhyme records but with less concentration and discrimination. His speech is clearly behind theirs—no sentences, and only 6 words (mole, gone, bell, Peter, light). His other sounds are not understood by his mother, so it was not just being strange to him. This is due probably to lack of contemporary society and good example. Marjorie speaks fast with a high tone and Roy has an indistinct burble. I found it most interesting. The welfare nurse came to tea on Wednesday and said their sentences were most advanced, more developed than their articulation of single words. They are inclined to be careless because they talk so much, especially Andrew.

A short raid with one burst of guns at 6.00 this morning.

Saturday 12th February 1944

On Wednesday, E came, though he is still below par after 'flu'. Andrew is better—less contrary and full of zest. He loves his big ABC bricks and combines them skilfully and symmetrically with the smaller coloured blocks to build houses, trains, walls, and bridges. Margaret loves to make cakes and to play babies with her dolls. She sings to herself a great deal. Andrew can almost repeat an 8 line 'poem' Hobday has taught him, but Margaret is better at the actions—Incy Wincy Spider.

The Germans have been attacking the Anzio bridgehead and the Standard today said 'degenerate'. It looks as if something went wrong after a brilliant start and a long period of quiet. Mr Hobday is due on leave on Monday morning for 9 days and Hobday is having 5 days from Tuesday onwards.

Saturday 19th February 1944

Hobday went off for the rest of her last summer holiday on Tuesday morning and comes back on Monday and I have had 5 of my remaining 7 days leave for the year to 29/2/44. She wanted it to spend with Mr Hobday on leave, but it could have been hardly less like a holiday for me.

It has been bitterly cold all the time without a glimmer of sun since Tuesday; dark, grey days with NE winds and icy rain or powdery snow. Moreover, on Wednesday Margaret appeared to have a heavy cold which got worse till E took her temperature last night and found it 102.4. I went for Dr Ross, found he had gone to his surgery the other end of Addiscombe, ran there, spent 15 minutes waiting in a most sinister dark little room and saw him. He promised to come and see her and arrived just before 8.00. He gave her M and B (American, which he said do not upset the tummy) to be given 2 at 8.30, 1 at 12.30, 1 at 4.30, 1 at 8.30! I decided to sleep in the shelter 1) to keep it warm in case they had to be moved into it 2) to be with her. I gave her the 12.30 one and was going to undress when the siren went. The shelter was warm so when I heard guns I transferred them both at once—fortunately, as it was a noisy and nerve wracking hour. Planes flew over quickly and low and seemed more numerous than usual. I was worried, partly because of the risk of carrying her out into the bitter cold with such a temperature, so I was glad to hear the All Clear at 2.00. I left them with me in the shelter till morning and slept little. Margaret was better and even asked for bacon for breakfast. Dr Ross called and confirmed it, though she was to have another M and B. He examined Andrew and said he had the tonsillitis that Margaret had but much more lightly. He need have only 3 M and Bs. They have been a handful, though very sweet on the whole. The difficulty is that they both want to sit on Mummy's lap. Today the problem has been partly solved by their sleeping alternately.

The only good day was Tuesday when I took the twins up to Charing Cross. We lunched with E (the twins would eat only a roll and margarine and chocolate trifle) and then fed the ducks in St James Park. They remembered going last time and were much more sophisticated—selected particular ducks to feed and were not at all nervous of the swan who ousted sea gulls, sparrows, pigeons from prior mention and the new order being ducks, swan etc.

Just to help, the coal is very low and consists of dust and big lumps forming the iron ration, and last night at 11.40 a soldier knocked me up to ask the way to the YMCA. I couldn't tell him but was glad to hear Sallie's bark in the blackout.

Saturday 26th February 1944

A wearing week, bitterly cold with east wind and dull grey skies every day except Thursday when cloudless sun cheered one's spirit if it did little to temper the icy wind.

All the week I have been struggling with a cold which developed last Sunday, no doubt due to the germ which made the twins ill. E too complained of a tight chest on Monday and Tuesday and gave in to the flu on Wednesday. He phoned me on Wednesday but couldn't get through again till this morning. He seems to have been very ill and the Dr comes again on Monday. I had grown rather anxious about him but was relieved to speak to him again. Finally, we have had raids every night this week except last night. The Alerts have lasted an hour— one and a quarter hours with an 'active' period of 30—45 minutes. They have been much heavier than at any time since the 40/41 blitz; numbers of planes flying fast, very determined, have caused quite a lot of damage. We have had bombs and incendiary fairly close—near Ashburton Park and on the garage and houses opposite Addiscombe Station, but everybody has had heavy raids and last weekend the NW suffered badly. There has been the usual crop of bomb stories and rumours—St James Palace damaged, Albert Hall just missed, Gordon's Gin factory burnt, Brands at Clapham burnt, Queens Rd (Thornton Heath) home burnt. These are a few I have heard. People have phoned to make sure we are all right. I was particularly relieved that last night was quiet as Margot was fire watching at Maida Hill. My lowest window pane at the office was smashed by shrapnel. E said that a home just behind him was hit and his windows were the only ones that escaped. His ceilings were damaged and his back door blown in. I have packed a case full of clothes and we have now decided to dress the twins in case of fire.

I have written to Reen to ask her if she can put up Hobday and the twins if things get any hotter. It is awful to see them so soft and vulnerable and unsuspecting. I should go to Purley during the week and see them at weekends. Everyone expects it to get worse this spring. I think it is still mainly propaganda for the benefit of Germans who are having a heavier and heavier blitz from us and the Americans. People are uncertain whether the 'second' front will make it heavier or lighter for London. Rosa came today, the first time for a fortnight, and there were great rejoicings. Her flu cold is better but she still feels it. She has begun cautiously to resume her activities—went to sculpture yesterday for a little while. I went to Purley for the night on Monday as the Hobdays came back in the morning. She was much better for her holiday and had had a good time. They went to Bridport for 3 days and said that people are afraid of rockets there! I went to Purley for dinner on Thursday as usual but Rosa sent me back at 8.15. I got home at 9.50, listened to the news and had a hot bath. I was just finishing dressing when the siren went at 9.45 and we had the heaviest yet raid since we came here. The twins are better, though not allowed out yet, hence we have not been able to get any lemons (we have had 2 given to us, though). Last Sunday afternoon

Margaret burnt her left hand, not badly, but we had to dress it as I am terrified of burns not healing well.

They are getting quite complex with their play. They have elaborate pretend games—feeding the ducks, which includes catching 2 trains, having pennies to buy tickets, collecting crumbs etc; 'going shopping', which involves taking one or other of the dolls in the pram, a handbag, pennies to buy sweeties, coupons and ration books and a latch key. They pick up songs very quickly; Andrew could say the last words of each line at the third repetition of 'Boney was a warrior', which is a favourite of his. The last line of each verse is 'Jean Francois' which he calls 'sandbox', which is his name for the song! They are very anxious to go out now.

Thursday 2nd March 1944

Still bitterly cold, but we have had dry sunny days. The nights were quiet till Tuesday night when we had a short burst of gunfire, an incredibly light raid. Last night, however, the siren went at 2.45 and we shuddered out of our warm beds. There were fewer planes than in the little blitz but a huge lump of shrapnel came down on the roof and we heard what sounded like a fire bomb. We could see fires glowing in the North West. The electricity was off for about 10 minutes. Margot was not fire watching at Purley but she phoned me this morning to say that the whistles blew quite feebly and pathetically and she went out to find a canister of incendiaries had fallen on the road. The Benbows had one through their roof, bedroom floor and hall floor just beside the Morrison, the Oxborrows had one through the roof, another set a garage alight; numbers fell in the road and in gardens. Margot said they weren't the explosive sort and though throwing a bucket of water on them made them fizz they soon went out. She lost their bucket but acquired a bigger one. She reported that costumes were very amusing—she wore a dressing gown, woollen hood and tin hat, Mr Benbow dressing gown and tin hat, Mrs Benbow fur coat and fur cape! Milner says what worries him is the way the planes lose height and seem to be steadily crashing on his roof!

Saturday 4th March 1944

No warmer in spite of brilliant sunshine and the wind NW instead of East. Today has been colder still and it was a relief to come indoors from the cutting wind. E had difficulty in phoning me at the beginning of the week—apparently an exchange was hit—but he has managed to get through every day. He is recovering from his flu very slowly and going out makes him worse. He managed to get over to see the twins yesterday for one and a quarter hours but he said today that his cough was very bad last night. We have had 3 quiet nights due, most people say, to the bright moonlit nights.

I went to the studio yesterday at lunchtime to see Rosa and her work and she said Reen had phoned to say she knew of a cottage and if I was interested I should phone her at once. When I got back, there was a letter written earlier saying the twins could come to her if the blitz gets bad. I spoke to her after an hour's delay waiting for the trunk call. The cottage for sale is semi-detached at Uffington on the Berkshire downs, with a good garden, in good repair except that it may need redecoration, has water laid on but no sanitation; electricity connected or available; 2 miles from the station on the main Didcot Swindon line and 4 miles from Wantage; *£200 freehold* I think. It sounds too good to be true. Hobday is quite thrilled and wants to keep chickens but draws the line at a goat. She wants to give up her flat and use the furniture to avoid storing it. This would suit me as I should need to get hold only of the remainder of equipment necessary. I could go down at weekends and possibly do 3 or 6 weeks farm relief at Swindon this summer. Reen said it was a good size and quite picturesque and Massingham says Uffington is one of the Berkshire villages influenced by the Cotswolds so it may be stone. With the summer ahead and the possibility of more blitz, it is attractive. Unless it is hopelessly decrepit or remote at that price one could hardly lose on it if one wanted to sell in 6 or 18 months. It is in Down country which I love, and just under the loveliest of the white horses and a fine camp, which I have long wanted to see. The twins flourish in chalk country and I should like them to grow up in such surroundings with the evidence of our long past around them. Reen is sending more details and I hope to see it next week. I have a superstitious feeling that if it continues to fall into my lap like this it is the right thing to do. Rosa is quite thrilled, though she carefully refrains from exerting any influence. Charles has the disposal of it and the furniture of the old lady who occupied it who moves out next week. I should miss the twins during the week (when I should live at Purley) but most Saturdays I could probably work at home and go down on Friday night and in the summer, anyway, come up on Monday morning. And if they are safe and in a healthier environment the advantages will probably outweigh the loss.

Saturday 11th March 1944

I intended to go with Rosa to look at the Berkshire cottage today but Reen wired yesterday to say, "Cannot recommend." I had a letter today saying it was in bad repair. I am still tempted to see it, however, before deciding finally against it. It depends whether one could get work done and how much it would cost. It needs a damp course and re-thatching at least, but it is freehold and detached with good garden and I am very drawn to the locality—375 feet up and near Uffington camp. E is still feeble from flu, though he came back on Monday. He wanted to come out today but Rosa and Margot came and he may come tomorrow, but is fire watching. He saw Mary yesterday and signed a codicil to his will leaving £1000 in trust for the twins if K survives him more than 3 months and £3000 if she doesn't. He is rather anxious about them when the 'second front' begins as he expects heavy air raids. He is not unfavourable to the cottage even now.

The twins are much better and Andrew, especially, is full of beans. Going out is stimulating his appetite and he has done very well this week. Margaret is having a difficult patch—clinging, querulous and self-willed. It is reaction of her illness and the effect of the raids. She is not sleeping well. Fortunately this week has been quiet except for a short alert on Wednesday when they didn't wake up.

I have finished a white wool and rayon frock with red smocking and buttons for Margaret, and she approves of it. She examined it carefully and observed that there were 4 red buttons on it, with approval! They love apples but will only eat oranges in the form of orange juice, and eggs in the form of dried eggs! They play elaborate pretend games with the dolls and Margaret loves to make cakes, covering them with a paper, putting them in the oven, trying them to see if they are cooked etc. Another fantasy is going to the office with case, train ticket, gasmask etc.

I have finished 'War and Peace'. It is magnificent in its breadth, normality and sanity and apparent simplicity. His most abnormal characters are more normal than Dostoevsky's most normal, but he doesn't penetrate the crannies and gulfs of the human mind. The one incredible thing, I found, was the later glimpse of Natasha who became rather a shrew, completely domesticated and a tyrant over her Pierre and the children. Why did he do this?

Sunday 19th March 1944

E and I were lucky not to have rain yesterday when we went to look at the cottage at Westcott but, though the sun shone at times it was not a genial day. We were 10 minutes late from Paddington and E shook his head despondently. The delay was due to a crescent bomb hole on the line which men were busily filling up. Apparently the signal system has been damaged as we were 45 minutes late back, though only 3 minutes late at Didcot. The delay was almost all from Westbourne Park to Paddington and we saw a burnt out train. We set out to walk to Sparsholt. It was a level walk along a quiet road towards the downs. E was disappointed in the almost dried up canal, and spring had not begun, but the birds were lovely. Sparsholt was a cosy village in a hollow with trees to soften the hills and a lot of thatch; 2 pubs, both clean and attractive, one shop and a good looking church. Westcott was half a mile further and 50–75 feet higher and was a hamlet of 6 cottages and a couple of farms. We found Mrs Wiltshore's cottage and confirmed it from the old soul next door. Not too bad repair, though the stone wall was cracked, the timbers of the roof not good and the thatch whole but old. It stood sideways to the road. It would have made a good weekend cottage in peacetime, but apart from its small size and the need for a good deal of work to be done on it, I felt it was too isolated and inconvenient for the twins and Hobday permanently. After a hurried discussion, we decided against the cottage and went by bus to Wantage, eating our picnic lunch on the way. We had 2 hours in Wantage where we revived 9 year's memories of the King Alfred's Head. The café where we had coffee on Whit Monday 1935 still advertised, but would not give us tea.

I left home at 7.40 and got back at 8.30 and the only bite I had was what I took with me. At Victoria, we had 20 minutes to wait and tried to get a cup of tea. At one buffet, one could get nothing but spirits and at the other beer or spirits. Why encourage people to drink? My head ached and my tummy felt hollow. I haven't felt so tired for ages and was particularly glad to have a quiet night. We had seats on buses and trains all the way except in the packed train from Didcot to Reading. To re-visit Wantage with its memories; to see Harwell again, and the chain of downs made 9 years slip away—yet not entirely; we looked at everything through the twins' eyes—Andrew could not sail a boat on this canal, said E—how they would love the ducks on the stream in Wantage, I thought. E came to see them this morning and they were in great form.

Saturday 25th March 1944

For the moment, all is peace. The loudest noise is the soft roar of the fire and the tick of the clock, and today the sun has been warmer after a slight frost so that I went out without gloves. A drowsy warmth, pricked by the song of birds, so last night's raid seems like some hideous hallucination. It was the worst I have experienced since the 4th May 1941 in Belfast—45 minutes' inferno with hardly 30 seconds lull. The guns were deafening but one is comforted by their protection. What made my stomach contract and my mouth dry was the swish and roar of the bombs and the sickening pause as one asked oneself—Where? And the crackle and clatter of the smaller missiles flying through the dark—was that a big fragment of shell or an incendiary?

Yet Andrew slept peacefully except when I crouched too low over his soft, appallingly vulnerable body and he protested. Margaret, in Hobday's arms, was awake but quiet and good and apparently calm. We said little and tried to control our fear. There was warning at about 11.00, after I had gone to bed, intending to leave the Hobdays (he was here on 36 hours leave) in peace. About 11.25 we heard what we took to be the All Clear and almost immediate gunfire. By 11.45, planes were over. By 12.30, it was virtually finished. Andrew woke up and had 6 cups of tea (small) and 2 biscuits. Margaret did almost as well and we went to bed. But it was nearly 4.00 before I was asleep and I awoke at 6.30 with a smell of burning oil in the room. We heard today there were 3 fires near us. We found a rug at the gate which we delivered to its owner today and a phosphorus bomb by the phone exchange. I was surprised that my train was more punctual than usual but Margot told me that the main line was hit between S and E Croydon. It seems to have been worse at Purley than at Addiscombe; many fires, far more activity during the raid. Rosa was very shaken when she came over for the afternoon. They were not hit but windows and floors blown open as were ours, and on Wednesday Rosa was alone because Margot was fire watching.

I saw E this morning and he agreed that the time had come to send the twins away. I phoned Reen (getting through in 35 minutes) and asked her if she could have us. We are to go tomorrow evening so I trust and hope we shall have a quiet night. I got the tickets today. The phone was indistinct but Reen said something about another possible cottage in the Hungerford direction. If so that would be fine and Rosa could go down till this uncertain spell is over. E said St Dunstans, Fleet St was destroyed but nothing much in the City. Milner said there were heaps of fires in Norwood, Tulse Hill and Streatham and Stringer of Dulwich didn't turn up. Today has been like a dream. I have been most inefficient, ending with cutting the top of my thumb! Elsie came on Wednesday for the night. I went to the London Centre meeting on Thursday. 400 people will be affected by the offer on the higher posts claim, but nothing more is known now. Mitchell put forward a resolution for the AGM for equal pay, making a witty little speech.

A queer thing happened yesterday. I had arranged to spend the night at Purley, to leave the Hobdays quite free. I even bought a paper for Rosa, but all through a harassed afternoon (2 cancelled cheques and an interview on Modiano) I felt oppressed with a mounting feeling of disaster. By dinner time, I said to Hobday, "It's no good, I'm sorry but I can't leave the twins tonight." A kind of leaden weight, insisting that I stay; no rhyme or reason and I even told myself it was superstition (having just read Phoebe Payne and Laurence Bendit and the psychic sense), but a conviction which I have never known wrong. It is seldom that I get it, but it cannot be gainsaid—a knowledge that seems direct as reasoned conclusions never are, and which leaves me no choice but to act on it. I wouldn't have been away from the twins last night for anything. Well, well. What is it?

Wednesday 29th March 1944

I am so tired. On Sunday, Hobday and I flew round packing and clearing up. Margot came at noon and we took the twins to the park for 30 minutes in the sunshine and saw a sulphur butterfly and 2 wagtails. E came to meet us and we went back to a hasty lunch. The car came at 2.00 and we took the cot, 2 cases, rucksack, wheelbarrow loaded with bricks and a box of rations to Addiscombe Station. It was a blazing afternoon, the hottest for the year and the beginning of 'Salute the Air' week so there were crowds everywhere. A woman porter coped with the cot and got us a taxi for Paddington. We went through Green Park and Hyde Park and the twins loved it. At Paddington, Andrew fell asleep and slept nearly till Reading. Margaret didn't sleep at all. E saw us off and we sank down, thankful that there was no change. We reached Pewsey punctually and Charles met us with the car. Reen awaited us and the twins were anxious for their supper. They seemed to remember the house. Charles and Reen had acquired 4 guinea fowls which made a small sawing noise of alarm. Rooks were building in the trees. Monday morning was perfect and Charles took me in the car to look at a bungalow at Collingbourne Ducis, a lovely thatched village in a shallow depression of the downs. Hideous, made of corrugated iron on a brick foundation lined with wood, with asbestos roof. They are fixing electricity and there is a lovely garden, big, a good shape and well cultivated with currant and gooseberry bushes, raspberry canes, apple trees and roses. The snag is water; the village is the first scheduled for a scheme in the area and the farmer promised to supply me. I offered him £275 freehold. He asked £300. I said £300 if he would put in the electricity, 4 lights and 2 power points. He agreed, so in 30 minutes I had seen the bungalow and bought it. I caught the 10.47 back from Savernake and had 35 minutes to wait (actually it proved to be an hour) at Newbury, so I had a coffee and then popped in to see McGhee and Oades. McGhee has got a move to Newport (Mon) assisting. He is fed up as it seems ominous.

Saturday 8th April 1944

I have had hardly a minute. Nearly every evening to Addiscombe to pack up and clear up, except twice; once when Oades came to see me last Monday and stayed till 5.30. He had been to Sardinia and gathered that the Ministry of Labour would not oppose his going to the Chamber of Shipping and the BIR released him. Big shipping people have seen Ritson and Loach and think he will be released. He was very thrilled—too thrilled—the new job can't be as good as he expects.

Last weekend I came down on the 12.30 on Saturday and returned by the 6.30 pm on Sunday. It seemed ages since I had seen the twins. Andrew had quite settled but Margaret was still very clinging. I came down on the 6.00 last night and learnt that she had been very querulous all the week; either the raids have affected her nerves more than appeared or she is missing me or is just feeling insecure owing to her routine being upset. This morning Hobday went off by the 8.00 train and returns by the 6.00. On Monday, I took the twins up to help Charles fence a field and it was chilly and fresh. Margaret tripped over the wire and scratched her leg. She was cold and cried a bit. Apart from this she has behaved perfectly since I arrived. E may come on Monday so I hope Charles will be out as they don't get on well together. Pickford want £24, £10 to move our small amount of furniture to Collingbourne. Electricity is being laid on next week, I hope. Last weekend I bought, second hand: 2 chests of drawers, one blanket and a kitchen cabinet, and a new small oil stove. Nothing else is really indispensable. The twins look fine and the air clearly suit's Andrew whose appetite is much improved. He needs no persuading to eat. They play elaborate air raid pretend games with the dolls and bears. They love the garden and the animals. Andrew gave me a long and correct account of seeing Brittania and Juno[58] yesterday. He has got quite used to the car and likes to ride. Margaret doesn't mind planes or guns in the day but is nervous of both at night. Andrew doesn't mind them at all. They both enjoy the great amount of military traffic and call out each type— 'Tank', 'Little tank', 'big tank', 'jeep', 'lorry', etc. Charles says the invasion is due to begin tomorrow (Easter Sunday). Today, after a chilly grey start, the sun has been lovely; perfect Easter weather.

Monday 17th April 1944

At last, we have had a real downpour and it descended on me in my best coat, walking from Savernake to Collingbourne on Saturday. Hobday had written to say she was going over there and would I come direct and picnic there? It was inconvenient as there was no bus till 4.17 so I walked from Savernake to Collingbourne Kingston where the bus overtook me, and when I reached Twinpath[59] no one was there. I phoned Hobday and learnt that Margaret had a tummy upset and so couldn't come. I was glad Hobday hadn't ventured, as to get soaked might have made Margaret really ill. Still, it was dismal and there was nothing to do but to get a bus to Marlboro' and from there to Pewsey— 16 miles to go! The buckle came off my shoe just to add to my troubles. On the road, before the rain, I had had a surprising encounter. An American soldier on a motor bike passed me and asked if it was the Tidworth road. I said 'yes' and he went on slowly; then, after a quarter of a mile, he came back, asked me where I was walking and with little more preliminary said, "Would you take a pound?" I said, "What for?" before guessing what he meant and saying I didn't do that kind of thing. He was quite a nice boy, naïve and childish. He reminded me of Andrew asking me to build a tower. I told him I was down to see my children and I was old enough to be his mother. He said, "That doesn't stop other girls, and I had a young face and he liked my walk and he wanted to know me; how much would I take?" It would only take 5 minutes, the other side of the hedge. I said, "No, he wouldn't like his wife to do it when he was married." He said he wouldn't mind if he didn't know. He didn't see any harm in it if you stopped at 2 or 3. A nice lad! What is the solution of the problem? I felt I hadn't been a bit adequate. Still, I didn't feel any fear at all.

---

[58] Horses of Charles

[59] The name of the bungalow, just purchased

Margaret was better, but not eating, and they both gave me a great welcome. It was lovely to see them. They had been talking about Easter Monday all the week. E came down for the day and we all went by train to Savernake—Smoke train, and by bus to Collingbourne, for him to see the cottage. They loved it, and were most demonstrative to him. On Easter Sunday, I took them to church, having taken them to see it the day before; pointed out the flowers and the pretty window etc. They behaved very well, Margaret with complete and grave assurance. Andrew had to be picked up and made his few remarks in a clear high treble. Margaret got left saying Amen once and finally wanted to wee. They stayed for a prayer and 2 hymns. I took them for a little walk so as to avoid Charles afterwards and I saw 2 swallows. The twins picked dandelions and admired the butterflies. When we got back, Andrew arranged the dandelions along Reen's kitchen sill, which puzzled me till I realised he was imitating the Easter decoration in church.

Monday 24th April 1944

So tired, but I must jot! We had 2 alerts last week, the first on Tuesday at 1.00. We had hardly got up when things began to happen; a bang vibrated right through my head and later we learnt that a landmine had landed just by the sorting office opposite the Royal Oak. It broke windows for a long way and blew our French windows open. The second was small but we could see a fire just over the golf links. Damage was done at Edmonton where Middlesex was hit.

I phoned Pickfords on Wednesday, in desperation about the furniture, saying I had to be out of 12 Baring Rd by the 27th. The girl was quite indefinite but first thing on Thursday they phoned and said Monday morning. This morning 4 men and the container arrived at 8.30. I had to scurry round and just reached Addiscombe before they did. I had arranged to have half a day's leave and got the gas and electricity men to come and disconnect. I couldn't sell the shelter so I got the ARP[60] to take it to the depot. The man said he had delivered 8,300 in Croydon and they had saved countless lives. I called on Gladwell and arranged with him to surrender the key and just caught the 12.02 from Bingham Rd to lunch with E. This evening we had tea and caught the 5.24 to put the house straight; carpet down and furniture distributed; no wonder I am tired; on the way back I called on Mrs Bryant to ask her to clean up on Wednesday.

---

[60] Air Raid Precautions

I went to Andover on Saturday and on to Collingbourne. Hobday had phoned me to say that Reen wanted them to go as soon as possible and Hobday was very upset. I was rather worried. She seemed fed up and grumbled about the cottage as well. The weekend was less strained than I expected. Reen said Hobday announced that Mr Hobday was coming for the night and she assumed (probably rightly) that Hobday meant coming to the Knoll. Reen said, No, Charles would not have it. Hobday was certainly taking a lot for granted. Reen said she was sulky all day. I said as little as possible except that, having second front complications, they ought to be out in a few days. Obviously Hobday is getting on Reen's nerves—she hasn't much insight, couldn't stand her all day every day. As it was Mr Hobday spent the night at YMCA—went over to Collingbourne with Hobday and the twins on Saturday, where he did some odd jobs. The garden was looking lovely—saxifrage just coming out. Apparently old Mr Brown was a gardener till he retired and the garden was one of the village sights.

The twins were in fine spirits, Margaret quite recovered. They have grown fond of Reen and stayed alone with her twice. Margaret a little nervous of Bimbo[61]. He is large. Andrew likes him even when Bimbo knocks him over. He is said to have gained over 2lbs in 4 weeks. We went up Martinsell Hill yesterday and picked cowslips and violets to send Rosa. The traffic, mostly lorries of English airborne troops, were continuous all day. Hitherto I had seen all Americans except a few RAF. The train was punctual and I got a seat all the way, though there were people standing.

I saw Jane Eyre (film) at the Regal on Thursday—shorter than I expected. I liked the casting and some of the settings but one loses any continuity. The early experiences at Lowood were good. On the whole, I was less impressed than I expected from Orson Welles.

Monday 1st May 1944

Last Wednesday we had 2 alerts when we got up and went to the shelter for 30 minutes. When we went back to bed, we heard a nightingale, not full song, but by the second alert it had grown richer.

I went to Collingbourne on Saturday alone, having had a wire from Hobday on Friday that the furniture had not come. I was very pleased to find electricity had been installed—4 lights and a power point, the cooker fixed—a fine, grey original unused cooker. After15 minutes I heard a man at the gate asking if Bates

---

[61] A labrador

was the name. It was the furniture turned up with no warning, from Amesbury, of all places. The 2 men were pleasant and helpful and thankful to have found me in. They put down the carpets and lino and put the furniture in place. There was great excitement when the toys were unpacked. We had tea all together off Granny's old mahogany table, bought 60 years ago. We had just begun to walk to Savernake Station when 3 men in a car offered us a lift. One took Margaret on his knee, and except for drooping the corners of her mouth twice, she behaved perfectly. She was looking perfect with a bloom of sunburn giving her colour a softness and a happy expression. She has quite settled down and likes the country. She told me of cows and sheep and lambs and horses and 2 baby birds—the rooks she could see. Andrew was rather overtired and more querulous than usual.

We went over yesterday to get tidy. It was a perfect day and the garden was looking lovely. Hobday and the twins had to go back to Pewsey as they were moving on Nicholl's lorry today. I put them on the 5.25 bus and caught the 6.09 from Collingbourne to Andover. I sat on Andover station waiting for the 7.42. It arrived at 10.38 at Waterloo. I stood with a crowd of other people in the guard's van—80% were army men. The train was packed. There was no10.53 so I had to wait for the 11.25 to Purley. I got in at 12.23 completely worn out.

On Saturday morning, EA was working at home and I opened the Head Office post. It included a confidential instruction on fire watching—all relaxations withdrawn—all incendiaries must be tackled at once wherever they fall. It is expected that they will be dropped as an indicator for a later concentrated attack.

I saw the house agent on Thursday and agreed the inventory. Almost all is intact apart from china breakages but I may have an argument. I was too tired and worked up to cope with the pram so E put an advert in the *Nursery Times*, £21, and it is in Addiscombe Station cloakroom.

On Thursday, my birthday, we went to see Madame Curie, a film based on Eve Curie's life of her mother. We enjoyed it and thought it good apart from a few sentimental touches. The French background is well sketched and the film really gives some picture of scientific drudgery and the thrill of discovery. Quite well cast with Greer Garson as Marie Curie.

There is too much material just now—I just can't get it down. I have said nothing of the satisfying feeling of owning a house, even a tiny one, and very little of the beauty of the country—the charm of goldfinches, for instance, that I saw from the bus and the misty, vivid green of the shooting flax.

Monday 8th May 1944

A lovely thing to open a new book. At lunch last week, we were talking about scientific eugenics and artificial insemination and E remarked, in parenthesis, "The supreme experience of life is to see one's children." And so it is.

A lovely weekend is gone. The twins are looking fine—good colour, good appetite, abounding in energy. I have a series of pictures—Margaret squatting down in the sunshine in blue sunbonnet and yellow woolly frock, a bunch of dandelions in one hand, gently touching the saxifrage flowers; Andrew running up the side path after putting weeds on the pile, stopping to look through the gap in the current bush row to call Rosa, "Hello Rosa!" and roar with laughter; Margaret sitting on Margot's lap, her arms round her neck, rocking to and fro, in an ecstasy of affection; Andrew skilfully walking front ways down a very steep slope, tottering but regaining balance two thirds of the way down, and then running the remaining third and turning round at the bottom, smiling at us in triumph; Andrew in bed with Rosa and me in the morning, singing 4 verses of 'Now the day is over' without a mistake in words or tune!

On Sat, Rosa and Margot had come down to Collingbourne. They loved the garden and liked the cottage. Hobday had got marvellously settled. The only snag seems to be the shortage of water. Margot took us all to Marlborough to tea at the Merlin and then she and I came back from Savernake. The train was packed and we had to stand. About Aldermaston I felt very queer—a cold stone in the tummy, giddy and weak at the knees. At Maidenhead, a man gave me his seat and a woman some smelling salts. I don't know whether it was just feebleness after my cold which hangs on indefinitely, or a touch of sunstroke. The sun was brilliant all day though it was bitterly cold at night. There was ice on the milk and a hard frost. The weekend did Rosa good. The air suited her and she got ravenous.

I have had 2 replies to the pram advert, one from Leicester, one from Ramsgate, so I hope it will be soon disposed of.

Monday 15th May 1944

Last week we had our first heat wave. It was warm even in the morning and the trains were like ovens in the evening. I set off on Sat morning in tweed costume and cotton blouse feeling I was over-cautious. When I came back last night, a bitter NE wind was blowing through me; it was piercing waiting 50 minutes in the sun on Savernake Station; today the central heating ban was taken off; we are sitting crouched over the fire.

I sent the pram off last week to Leicester but haven't had the cheque yet. I polished it up in the ambulance room at Addiscombe. It depressed me intensely to go to Bingham Rd. station. Every inch reminds me of the twins. The boy wouldn't accept it in the evening so I had to get up early to catch the 7.49 and get it off in the morning. The girl clerk said he was hopeless—he could quite easily have accepted it. I was glad to see the last of it. On Friday, I bought an immersion water heater and a small electric fire. The train arrived 15 minutes late on Sat and the twins were waiting on the station. They looked fine, though Andrew had been 'naughty'. He was so excited he left Pink Bear on the seat. They were sleeping in the new bed to give them more room. Andrew loved it but Margaret seemed to miss his close proximity and lay awake a long time when I went to bed. I took Sally as far as The Shears at dusk. She loves the country smells—just stood still in the grass under the hedge wagging her tail. The woman next door is letting us have a pail of water from their well every day. In the afternoon, the sun came out and we gardened. Andrew stung his leg on a nettle and was already tired. So I sat him on my lap and he just relaxed for half an hour. I sang to him his favourites—'Now the day is over', 'To be a pilgrim', 'The water is wide', 'I will give my love an apple'. Lovely. Margaret sat on the stool beside me and said, "Andrew going to sleep?" and watched the gambols of the horses opposite with great amusement. They came in my bed in the morning and we looked at books. It is odd how they each see different things in the same picture. Margaret liked my cotton frock with flower pattern. Andrew liked my check blouse (graph paper pattern) and remarked, "Windows."

Lunched with ES today. He looked fatter but is still very languid and not interested in anything. Had tea with E.

Tuesday 23rd May 1944

It remained bitterly cold all last week and the ban on heating is only being re-imposed tomorrow. When I went to Collingbourne at the weekend, I found a third of the gooseberries and half of the currants spoilt. Lupins and peonies still in bud as a week earlier. E went down last Wednesday to see the twins and was rather concerned at the smallness of the cottage—"No elegance is possible," he said—and the way their toys are getting dusty in the play-room. They were most demonstrative to him and clearly quite overwhelmed him. I felt rather depressed towards the end of the week. I can't help being anxious about the twins when I don't see them, although when I do see them I realise it is foolish and that they are quite alright, and anyway it is useless to worry. They are much better off for the next few months away from London. E heard of an RAF man, now a night fighter over London, who insists that his mother stays in Wales for the present, being sure we shall have a bad time.

Wednesday 31st May 1944

Whitsun over and no invasion. E didn't risk coming to Collingbourne in case he couldn't get back. I went on Friday and had an easy and comfy journey. Margot and Rosa came down on the 4.00 on Sunday and had seats and a good journey except for the heat wave. Rosa and I went back yesterday and got in just after 11.00. As I closed the door E phoned but I couldn't say much as Rosa was at my heels. We had a sudden heat wave so that all the gardening I did was to cut three long edges' grass in 4 days. Monday was the worst as it was so heavy. All we could do was to sit still in the garden. I didn't go outside the gate till yesterday when Margot and I walked about 4 miles over the downs. It was lovely—on top of the world and we saw a wild rose bush in flower. The wind over the green corn was exquisite and although it was hot it was fresh.

The twins were lovely. They have new pretend games. He calls the skittles 'milks' and plays being milkman delivering 'milks' and collecting bottles. She has washing, sews and irons etc. They both still make 'cakes' and 'pudding pies'. They come into my bed after morning tea and cuddle and look at books—'The Pink Book' (de la Mare), the Puffin Insect Book and Ship Book this weekend. Andrew can now give a detailed account of what he has done—e.g., Rosa and Margot and I took him for a short walk along the road and up a cart track to the gate onto the downs. He told Nannie and Margaret all about it on our return and enjoyed the walk very much—'up big hill'. He is very venturesome and runs up and down slopes recklessly. He climbs over the arm of the garden chairs and sofa. Rosa thought his head had grown a lot and changed in shape. It looks higher at the back and his forehead seems higher; but it may be the way his hair is cut. E thought when he went down a fortnight ago that his hair had grown coarser, but the hairdresser said he would never have a good 'head of hair'—but of course it was a beautiful colour. He likes to wrap his toys up in parcels—he stole *The*

Sunday Times to wrap up the dolls' bedclothes. He begins to show off doing his 'wee's' and has in the last week developed a queer kind of showing off—he groans and will not eat or speak—just to attract attention. He did this several times, though not for long. One soon hears his ringing peal of laughter again when Margaret says something nonsensical like, "Rats!" which amuses him. They have several nonsense words with a hidden meaning they both share and both roar with laughter as they shout them to each other—a kind of play with sounds. It is lovely to see him 'helping' again after his enforced inactivity at Reen's. He participates in the washing up, peeling potatoes etc. His final remark after washing up yesterday: "Andrew can empty tray, Andrew big boy now," and he did drain the tray and stand it up. He can practically undress himself and struggles manfully to put his sandals on and take them off. Margaret doesn't bother about dressing, though she likes to brush and comb her hair and they both love to wash—washing hands is great fun before meals and after and on Sunday they had a bowl of soapy water in the garden and played with spoons and strainers and bubbles for a long time.

Monday 5th June 1944

A red-letter weekend! E came down to Collingbourne and we had a lovely, lovely fuck! I had gone to sleep thinking of him on Thurs and Friday but hardly daring to anticipate—things are so precarious—so much might interfere from K falling ill to the train being taken off or the invasion beginning. But no! I caught the 5.58 from Balcombe, where Rosa and I had gone to spend the afternoon with Johnson, and the 7.35 to Andover. The connection only went to Ludgershall and I had three miles to walk home. I was just collecting my memory of the route when there he was waiting for me round a corner with a wild rose in his buttonhole. The walk was lovely with a lurid windy sunset. We got in at 10.30. Hobday had got me a salad with egg and tomato and a blancmange and cream. At 11.00, there were bangs and we looked out to see flares. I wondered if it was a real raid as there is no local siren till I saw a plane with its lights on. We went to bed, the twins being asleep, and E took off my vest and we loved till nearly two, mainly by E's careful management (though through my fault we missed the final climax). How to indicate the sweetness—the lovely rhythm of feeling rising and falling! E tried new things—he told me in a whisper a verse he had made on 'Now the day is over'—"the best since Harwell, of 'lingering sweetness long drawn out'," he said. The only small fly was that we had to turn off the light in case Margaret awoke. As lovely as anything else was the peaceful quiet when I fell asleep in his arms. So much happier than having a train to catch. We are still enjoying the glow.

The twins were lovely—we took them up to the downs before dinner in the sun and wind. Margaret picked flowers—she found lady's slipper and one or two poppies ('red pobbies', she called them) and Andrew pranced about and made us each walk on our own path. He played the milkman again in the afternoon with fine realism. They still make up nonsense words together. "Bummie" was the funniest this time, being a portmanteau word for Bill and Mummy.

The SI and PI and HG list came out last week amid great excitement. Holden has got his SI and Miss Bennett and Miss Langwill HGs. There are now 6 women Higher Grade.

Rome fell yesterday—it is a landmark and a symbol but no one is making much fuss with the thought of so much more to do.

Friday 9th June 1944

The invasion began on Monday night/Tuesday morning having been postponed 24 hours by weather. So our suspicions were justified! So far so good but how appalling! The stories are dreadful—of lives lost, of courage, hysteria, and relief. And we have bombed Caen with its lovely churches. The only reflection here is 1) less military traffic in the city, 2) more (if anything) planes about, 3) the trains are half empty. I spent Wed evening with Elsie in Pimlico and caught the 9.48 to Brighton home. It was most comfortable and all those trains have been packed for the last 2 or 3 years. Holden took us all out to lunch on Wed at the Strand Palace. I had tea with E and walked to Blackfriars with him. It has been nice all this week—a kind of afterglow from last weekend still. Got the photographs today—disappointing, as always, but a few good ones.

Friday 16th June 1944

A new development in air raids—the Germans have sent over pilot-less, radio-controlled planes. We had three short odd alerts on Monday night and I heard a plane was brought down on a railway line in the east of London and damaged 100 houses. Then, last night, the siren went at 11.35 and we heard gunfire and the engines of single planes coming over—on and off, near and far, all night. We suspected they were not the usual sort of bombers and we heard from the post this morning that 58 had come down over a 40 mile radius. We heard three falls in our neighbourhood during the night, ending with one on the golf course, which had been hit by a gun and crashed with masses of black smoke. We had little sleep going from bed to shelter and back and I felt most jaded all day.

Ten minutes after I got to the office the alert sounded and then the imminent danger signal was given. We went down to the shelter, which we found locked, and in darkness. We were told we could resume work but we should keep away from windows—an impossible injunction except in the corridor. We heard guns now and then through the day and when I got home I found that Rosa had been shaken up this morning by one of the planes falling on the row of cottages by the Royal Oak and exploding. The blast blew our French windows open, tearing off and breaking two metal catches and a piece of the wooden frame. We have already had one alert this evening, listening to the engine—now growing familiar—and gunfire. E felt he could not leave K for the weekend so Rosa and Margot are coming for the weekend, trains permitting.

Monday 19ᵗʰ June 1944

Friday night was worse than Thursday night. We had an alert about 9.30, went to bed until 12.45. From then till 2.20, we were in the shelter. There was gunfire and we could hear explosions but not much near. The All Clear went and we had just gone to bed when the siren went again. Before we could get to the shelter, we heard the p-plane zooming. Rosa was at the door and took the opportunity to look well at it—"like a fish, a malicious fish," she said. But she felt better for seeing it. We then went into the shelter and stayed there till nearly 6.00. They were coming over fairly regularly and we heard several explode in our area. Although we had a worse night, I was less jittery and exhausted next morning, mainly because we were learning what to expect.

On Saturday Rosa, Margot and I went to Collingbourne. We persuaded Rosa to stay at least for a few days. It was bliss to sleep securely and to please Rosa we stayed until this morning. We had to get up at 3.30 and leave just after 4.00 to walk to Andover to catch the 7.15 train. Half a mile past Ludgershall an American driving a lorry offered us a lift and dropped us at Andover that we reached at twenty to six. Hobday had given us coffee and biscuits so we sat in comfort in the waiting room. The train was a quarter of an hour late. It was clear that London had had more P-Planes but I was surprised to find Ibex House in chaos. A P-Plane had directly hit the building on the corner opposite City 6. Milner had been fire watching but was luckily on the ground floor and had not been hurt. The porter had been flung on his back by the blast and several people were killed in the direct hit. I spent the day sweeping up glass, moving furniture, dusting and cleaning and telling the men what was wanted. E phoned at 11.00 and said he had nervous indigestion and they had had a very bad night at Kingston. Apparently Saturday night at Purley was worse than Friday but last night was better with no guns at all. During today I have heard explosions and we have had several alerts. They are horrid but on the whole they annoy me more than they terrify me now—at any rate in daylight.

The weekend was perfect, by contrast, and the twins lovelier than ever. We took them for a walk over the Down and they picked lovely bunches of tormentil, ladies' slipper, poppies, meadowsweet, honeysuckle and wild roses. Margaret was dead tired when she got back, so tired that she cried and had no tea, just went to bed, but Andrew kept saying as we went back, "Andrew wants his tea," and ate a large one. Neither asked to be carried and both enjoyed it all and could hardly be persuaded to sit down to rest halfway.

Tuesday 20th June 1944

We have done a more or less reasonable day's work. It is very cramped in our new quarters—no phone, no bells, no filing cabinets and nowhere to put anything. I found a nail and just put it in enough to hold my towel. All the files have bits of glass however much one shakes them, and the furniture has got a perpetual film of dust however many times one dusts it. Still, it was something to work an account and do an EPT computation. E was feeling better. Margot and I slept in the shelter last night except for half an hour from 2.20 between alerts when we relaxed in bed, and from 6.30 when we awoke after failing to hear a doodle bug go off 10 minutes' walk away, and also the All Clear. I felt sure I should oversleep and I should have if I hadn't been awakened at 7.15 by a p-plane zooming over. Worthington later told me he watched it and it seemed immediately over us. I heard it fall in Wandsworth. Milner came late having packed his wife and the baby back to Leeds after a very bad night at Streatham. We had an alert this afternoon—immediately all the city roofs and windows produced heads craning out. We have had two or three more alerts this evening. There always seems to be one when I pick the cherries. There are even more balloons out in Oxted direction and the search lights were all moved out too. They were a marvellous sight.

Wednesday 21st June 1944

Bitterly cold; low, threatening clouds, grey dark sky, cutting wind—for the first day of summer. The weather depressed me as much as the continuing series of raids. We got up this morning stiff, cold and aching and unrefreshed after a night (from 12.20) spent in the shelter. The first half of the night was noisy and we heard one after another P-Planes come over. Later we could still hear them cut, though they were further off. Milner got Mrs M. back to Leeds yesterday morning and is now on his own again. The office is functioning, though with difficulty, but I have overtaken the day I spent helping to clear up and more. E is still depressed and hates to think the twins may be completely orphaned. I told him that my regret was that we hadn't any more! All our eggs in just two baskets, as it were!

Thursday 22nd June 1944

Last night was quieter till 5.00 a.m. We slept in bed from 11.15 to 12.15 and from 2.30—4.45. In the first alert, there was nothing near but from 5.00 a.m. onwards the bombs were coming over one after the other and sounded just over the chimneys. They went on after we had gone for the train and we heard a plonk just by Sanderstead station. Over and over again I am thankful the twins are away.

Rosa phoned last night to know if she could return today. I said no, certainly not. She said the twins were splendid. Andrew had asked her to stay a long time and Margaret had four helpings of a pudding she had made. E said today, rather extravagantly, that if what I paid for the cottage had been rent it would have been worth it.

Monday 26th June 1944

The raids have continued off and on though we have had more sleep the past few nights. There have been some nasty periods in the daytime. On Friday morning when a p-plane hit a bus queue at Waterloo, Miss Rochford was hurt. This afternoon we had several imminent warnings and I was told one had fallen in Finsbury Square. I can't help worrying about Margot. She was on duty all night on Thursday night and phoned me first thing in the morning. Hobday said Rosa was worried about us very much but she wasn't looking bad on Saturday. E saw us off from Waterloo and got very edgy because Margot cut it fine. We went on the 12.45 to Woking and stood to Andover. Rosa and the twins were waiting on the platform.

The twins were lovely. Andrew, with his skittles—first they were skittles, then, standing up, they are 'milks', lying down they are bombers. He made a train with bricks: "What train?"

"Goods train."

"Where is the smoke?"

"No smoke—bricks!" He can clearly distinguish fantasy from reality. They have a passion for poppies—picked a bunch, which they offered to Margot to take back. They love having Rosa down there. They helped me peel potatoes and pick gooseberries and blackcurrants. Margaret found some blackcurrants but not many, so she said, "Nimmie pick gooseberries now and pick greencurrants."

Wednesday 28th June 1944

I was so tired on Monday that I went to bed at 10.00 and didn't hear any sirens—only explosions. Nights have been better but days worse. This morning we had 8 imminent danger warnings, which means we go into the corridor to be away from the worst glass till we hear the explosion. On London Bridge platform tonight, the alert went and we heard three flying bombs come over. One was so near when its engine cut out that everyone ducked (I was more or less under a barrowful of mail bags!). Southwark 1 and 2 were destroyed by a direct hit at 7.00 on Saturday morning and Bryan (SI, temporarily retained) and 2 clerks killed. Puttick came over to see us today and told me 70% of the papers were salvaged. Everyone seems to have had more or less.

I can't help worrying about Margot working in Waterloo, Lambeth, and Kennington area. One trouble is that it is difficult to think or talk of anything else, though Cherbourg has fallen. The Russians are in Vitebok and going hard for Minsk. Weather is foul—wet, cold and windy. Yesterday afternoon we had a violent thunderstorm. Margot and I went to the Prom (Berlioz and Mozart). She said she didn't like being in a crowd but I think the music seemed more sharply beautiful with the realisation that any note might be the last one would hear, the constant contrast between the ideal world of beauty and the material hideousness more pointed than usual. We stayed till the interval and as we came out there was a vivid rainbow.

Monday 3rd July 1944

I have a drumming headache and have kept falling asleep and jumping all day—in trains, after dinner and so on. After a weekend free of flying bombs, I am usually worse on Monday. It is partly the weather this time. It is heavy as lead and has rained without cessation from midday yesterday till this evening. The water butts are overflowing and it was too wet to pick any flowers or fruit to bring back. We still need rain in the garden, though it is late, but the weather has certainly played Hitler's game since the invasion began 4 weeks ago. The bombs still upset one's sense of proportion. This afternoon we had two Take Covers (which means that we get away from the window) in 5 minutes and the second bomb hit the building next door to Adelaide House. I felt the blast in my right ear. This evening we have heard 8 or 10 explosions. The balloon barrage is on Riddlesdown now, where two incoming routes converge, and is said to be catching bombs successfully. It is rather disturbing for Purley, though, and Worthington has had his boarded up windows blasted again. Mrs Endacott saw a spitfire explode a bomb on Friday over the golf course. I was scared in Croydon on Friday evening when they announced on East Croydon station, "Enemy aircraft approached—or passed" from the microphone.

I went to Collingbourne on my own (standing all the way). Rosa was getting fed up with Hobday who is exceedingly tactless and most moody and temperamental. Rosa is very restrained though she finds it difficult. It was lovely to see her and the twins; what a relief to feel they are safe. I heard that a number of people have come to Collingbourne from London, and of one place where an RAF man and his wife have been charged £7/10 per week for two rooms without food. Margot says evacuation is to be resumed. I had instructions to assist at Stroud for three weeks, which is no good at all for trains. I phoned Robertson this afternoon, but he said Swindon is no good, so I don't know. There was an awful mess last Friday when a bomb damaged Bush House and Astral House and City 20. E seemed a bit better. Meanwhile, if one could appreciate it, the Russians have taken Minsk and the Americans are attacking Cherbourg and we have Siena. I think the war in Europe may be over by the end of October (for those who live to see it).

Thursday 6th July 1944

Today has been a summer day with a sparkling summer morning and blue sky all day. So, apart from a warning this morning, while I was walking over

London Bridge, which resulted in a bomb on Kennington Park Road whose smoke I saw, and another warning at lunchtime, when I heard nothing but a distant bang, we have had freedom since early this morning. Last night Elsie came and stayed the night. Margot and I slept in Rosa's room with the curtains back. She was dead tired so we didn't go to the shelter even though once I was awakened and opened my eyes to see a bomb going past the window with its bright tail light. Nancy phoned me today to say the Proms have been 'indefinitely postponed', though it has not been publicly announced, and the Royal Exchange concerts cancelled. She said a bomb came down on Merstham village last Friday. Margot has been very busy yesterday and today on medical and kit inspections of evacuees. It is clear that Brixton is about the worst area. She had 205 yesterday and 850 today, and was worn out. She has to work on Saturday afternoon. Elsie was rather upset by seeing the Peabody building in Pimlico just after a bomb hit it, and last Sunday she went to see a friend in Kilburn and found her flat gone and her piano in the wreckage. She enquired at the Police Station and learned she had been killed. E told me Kingston Hospital had been hit yesterday at 5.15. Herrick said he and McCreath were golfing in Barnet last Saturday and a bomb dived silently down 200 yards away. They threw themselves down and just felt a wind, but it broke windows three miles away.

Monday 10th July 1944

The weather is really atrocious. Saturday tempted me to go to Wiltshire in a linen costume. There was a lovely sunset—deep gold and purple. Hobday and I watched it from the Downs where we were looking for mushrooms. But yesterday morning Rosa and I got soaked and by evening it was blowing a gale. This morning, when Margot and I went out to catch the 7.22, it was pouring again. Margot was completely worn out by Saturday, so much so that although she was supposed to work yesterday she said she couldn't. She was quite dazed and couldn't sleep on Friday night—just saw queues of children and suitcases - arrived at the cottage at 6.30 and just slept and slept. She was a bit better by the evening and tonight she is fire-watching, so I am alone. The bombs continue, though during the day they have been fewer. Two have gone over this evening.

Rosa keeps agitating to come back, and I think she will next week. I have to go to Yeovil for 3 weeks. It will be pleasant to be quiet but I would rather not go now. It isn't as if I can stay at the cottage. I have to find somewhere and I wrote to Heyhoe about it today.

E sent Andrew the Railway Magazine and he was very pleased. Insisted on looking diligently all through it over and over again. He is still mad on trains.

It is lovely to see the procession of flowers week by week; this time wild roses and rhododendrons are finished, mallow, cranesbill, scabious and poppy are at their best and knapweed, harebells, heather and toad-flax are beginning. The garden was a mass of white campanula, delphiniums and sweet Williams with some cornflowers, pinks and pansies.

Wednesday 12th July 1944

A most unpleasant day after the first quiet night (not evening) we have had since the flying bombs began. First, one shook the house and induced me to put a pillow over my face at about 7.30 a.m. Next, out of New Cross Gate, after crawling through the south east suburbs, my train put on speed. Suddenly, the crack of an explosion, and my left ear popped. A woman in the corner said, "Did you see it come down, just by the line?" Then, waiting on London Bridge platform for a Cannon Street train to meet E for a coffee, an explosion hit the station and the crowds on it. The cloud of smoke looked as if Ibex House might have been hit, but it was actually a barge on the north side of the river just by Tower Bridge. Traffic was diverted. I heard there was one man on it. These three incidents shook me up a bit but I had picked up alright and done some work before the Alert this afternoon, which went about 3.00. We had seven Imminents between then and 5.00 when I went home—nothing near, but I didn't enjoy them. When you hear a terrific roar, you think will it go over?. When you hear a distant buzz cut out, you wonder if the thing will glide on to Ibex House, but you say nothing.

Tuesday 18th July 1944

Settled at Yeovil for 3 weeks. The office found me digs with a Mrs Green and her old mother and so exquisitely clean and looked after and highly respectable. The old lady is sweet—daughter needs humouring. Old lady was House Keeper to Mrs Taylor, widow of the former proprietor of the best shop in Yeovil and sister of WE Cox[62]. Daughter worked in the shop. They know the Cox family well—talk about 'Willie' Cox—would have been CI if he had been a few years younger. They welcomed me when they heard I had played one of his daughters in Hobson's Choice. They work very hard running the house and garden and taking boarders in the spick and span council house. Very

---

[62] Someone who became very senior in the Inland Revenue

comfortable, and it was a relief to find a bed, though Mrs Parsons[63] had written and wired to say she would put me up. I am going to see her tomorrow evening, trains permitting.

I got to Yeovil about 4.45. Heyhoe is nice but overworked. Whiting, who assists, works hard and is expecting to be reviewed for Higher Grade in two years—Hoey's group.

Wed 26th July 1944

- broke off to hear the news. I have worked very hard—133 accounts so far, most of them small, and yesterday I did the claims and interviewed a farmer.

I went to Collingbourne for the weekend and was the only visitor. A dull weekend but little rain. We took the twins over the Downs twice. Andrew was sweet and found two feathers which he sent "Bill." Margaret picked lady's slippers and harebells for him. She had fallen on a bath of water on the Tuesday before, which they were playing with and in, as it was hot. She bruised her chin and cut her lip on her teeth. Hobday took her to the doctor in case she needed a stitch but it was alright except that it shook her up and she was rather tottery at the weekend, fell over easily and made a fuss when she did. On the way back, they waited for a train and an American troop train ran in. The soldiers made a great fuss of her and one threw her a sixpence. In a minute, they were all throwing her coins. She picked up four and threepence halfpenny, four shillings of which Hobday was putting in war savings, two shillings each.

Much excitement at the end of last week due to the plot against Hitler. Mrs Whiting came up to say that on the 10.00 news it said that there was civil war in Germany. It is interesting and significant for what it implies i.e. that the army thinks it hopeless to continue fighting, but probably we shall make a more complete job of the war if the Nazis retain power.

Last Wed. evening I went to see Mrs Parsons. The train was slow and late and it was two miles uphill from Axminster station and I didn't arrive until 7.30. It was nice to see her after 4 and a half years and she was looking better than I expected. Jack is growing deaf and can't hear traffic on the road. Dinah, lovely as ever, still catches rabbits. The house is quite palatial with a lovely view over half Dorset and, through a gap in the hills, to the sea six miles away. Lennard has separated from his wife and lives with a French ex-secondary school teacher who has improved him enormously according to Mrs P. After getting invalided

---

[63] A friend who lived in Dorset

out of the army, he bought a lorry and soon had 5. The French woman helps and bought the house out of her share of the profits. Lennard makes Mrs P an allowance, gives his wife £2 pw and keeps the girl at a boarding school in Seaton. So the Parsons seem to have struck lucky at last. She was very cordial, said Margaret was the bonniest child she had seen, and wanted to know all about them. Did they walk? and talk? and quarrel? and get up to mischief? which was quicker? which was Andrew like? I left it late to start back but the train was 20 minutes late and a girl overtook me on the hill and gave me a lift so I was lucky. Axminster is a small place arranged along a hill like china on shelves with a huge church in the middle.

I get very tired in Yeovil—the air is soft and relaxing and I just want to sleep. However, I shall probably brim with energy when I get somewhere bracing. I felt quite different when I got out at Ludgershall. Last night I dreamt I heard the Alert and awoke in a fright to hear planes flying low and singly overhead. I had thought in my sleep they were flying bombs. There is water shortage here. Last week it was turned off at 5.00—this week at 4.00 and it tastes horribly of chloride of lime. Even in peacetime, I gather, it is short and yet there are heaps of streams and rivers.

Thursday 3rd August 1944

Mrs Cox and Mrs Taylor have been to tea and we have all been on our best behaviour. I put on my new linen blouse for the occasion. Mrs C., retired biologist, now teaching Maths in a girls' boarding school in Wilts with no water, is sweet—lives at Hampstead in peacetime. She is just worn out now. She is very like her brother W.E. Mrs Taylor, the youngest, is not a bit like him—she is witty and dry and very sharp.

Last night I went to Axminster to see the Parsons and took them some fish as they can't get it. I aimed at the 3.55 from the Junction. About 15 little boys got off with labels and pillowcases full of clothes—evacuees. They looked so lost and forlorn walking across the line to their bus and going off to the depths of Somerset. I got to Axminster at 5.00 and looked at the church—a big decorated building, very light with a Jacobean pulpit and reading desk, three good sedilia and a piscina and a lovely medieval effigy of a woman with a tiny child clasped between her hands—?her soul. I have never seen this idea before. The walk up to the house was lovely as it was a bright sunny evening, too hot for the steep uphill but there was a breeze as one got up. It was almost too misty to see the sea if one didn't know it was there and the hills were softened with mist. But the smell of the fields and hedges was lovely—the hedges so thick and just full of flowers, bushes, birds, butterflies, moths, bees and flies. Mrs P. was very cordial and gave me a boiled egg for tea and a fried egg and bacon for supper one and a half hours later! Tea and cider and a huge piece of homemade cake and apple jelly. She had saved a dozen huge brown eggs for the twins and also gave me a lump of country bacon.

The weekend was mixed. I got to Twinpath half an hour late about 11.00 and E arrived half an hour late on Saturday afternoon. He was worn out and still on edge from the bombs. We intended to go and get mushrooms after the twins had gone to bed but it poured with rain and continued even after the sun shone yellow just before it set so that we had a magnificent rainbow. We went to bed early and I didn't intend him to do anything but sleep—we had a half love and then slept till Andrew woke at 6.30. They were thrilled to see him and he chopped wood in the morning. In the afternoon, we took the twins over the Downs.

Rosa had been upset by the bombs at the weekend which were very bad. One fell in Woodcote Valley Road while Margot was getting the meat at Sainsbury's. One fell at lunchtime on Sunday in Brancaster Lane and broke our dining room windows. She had just heard that Fred Bell and his wife had been killed the Saturday before. Having heard this I felt so worried that I gave myself a little sty on the eye. Yeovil seemed intolerable. I felt I couldn't stay another hour. I phoned in the evening and got through after 2 hours. Margot was in her bath but it was lovely to hear her. I just cried with relief. She was going to Digswell last night and I was glad she was when the 8.00 news (said) "a rather heavy attack" last night—800,000 houses damaged, according to Churchill, and the only hope is to re-conquer France, and we may get rockets. Not a pleasant outlook. Still, the Russians are almost in East Prussia and Warsaw and at last the Americans and English have broken through in Normandy and have even turned the corner into Brittany. For those who survive, the war in Europe may be over by 31st October. I have worked 236 accounts in Yeovil and have exhausted their reservoir of work. The water is to be turned off at 2.30 henceforth.

Wednesday 9th August 1944

Back at Purley again and Margot is fire-watching tonight. She came down to Collingbourne on Sat but got taken on to Salisbury because the train didn't pull up the back at Andover. She got a seat and brought Susan. She said that a bomb dropped in Mitchley Avenue on Friday afternoon which brought the landing ceiling down and knocked some more glass out of the dining room windows.

We had a lovely weekend with hot weather, but not oppressive. Indeed it was chilly in the early morning. Everywhere the harvest was in full swing. We went over the Downs and watched the big cornfield being cut. One of the workers was a real cockney from Edmonton who welcomed a chance of a rest and a talk. He told us bomb stories as if they were funny stories. "On the station, they suddenly called out 'duck!', so we ducked our nuts; but she came down in Dalston." He had been bombed out three times in all and didn't want to go back.

When I got to the cottage on Friday about 8.30, (having caught the 4.05 from Yeovil), I found Rosa decidedly cool and still looking very worn and strained. Andrew had been very sweet to her. She seemed much better by the end of the weekend with no one to worry about for a few days. We took the twins to church on Sunday afternoon and had a lively conversation with the vicar's wife and sister and had to cope with some questions! On Monday we all went for a picnic on the downs. The twins loved it and walked valiantly and drank all there was but ate little. Margaret found some reddened haws which she picked and put in the empty milk bottle. A was much intrigued and at one point called them 'ladybirds'. I sat on a 5–bar gate in the shade and they had a great time climbing and climbing on it. They are both very good at 'sharing out'—leaves, tickets, beans, berries etc.—"one for Nimmie, one for Andrew" and so on. I got Andrew an ear-cap in Yeovil and by cracking it up as a 'bed-hat' we have got him to wear it with great pride. Margaret was much drier—going round showing her knickers to everyone—"quite dry!" She seemed to be trying more.

I said goodbye to the Evens with great affability on both sides. They said they had never had anyone whose departure they so much regretted and I should always try to stay with them. They gave me four snaps of the old lady and two pieces of cake for my tea and didn't charge me for my last bath.

Plenty of work at the office and I heard about 3 bombs which fell very near last week. A letter from E saying he intends to come back tomorrow. We make progress in France—almost all Brittany—and today the Americans in Le Mans and nearly to Angers. For once, the weather has been good. The Russians seem to have slowed a bit. Last night we slept in the shelter as I heard my first siren just before bedtime—a few bangs but not near. I found the shelter very hard after three and a half weeks of beds, and didn't sleep well. A short alert between 6.30

and 7.00 when I heard about six bangs, one fairly near, but the day was quite quiet. Saving up, or getting the rockets going?

Tuesday 15th August 1944

Still the weather holds, though for 2 days there has been a fresh east wind. At midday came news that we have landed in the south of France. In Normandy, it seems as if we may surround the main German forces. Anyway, France is probably ours in a month. Since the weekend flying bombs have been more troublesome—about 6 alerts today and perhaps four near enough for me to see the smoke, one at ten to six at West Croydon fused our power and stopped the clock. I still can't get the radio going. Last night I slept at the Benbows under their stairs.

A good weekend—Rosa was better but not recovered. Twins were sweet. Their language progresses. Andrew uses the prefix 'un' correctly—'unlate'. Hobday put the fireguard outside to clean the room and they seized it to play with. The dolls became corgies which Andrew wanted to leave out at night! They play houses with elaborate make-believe making tea, washing up etc.

A letter from Miss Green—most uncharacteristic. Her latest lodger has money but no polish! Uses one knife for bacon and toast and doesn't use the butter knife!

Thursday 24th August

I have been on holiday since last Saturday and very quickly it has gone. Hobday went off to Bridport on Tuesday morning, much to our relief and her benefit. Margot arrived on Sat, just after 6.00 and I got to Twinpath at 3.30 It was very heavy and hot with a damp heat. I stood to Woking but unaccountably got a seat to Andover, though a small, squashed one vacated by a little boy. Hobday, Rosa and the twins were waiting. We spent the weekend as usual and on Monday Rosa, Margot and I took the twins to Salisbury by train to Ludgershall and by bus to Salisbury via Tidworth, Bulford and Amesbury. We lunched at the British Restaurant but by teatime we were rather jaded so we had a luxurious tea at the Green Bay Tree. Andrew and Margaret were most impressed with their tea knives and pastry forks. They ate a large tea and behaved perfectly. I got Andrew a pair of shoes and a pair of brown cloth leggings (14/3d). There wasn't a pair to fit Margaret. I was tempted to get them stone coloured coats with brown velvet collars but there was only one size. I also managed to get the orange juice after enquiring at three different places. We also looked at the cathedral. It is as cold as I'd remembered but lovely—a perfectly unified style. I hadn't remembered the 5 lovely jewel-like windows of the Lady Chapel. The Chapter House is not open. I peeped in and heard an infant's wail.

On Tuesday, it rained in the morning but Rosa and I left Margot in charge of the twins and walked to Ludgershall and caught the train to Andover. The town has more character than I expected. We went to see the first 2 and a half hours of 'Gone with the Wind'. I still don't like technicolour and the Americans do exaggerate. However, we enjoyed the film and were sorry to miss the end. The News Reel was moving—the Land of the Free French army in France. Typical crowds, especially the women. Yesterday Margot and Rosa went to Cirencester and enjoyed it. I stayed with the twins and had my hair cut.

Friday 25th August 1944

The nicest thing the twins have done this week was on Wed I think. I was peeling new potatoes at the back with them helping. Margaret decided she wanted a seat and fetched her stool. So did Andrew. I took a snap of them peeling potatoes. After a few minutes, Margaret said with no prompting at all, "Must get Mummy a seat"—and appeared a bit later with a large cushion for me. She was very pleased when I sat on it. They play together well and co-operate and begin, just begin, to be thoughtful for each other and other people e.g., Andrew wanted more pudding and enquired if there was some more for Nimmy.

Monday 28th August 1944

It poured with rain the last ten minutes walking into Ludgershall with Margot this morning to catch the 6.43 bus to Andover. I caught the morning train back to Collingbourne. Margot's week went very quickly. We had two perfect days to finish—Saturday and yesterday. Brilliant sun and hot but a fresh breeze and chilly mornings with mist and dewy cobwebs, crimson and gold sunsets, with the growing moon brightening over the downs. Each night we took the dogs out and found one or two tiny mushrooms for breakfast.

On Sat, we went for a walk over the downs in the morning and stayed in in the afternoon. Yesterday we all went over the downs and Margot and Rosa went to Collingbourne Kingston church in the evening. Today I intended to take Rosa and the twins to Avebury but as it rained we stayed in and I washed some clothes and gardened. Yesterday a training plane came over very low making a deafening noise and frightened Margaret. She was afraid to have her tea in the garden after it. Today it came over, but not so near, when she was near Andrew in the garden. I looked up from cutting down delphiniums to see if she was alright and found her with her arms round Andrew's neck—each consoling the other.

Friday 1st September 1944

The weather has been unsettled but has not kept us in and we have not got unduly wet any day. On Wednesday, we caught the 1.21 bus to Marlboro' and the 3.10 to Avebury. It gave us just an hour there which wasn't enough for Rosa or the twins, who loved the green circle—running up and down the slopes. We had tea first at the Merlin. So yesterday we chanced the weather and set off for a picnic on the 9.21 bus. We looked at the shops and had coffee at Polly in Marlboro' and then caught the bus to Avebury. On the way, Rosa suggested going to Calne and stopping on the way back at Avebury. It was a good idea as it would have been chilly to spend the whole day at Avebury. The bus ride was lovely. We had a good view of Silbury Hill and then on the Bath road to Calne. The road rises to nearly 600 feet with wide views over the downs before it leaves the chalk behind to drop down to Calne, only 19 miles from Bath. It suggests the Cotswolds, with a big grey church and plenty of grey stone houses and slated roofs. The place is dominated by the bacon factory but there is a pleasant little river, the Bristol Avon, and some marvellous yews cut into arched avenues in the churchyard. We ate our sandwiches in the churchyard and while we were inside it rained. Then the sun came out and it rained while we were in the bus going back to Avebury. We had our tea on the ring. We had just got back to Twinpath when it poured with rain followed by a vivid rainbow. Today we had an early dinner (steak and kidney and mushroom pie, boiled potatoes, peas, rice pudding). We waited for the Friday train and caught the 2.00 bus to Salisbury—had tea at the Bay Tree, bought books, and had a short look at the cathedral. It had a warmer beauty with the sun on it and the lawns of the Close looked exquisitely peaceful with swallows swerving over them and wagtails gliding along.

Flying bombs seem to have increased this week. I am not looking forward to going back on Monday but we are racing ahead in France, almost at the Belgian frontier; Rumania and Bulgaria out of the war; Hungary likely to be.

Tuesday 5th September 1944

Back at the office. We have moved back to the rooms blasted in June, but they are far from restored. The windows are merely scrim-nailed to bits of ill-fitting wood and let in wind and rain. The whole place was damp and cold yesterday—one stuck to one's chair—one's hand slipped on the slimy damp tables. Rain dripped through the ceiling. However, there is more room. I found a great deal of work—far more had collected in 2 weeks' leave than in 3 weeks at Yeovil.

It looks as if flying bombs are nearly finished. It has been quiet (except for an alert this morning early when bombs fell at Ilford and Southend) since Friday. Some more of our landing ceiling came down last night. Brussels free and we are in Holland—reports that we are in Germany near Saarbrucken (where we began the war). It seems incredible. E is cheerful but limp—tension relaxed, but 'dying to see the twins'. He wants to come next weekend but is fire watching on Saturday and Rosa won't be back probably, so it is patience again.

Margot came down to Twinpath on Saturday and Hobday returned in the evening. Hobday was most impressed with the tidy and clean cottage, but I fear it will have a short effect. I miss the twins very much. Oh, to have 3 or 4 years with them—till they don't need me, or need me so much.

Tuesday 12th September 1944

The weather improved at the weekend. We have had 4 days of unbroken sunshine and brilliant starry nights—biting cold morning and evening, but warm sun at midday. Margot and I had a lovely weekend at Collingbourne. In the afternoon, Hobday and I took the twins on the downs and Andrew loved it, enumerating as we returned to tea all we had found—blackberries, sticks, mushrooms, toadstools, acorns, feathers, harebells etc. On Sunday night, he had a tummy ache and finished up in our bed where we were squeezed like sardines.

London is full of rumours. There was an explosion in Chiswick on Friday at 6.45 pm. I think I am the only person who didn't hear it. Five people were killed and 8 houses destroyed. I have heard it was 1) a gas main, 2) an unexploded bomb, 3) a bomb dropped by accident by an American. There was heavy gunfire at the weekend, probably in the Channel, audible because of the weather. This morning there was an explosion at 6.00 am (which didn't wake me but was very loud)—I have heard it was a rocket at Kew Gardens or Mortlake. Another at 8.50 shook my train and was at Upper Warlingham. Another reported by Rosa at

10.00. I have been told there was one at Dagenham and one at Sidcup. It seems as if something is coming over with no warning. Whitton said there was an Air Ministry warning at 8.30 am today but we have had no sirens. Taylor came to see our war damage and discuss repairs and told Rosa we ought to sleep in the shelter. He preferred flying bombs—"you knew where you were with them— you could be 10 yards from them and alright if you lay down." I fear last week's optimistic announcements were premature. It is a pity people have come back in such numbers.

An interview today with Setty—an Irakian Jew who thinks £750 reasonable remuneration for his son of 19 and £500 for his daughter of 16–17! Last week I saw Sanderson, now of Yeovil, who told me an incredible story of Salzmann and the BATL. He was offered secret commission of £30,000 and resigned. He has exposed the [offer] to the FO, who have done nothing as members of the Turkish government are involved.

Tuesday 19th September 1944

I caught a cold, probably from Rosa, possibly from the twins. It developed on Sunday and was at its worst in the evening and yesterday. E and I went to Twinpath reaching there only half an hour late. The twins gave him a great reception, especially Margaret who kept looking soulfully at him, murmuring, "Bill! Beel! Beel!" In spite of colds they were in good form, though Andrew played up at breakfast. Did he resent another man to challenge his monopoly? I didn't enjoy the weekend much because I had an underlying anxiety all the time about Rosa. I phoned at 12.30 on Sunday and Margot said things had been fairly quiet. But when I got back in the evening I heard that a rocket had dropped at 1.15 just by the golf links. Margot said it was the loudest, longest noise she had heard since 1939—the house rocked and some more glass fell out. There were also a few flying bombs. The feeling I had was of the same quality as that on the Friday when I couldn't leave Addiscombe in March.

The weather was perfect: misty, cobwebby morning, sun so warm that I wore my green shantung dress and no coat to phone, cloudless sky. E and I went to the mushroom field on Sat evening and picked two bagsful so we had a feast at breakfast and dinner. We all went on the downs in the afternoon and Hobday and I left the twins with E while we picked another basketful to bring back. The twins grow. We measured Margaret for leggings—23" waist, 29" hips, 14" inside leg, 24" waist to foot. They begin to develop fantasy. Margaret talked at length about 'my little boy Geoffrey'—who wetted his bed, had a bath, had his hair washed, had various meals, was good, wanted this and that etc. E made Andrew a signal which intrigued him—he had liked the signals in the train book E took him even more than the trains. I did some gardening—pruned and tied up the loganberries, tied up raspberry canes, cut grass, cut down dead flowers. E made a bonfire which pleased the twins.

Monday 25th September 1944

It has turned blustery and cold with squally showers. I have been too cold to concentrate in the office in spite of wearing a woollen long-sleeved jumper, a thick brown cardigan and a firewatcher's blanket wrapped round. The weather has not been favourable for the fighting in Holland. Everyone has seemed anxious—there is a sense of decision about the Nijmegen and Arnhem fighting.

I went to Collingbourne on Sat. The train to Woking was packed but I got a seat in the 12.50, reaching Collingbourne about 3.20. Margaret had crashed into the front door on Friday chasing a marble and had bruised her nose badly. It shook her up and on Saturday she was blinking nervously. I was rather worried. But yesterday the blink had almost gone and the bruise was coming out. She elected to come for a walk over the downs in spite of the wind which she dislikes. She stood up to it quite well, encouraged by a bunch of elderberries and some late scabious. As the weather was wintry we gave Andrew and Margaret their 'best' bricks. They were thrilled as they hadn't had them since they left Addiscombe. Andrew built houses, trains, bridges, etc. with his; but Margaret, though she asked me to build her a house, used hers mainly to symbolise—she arranged them on a cloth and then called the dolls—"dinner ready"—sat around and pretended to eat. In the middle of our dinner, Andrew fell asleep sitting in his chair and we put him to bed and he slept for an hour. In the afternoon, I dug some potatoes. The journey back is wearying and dismal these dark evenings. The train was 35 minutes late from Andover. I got a seat at Basingstoke. Round Woking to Surbiton it lost time and as I got out to get a slow to Clapham I heard a zoom and looked up to see a doodle bug going slowly along from east to west. The best view I have had at night since I saw one going past the bedroom window at Purley. The searchlights followed it until its taillight went out and a second or two later I saw the flash of the explosion. The train from Wimbledon to Clapham was in dense darkness although the All Clear had gone.

Wed 27th September 1944

Yesterday Rosa and I were awoken by a bang—at 4.00. Five minutes later I heard a distant All Clear. Heard nothing last night. E said the doodle I saw at Surbiton hit an RC boys' school at Chertsey and killed 9. We have withdrawn the survivors from Arnhem. It is most moving. They succeeded to a great extent but just missed complete success owing to the weather.

Mon 2nd October 1944

The weekend was perfect weather. Saturday sunshine and warmer than any day last week—rain at night. Brilliant sun and wind yesterday.

The twins were at Andover to meet me. I didn't see, being deep in thought about my train. Hobday had been to Andover to get them hankies and a picture for their birthday and two kettles for the electric stove. Andrew was thrilled with the trains and scandalised with the half full cups of tea lying round the station. Margaret's nose was better but 'not quite well' as she said. She had stopped blinking. I went to see whether there were any mushrooms but there weren't. I picked enough blackberries to colour the apple juice and a big bunch of berries which Margaret liked very much and wanted for her pies and cakes. After breakfast, she suggested taking Sally over the downs. Andrew asked if Nannie was going. No—she was going to cook the dinner—he'd stay with Nanny, not go out.

So Margaret and Sally and I set out. She enjoyed it thoroughly—found a worm drowned in a pool, admired chrysanthemums and yellow daisies, watched the big flock of rooks working the grass, wheeling in the sky, bathing in the puddles, looked at the various toadstools, observing unprompted that the cornfield had gone brown ('ploughed up') and later, having watched the tractor, that the tractor was making the field brown; asked for elderberries and acorns to take home, some for Andrew as well. Andrew had meanwhile stolen bits of pastry so with the combined ingredients they made 'acorn cake'. I warned Margaret not to spill elderberries on the floor but she upset some on the chair. I remonstrated and she said, "Dear me—it's boiled over!" Andrew was intrigued with my green costume coat—thought it was 'Rosa's coat' first, but then remembered that hers had a lot of buttons and mine only one. Margaret wore her new nightie and was very anxious to keep it dry. I took her a new pink sleeping vest as well and I heard her later telling Topsy, "Here is your sleeping vest—it is pink!" We took the twins to the Children's Service but it was rather unrewarding. When we got back, I dug some potatoes—2 bathfuls. They have done well, though some plants have only one or two the size of acorns and others have a few pounds of big fine ones. Andrew was interested in the worms that appeared and picked them up to make a worm heap. While we were there a big formation of about 50 large planes came over low—an enormous triangle. A quarter of a mile away they released paratroops—18 each—it was a lovely sight to see the parachutes open, nearly all white but a few wine red or brown. All the weekend there were manoeuvres—the 'Germans' were holding Collingbourne and the Americans attacking. One would hear bursts of gunfire, see soldiers creeping along hedges, meet tanks and lorries with a cardboard swastika in front and soldiers on light motorbikes whizzed about. These motorbikes are like scooters and the twins were much amused at them but dislike the noise.

Monday 9th October 1944

I had a very bad headache yesterday, so bad that I retired to bed for the afternoon, to my own disgust and the twins' concern. Margaret had offered to stroke my headache and Andrew had kissed it. She told Margot, who was digging potatoes, that it would be better 'after tea' and later, less hopefully, 'after supper'. It had ceased to rage by the time we got home (11.30) but all today it has been sore and stiff and I have felt tired and achy. After the twins were in bed, I went with Hobday to look for Zebedee the wireless man and we met a woman with a friend who asked me to let her know if I ever wanted to let the cottage as she wanted one that size. I said I might want to sell it if I were not keeping it. She would consider that if she had any money. The other woman showed us her cottage—200 years old, two rooms and a kitchen with a window and two bedrooms. She is paying 12/6d p.w. which is more than the restricted rent. No main water or drainage but electric light. She has been there 5 years and the landlord recently failed to turn her out.

I lunched with Oades last Tuesday and we bickered about shipping very pleasantly. E was lunching at the same place with Osborne and was rather displeased that Oades took me there! A letter on Friday from ES with a cheque for the twins' birthday—sweet of him to remember. He is a dear!

We had alerts of Thursday and Friday evenings before 9.00 and one last night at five to one. Each time we heard flying bombs, but not very near. There was one at Old Jewry on Friday about 8.00 which broke windows in E's office and damaged Price Waterhouse, Peat Marwick Mitchell and Whinney Smith and

Whinney. I was told there was a rocket between 3.00 and 6.00 this morning but I didn't hear it. Next door to the office this morning there was a small explosion and fire when the demolition of a bombed building damaged a gas pipe and on Friday afternoon I got a shock when one of the windows blew in with a crash when I was concentrated on Paterson Symons EPT computation.

Monday 16th October 1944

Yesterday was lovely—warm and bright. I took the twins over the downs and we found 2 mushrooms, acorns, out of their cups, now, to A's surprise, blackberries, hosts of toadstools, little white slimy wet ones, vivid scarlet and yellow ones, and the usual puffballs and brown champignons; flocks of rooks and starlings. Hobday came to meet us as Andrew would only come when he was convinced that he couldn't stay at home alone. Margaret suggested the walk.

After dinner, I rushed to the end of the road where an ambulance picked me and 6 other people up and took us to Collingbourne Kingston for taking blood. It was an army unit from Winchester, most efficient. After our tea, we were taken back. Hobday explained where I was to Margaret who was most interested and asked me if 'the soldiers' legs were better now?' When I got back, I dug three rows of potatoes and one was the largest I have ever seen—about 6 inches square and 2 and a half inches deep! Hobday had been ill from Tuesday—nerves, the doctor said. Anyway, she stayed in bed and Mrs Blackmore and Mrs Reeves helped with the twins.

They had tea alone one day and Andrew finished and got down. Margaret: "Andrew, you've forgotten something." No answer. Margaret: "Andrew, you didn't say, 'Please Nimmie, can I get down?'" And he did! I took Andrew the mosaics and Margaret a bodkin to sew with but she looked expectant so I gave her the dominoes. Andrew learnt the word with one hearing but Margaret mistook it and called them 'baminoes'. Andrew is very good on vocabulary. He tackles 'Michaelmas daisies' and 'diagram' and 'mosaics' without an effort. Margaret's articulation is better but her memory not so good, e.g., she mixed up 'blue tit' and 'tulip' and called Cheltenham 'Cheltming'.

Monday 30th October 1944

It has turned cold. Sally's water dish had ice on the top. The north wind cut through my porridge coat and today in the office I have been cold. But the sun has shone all day. It was fine all the weekend with pale blue sky and warm out of the wind, except for a short hour in the afternoon when the sky grew leaden and it looked as if it would snow and it actually rained icy rain. Yesterday it came down as we were returning from the station and seeing off Margot and Jock. The twins kept under their macs and I carried Andrew since he said, "Can't walk in the dark!" Hobday went to Bridport for the weekend and got back at 12.15 last night having gone to Reading on a train that didn't stop at Savernake. It was lucky she could get back—by train to Basingstoke—Andover—Ludgershall, and walked from there (with an American soldier).

Jock and I went down on Friday evening. Margot and Rosa arrived on Saturday afternoon. It was an enjoyable weekend with abundant good weather and a pleasant freedom. The twins were good except for Andrew when Jock and I took him through the village and he fell over and cried nearly all the time. They had good appetites—in fact he had three helpings of crackle pops for breakfast, followed by bacon and omelette and milk with a dash of tea. On Saturday for dinner, he had soup (not finished), bread and butter and cheese and rice pudding (two helpings).

I got up at 6.15 this morning to catch the train to Savernake. It was dark as the moon had shrunk but Sirius and Orion twinkled fiercely. The trees are nearly bare and as the light grew the whole world seemed new. Just outside Savernake we waited 10 minutes by the canal. Opposite was a beech glowing rust coloured in the morning light, next to a pine. It was exhilarating—but when I got to the City the enchantment faded. No word from E and I grew uneasy about him. Rockets have increased. Rosa and Margot were disturbed on Friday night by two at least, one of which shook the house. Rosa couldn't sleep and got to Twinpath quite worn out. Today I have heard at least four (two at 11.30, one at 4.30 and one this evening). Mrs Benbow called about the play-reading and told me there was a near doodle bug on Sunday morning at 5.45 am. Rosa is staying away for a time and the twins are enjoying her. Margaret observed to Rosa yesterday, "You haven't got so many eyebrows as Nannie (who certainly has very heavy ones)."

Friday night was the first of a dream recounted—she woke up crying and said, "There was a big worm outside the house and it came on my shoe." Andrew is beginning to know the small letters—has gained interest both in the station posters waiting for Rosa and Margot and in the book Jock gave them. He also played dominoes with her and has quite got the idea. A queer instance of possessiveness—Margaret fetched the bells, "To play my wireless." Jock asked whether she could try it. Margaret said no—and took it right back in to the bedroom. Andrew fetched her his best book ("my train book, Bill did bring me from London") for her to see. They both liked her—from the first, when Margaret opened one eye on Friday night and said, "What's that?"

Sally has had seven puppies—very healthy and vigorous—six dogs and one bitch—4 brown, two black and white and one brown and white. She is very maternal but was very glad to see Susan.

Tuesday 31ˢᵗ October 1944

Things get noisier. A rocket at 3.00 am and at 6.50 am the siren woke me. I decided to stay in bed a) because it was cold b) because I should probably not have time to get up. Sure enough I heard a doodle bug as the siren died away. It came over very low and reverberating. I was just thinking it was passing when it cut out. I put my handbag over my face and the eiderdown over that, held my breath and felt grateful I was the only one in the house as I heard it whistle down. The whistle seemed interminable and then the explosion—much shorter and less noisy than I expected. The house shook but less with blast than with the heave of the ground. No windows went   we were protected from the blast by the rise of the ground. Then I saw flickers of fire against the curtains and heard bells of fire engines and ambulances. It fell, apparently, just over the brow of the hill— Worthington's latches were blown out though he is much further away. Purley station lost windows and roofs. Another alert about 8.00 am and I heard a rocket at breakfast. I was glad when Margot phoned that she was alright. I went to Sainsbury's for the meat ration and the siren went again as I got into the train. Heard rockets at 11.30 am, 6.20, 6.45 and 8.30 pm. They are getting a nuisance. Whitton was annoyed because no one has made a 'statement' on them but EA and I agreed that it would be folly to convey to the Germans anything even if we suspect they know where they are dropping. I heard that 2 went off in mid-air, that one landed at Palmer's Green covered with ice and didn't explode and that 25 people were killed and 95 injured by the one that hit Peek Frean's biscuit factory on Thursday morning.

At lunch, I went to the Haymarket to try to get seats but learnt that there is nothing under 10/6d for Hamlet. I went into the Nat. Gallery as I was passing and looked at Hogarth's Calais gate and at Tom Monnington's picture of 'Southern England, 1944'—a lovely landscape with bombers and white trails against the blue sky. I loved the right hand of the picture—a thin clump of trees on rising ground with a bit of the weald glimpsed behind them. An elm on the left I did not like so much. A farm cart crossing a ford in the foreground was attractive.

It is horribly cold at the office with no windows. E phoned this afternoon—he is better—may be back tomorrow or Thursday.

Monday 6th November 1944

It is lovely sitting by the fire after a good dinner, too tired to play the piano. We got up at 5.00 am and walked to Ludgershall to catch the bus to Andover for the 7.15 train. Twice we felt a few stray drops of rain and the road was drenched but we were lucky, especially as I had no mac. The dawn began as we waited for the bus. We saw the raindrops on the grass gleam in the moonlight. I don't remember noticing this before, though it is common in sunshine. It was too wet for a bonfire yesterday for the twins. We went over the downs in a gale which Andrew thoroughly enjoyed. He ran after my cap when it blew away and ran before and against the wind. After dinner, it rained and we all did modelling with Glitterwax. The twins enjoyed it and continued till tea without stopping. Andrew was then worn out but didn't want to stop—he got himself into a state and had tea on my lap.

On Friday evening, we went to the Benbows to read 'Dear Brutus'. I enjoyed it as they gave me Narrator and Margaret, both lovely, to do. It is Barrie's best play, I think, and I was again struck with his technical skill. Mr B. and the vicar as Matey were both good.

On Friday, I heard the fatal casualties in the Purley hotel bomb last Tuesday were 19 (out of 42 in the building). The vicar was burying 4 today. Banstead Asylum was hit but luckily only the dairy—4 killed altogether.

Wednesday 8th November 1944

There is still a restricted service to London Bridge—yesterday I was 35 minutes late, today 20. We creep gingerly by the chasm where the rocket hit the line on a bridge. I heard today that a troop of scouts were under it a minute or so before the explosion.

Milner came back yesterday with the Leeds chatter. He had heard that the rockets came from Holland, that we know where they come from as a man he knew on CD had a warning—expect one in 5 minutes, and it came. The Germans announce today U2 is falling on London. The great news, though, is the re-election of Roosevelt for a fourth term which I feel is only slightly less important than his re-election 4 years ago which was perhaps one of the conclusive factors in our survival and the defeat of Germany.

Monday 13th November 1944

The weekend was wet. It is the first time I haven't been over the downs at all. Margaret slept for an hour after dinner as I played dominoes with Andrew. He has completely mastered them. We then built houses and bridges and stations till teatime and he continued two thirds of the way through tea. In the morning, they had a little piece of pastry each and made apple turnovers and tarts. Andrew always insists on eating his efforts. Then they brushed the bedroom.

I was glad to go for a little peace. Until Friday it was quiet but then there was a rocket on Middlesex Street, just behind Aldgate. Five minutes before I had been in Aldgate High St buying sweets. The noise was deafening and seemed to last an eternity and the building rocked. The windows blew in and the fire watchers' milk was blown off the shelf and the blackout was blown out. The rocking was most pronounced, like being on a ship at sea. EA's ceiling dropped bits on the floor and the cracks in the walls gaped and closed. I heard today that Brook Bonds factory had been blasted and there were casualties. It shook me up so that when, at 10 to 2 (am), the siren went and some doodles droned I was quite jittery. My heart pounded and I had a short violent headache.

Thursday 16th November 1944

It has been bitterly cold, gloomy and damp this week with pitch black nights. Tuesday night was awful. We heard a rocket at 10.30; at 12.15 the siren went and a flying boat droned into hearing so we came downstairs as it cut out. It must have been gliding towards us, for a minute or two later it went off (somewhere in South Croydon, we heard) and shook the house. We went back to bed and had just got warm when another could be heard, but it went off further away. When we got downstairs, the All Clear went at about 1.15 but we had another siren at 5.45 and another flying bomb. After that, we overslept and didn't wake till 8.00. Also, the electric clock stopped at 1.20. No wonder I felt depressed and low and tired all day yesterday. Last night was quiet but I heard rockets at 12.55 and 5.20 yesterday near enough to make me jump. A letter from May to say a girl in her office would like a brown dog puppy—4 of them are gone.

Monday 20th November 1944

A damp, mild weekend with a boisterous west-south west wind—not so wet that we couldn't go for a walk yesterday morning. Andrew was consoled for coming by bringing his little bit of pastry (raw) with cheese in a paper bag and doling out small bits to everyone, including the dogs on the way. When we got on the downs, the wind went to his head and he capered about in the wet grass with great enjoyment which reached its peak when his white woolly beret blew off! He plays up at weekends when I am there—makes a fuss at meals etc. He wetted the bed so I hardened my heart and wouldn't let him come into my bed yesterday morning with Margaret to look at books. He was quite docile and stood by his bed until it was time to dress. E sent him another railway magazine 'to lend' and he was terribly thrilled with it and chose to look at it for his bedtime story and dressed and washed with record speed so as to look at it again before breakfast. He and I spent the afternoon building with the 'new warm bricks' (wooden) and the 'cold' bricks (stone effect). When he had 6 pieces of bread and butter on his plate, I said, "How many?"

"6!"

"How many when you have eaten one?"

"5," he said without any hesitation and so on down to 'Anything', which is like the French "Rien"!

Rockets continue—I heard one this evening about 7.00. I heard there was one on Gaumont cinema at Peckham yesterday morning; EA said they heard one at 1.00 am; Bushell said they had about 20. Milner saw one—an orange ball which lit up Streatham and 10 seconds later the explosion, not very loud. Are they reducing the charge as they get pushed back? Rosa is staying at Collingbourne another week. The western front is moving east again. The French are a mile from Basle and on the Rhine.

Friday 24th November 1944

Last night I met Ella and we had a quick meal at the Corner House and then went to see Peter Ustinov's play, 'The Banbury Nose'. It is better than the last and is amusing and quite stimulating—except that the point needs no labouring for me. But it was pleasant to see—I liked the way it went backwards from 1943–1920–1900–1885. Roger Livesey was excellent as the old general getting younger and younger. We went in the gallery having found that the Pit has been abolished and is bookable, and persuaded to the gallery by the commissionaire.

In the second act, a rocket went off not too far away—distinctly feel-able and audible in the theatre. Ella said her flat at Pinner was destroyed at 1.00 am on Monday by a rocket falling immediately behind it. Hers and the one below were worst but the whole block is coming down. Her piano had its top blown over and it was filled with glass and rubble and that was the least of the damage. The flat collapsed into the one below. No one was killed and 6 injured but not badly. Her tenants had been in a week and were in bed. Mr P. slept through it so that Mrs P., emerging from the wreckage of her bed, thought he must be killed! No one in the block heard the explosion but of course it shook up Ella who was at Kath's a mile away. Ella loses her furniture, has the expense of the war damage claim, loses her sub-let rent, loses the cost of the agreement, etc. with the tenants as well as the flat. She was surprisingly calm about it.

A very good letter from Margaret yesterday, quite a good imitation of a real letter—even to the address and date! Andrew was 'too busy' to write. It has been damp and mild the last few days.

Monday 27th November 1944

The weekend was lovely. Hobday was very pleasant and Rosa more cheerful and the twins in good spirits except that Margaret had tummy ache on Sat night and yesterday morning. It did not diminish her appetite, though, so I am not worrying. On the way to the station, I asked her if she would send her love to Bill. She said, "Certainly, I will send him a letter if I have the time. But I have to go to Cheltenham with baby Sandra this week!"

There was a rocket on Sat. morning at 11.30 on Leather Lane which rocked the office. There was also a dreadful incident at New Cross when one crashed on a crowded Woolworths. We have heard a distant one this evening. We had an alert on Friday evening and heard a flying bomb a long way off. I went to the library on Sat morning and got de la Mare's anthology 'Love' and Coulton's autobiography—lovely! E borrowed Coulton for the weekend and enjoyed it. He said it was clear that Arts needed a finer mind than Science! From him! What a progression!

Monday 4th December 1944

It's late and I am tired and surrounded by family but I must note briefly what a lovely weekend it was. Rosa came back to Purley on Thursday and I let E know at once as I knew he was fire-watching on Sat night. On Friday, he said he had changed with someone just on the chance so we caught the 12.50 on Sat. The twins weren't expecting him—indeed, when she went to bed, Margaret said, "I didn't know Bill was coming today"—but they welcomed him. We went to bed at 11.00 and had a lovely time for an hour. Afterwards, when we were quiet, he said, "Music and sexual intercourse must be closely connected—the same changes of tempo and intensity—rhythm, pauses, leaping crescendos." We bickered pleasantly. Andrew woke first, at 5.00, and his bed was dry. He was full of pride and he came triumphantly into our bed after his tea. In the morning, we played indoors as it was wild and stormy. After dinner, we walked over the downs. The twins played ball and threw stones in puddles and listened to the telegraph wires.

Still a few bangs—there was a rocket in the river that broke the windows of Somerset House at the weekend.

Monday 11th December 1944

It has been so cold in the office that I have found it almost impossible to work. I feel as though I had a piece of ice in my tummy and my head aches with the cold. EA is trying to get the windows put in. If he does, I suppose they will at once get blown out again. On Saturday morning, I was so miserably cold that I suddenly cried in the underground going to Waterloo with E.

The twins met me at Andover where Hobday had been to buy a new dress. Andrew was more interested in the train I had come off than in me! Margaret kept her bed quite dry and Andrew did his best so they both came in my bed. Andrew looked at the two railway magazines and de la Mare and Jock's ABC book and Margaret at de la Mare and 'Water Rat's Picnic'. They had good meals and an orange between them and an apple each after dinner. I came back Savernake way and found the waiting room with no fire and only a hurricane lamp—like the setting for a murder play with sinister dark shapes sitting around.

Monday 18th December 1944

It was cold till Friday night and then the wind changed and we had gales and rain, though yesterday was sunny so we could go over the downs playing ball and collecting holly and wood. E came down and the twins met us at Andover. The twins were good and they both wrote letters to Margot. Andrew put his in a large brown envelope with string round and handed it to me through the carriage window. He planned all this most deliberately. The puppies still give the twins great pleasure and they want to keep Finn. I brought Monty back last night. E and I had a lovely night though I was depressed and shaky from the Borough rocket beforehand. I suppose it is good and keeps me balanced. In spite of having had only about 4 hours sleep, I felt most exhilarated this morning and even after hearing the Endacotts' complaint because I play 4 times a week (at most), sometimes up to 10.00 (will I only play between 8.00 and 9.00—"otherwise we have to wait till 10.00 before going to bed!"), I still can't feel depressed. It was a good time though I wish we could have the light. E fixed up the lanterns and decorations and we decked the tree, though the tree lights wouldn't light after 3 or 4 flickers. The twins liked them and were thrilled—"one week to Christmas."

1945

Bill with Andrew and Margaret at Collingbourne

Monday 1st January 1945

Still bitterly cold, though on Sat the wind went west and the ice thawed. Yesterday the wind was north and it was as cold as ever. Travelling was so bad last week that I wired Hobday that I might not be able to get down on Sat, but things improved and my train was only 10 mins late.

The twins went to the village party on Sat. We left them sitting at the table waiting for their tea. They had good teas and stuck it for one and a quarter hours and then a boy came to say they were crying. They seemed alright when we arrived for them, though Andrew looked flushed and had been upset. When she was dressed, Margaret went back to the party and sat on a chair by herself, in the middle of the room, and Andrew was prepared to stay if Hobday and I stayed there. They were given an apple and a half crown each. Margaret saw some badminton rackets and remarked they were what the girls played with in the park at Addiscombe. It is probably over a year since she saw tennis being played. Andrew can do his jigsaw and still enjoys it. When they got back, they helped me to eat my high tea of plaice and chips, even Andrew, who asked for 'just the crumbs of fish'. They looked very nice; Margaret in her pink Dayella and Andrew in his new, soft jade jersey and knicks.

We took Finn on the downs yesterday, mainly to encourage Andrew, who had burnt his lip running into the hot baking tin. Finn is going to Plymouth today, to the twins' sorrow, though Margaret is philosophical—"Spect Sallie will get some more puppies out. I wonder what they will be like," she said yesterday.

Monday 8th January 1945

Rather depressed, tho I have been cheered by finding Young's have delivered some coal and a few coke nuts for the boiler. We were reduced to our last knob of anthracite nuts and all the weekend there has been a gusty NW wind. The office has been bitterly cold. Last Tuesday I stayed in bed to try to get rid of a chill. It was pleasant, and I felt better after it but not for long. Also we had several rockets. Wednesday was quieter but Thursday was very noisy and Rosa got very shaky. On Friday, we had a play reading of 'At Mrs Beams' here, and about 10.30 we had a siren and heard a bomb coming. It went off, apparently in the air, with a great bang and a few minutes later we heard another which went off further away. Just after the All Clear we heard a rocket too loud to be nice. All this persuaded Rosa to come down to Collingbourne with me again. She had got nervy mainly because she couldn't sleep. She didn't want to come to Waterloo to catch the train and I held my breath all Saturday morning. Luckily it was quiet after an early one, which went off a long way away, while I was getting the coal and admiring the sky. She improved at once and began to relax—sleeping at once on Saturday night. Margot had Jock for the weekend and also acted as plumber's mate from 9.15 to 3.30 yesterday while our pipe was mended. The man then found an airlock but the water is functioning now. She said there were 3 or 4 noisy rockets on Saturday afternoon. Margot said there was another when I was in the train. London Bridge was upset—huge crowds flocking from platform to platform; no sign of the 5.35 and 5.40, and 5.50 was cancelled. I came on the 5.44 to Coulsdon, packed like sardines. Still, I got home at 6.45. Felt better after finding the coal, still better after dinner and listened to Russell on Civilisation, and best after I played till 9.00.

The twins were fine. E sent them an orange each and they were bowling them about on the floor. I said to Margaret, "If that were my orange, I shouldn't play ball with it." "But it isn't your orange," said Margaret logically.

She was telling a tale in bed about going for a walk with all the dogs she knew—Susan, Sallie, Jock, Bimbo, all the puppies, named one by one, then the horses—Joey, England, Prince etc. Andrew added 'and Margot', but she wouldn't have that incongruous member among the animal companions. Andrew built me a very good house. He looks carefully at pictures—remarked that you could not see the end of that train because it was behind the tree. He ate fine meals with enjoyment. Margaret went into Rosa's bed yesterday morning and Andrew remarked, "Fine games Nim and Rosa are having." Hobday had been to Andover and bought them a pair of shoes and a pair of sandals each £2/7/3d altogether—all very good, but how do people manage to shoe a lot of children? E paid for them. He said prosaically last week, "I may be rationalising but I feel reconciled to sudden death now. It is the thought of leaving the twins alone that bothers me."

Tuesday 16th January 1945

Margot and I went to Collingbourne for the weekend. We just got seats on Saturday (I had inadvertently left my bag at home at Riddlesdown so went to the office with my season ticket and a threepenny bit!). Next to me sat an old parson who began to talk by explaining that he had cress in his sandwiches and so could not give Susan any bits. He was called Chalmers and was vicar of a Chelsea church. He had lost his vicarage, church (except for the tower) and the larger of the 2 halls in the blitz, but had services and had produced a nativity play in the surviving hall. He did not approve Fisher as Archbishop—"Mrs Fisher is the man of the house." She is secretary of the Mothers' Union, a job that should go to a clergyman's widow at £300 pa—though she is honorary. But she isn't domesticated, he isn't strong enough". Chalmers had been 15 years in an Australian parish 140 miles long where he got about on horseback. He was most entertaining and quite overcome to learn that Margot had evacuated some of his flock in September1939.

Rosa was rather depressed by her birthday. Andrew and Margaret had bought her a hankie each, going off to Saunders for the purpose, each with a 1d in a handbag! They were both looking well, though Margaret had little dinner on Sunday. We had high tea—roast chicken and Christmas pudding on Saturday to celebrate. They thought it a very funny tea, but Andrew had 3 roast potatoes and gravy followed by Christmas pudding and Margaret had roast potato and breast of chicken (which she enjoyed and encored) and birthday cake. They awoke early on Sunday and sang. Margaret begins to get the tune of Good King Wenceslaus at last.

Once she paused halfway to invite Andrew to 'sing with me'. He did. He has a queer habit of projecting mistakes on to Pink Bear: "It's Sunday today."

"Yes it is, Andrew."

"Pink Bear says it's Saturday!"

I took them the 2 books Mary had sent them—'Copy Kitten' for Andrew (he liked the dust cover as much as the book and took it on and off) and 'Lucky Lamb' for Margaret (the theft of the train by the lamb and the small boy's distress was the most popular episode). It is a privilege to watch their minds growing and unfolding like flowers. We walked on the downs:

Me: "These are gorse flowers."

Margaret: "They are like ladies slippers." (An acute observation)

Me: "Yes."

Margaret: "When will the ladies slippers come?"

Me: "In the summer."

Margaret: "When will the summer come?"

Me: "After the spring; it will be spring when the mornings and evenings get light."

Andrew: "When the daisies come."

Margaret: "I saw some daisies last Sunday on the downs." (True.)

Andrew: "Daisies will come to Twinpath when the spring comes."

Cooking is still a favourite game but they both play with dolls.

Andrew: "Pink Bear is ill—he must stay in bed—I must wrap him up."

Me: "What is the matter with him?"

Andrew: "Just ill." Later: "He has a pain in his tummy."

Margot and I walked to Ludgershall for the bus to catch the 5.50 and Rosa came in with us. She thinks Hobday is too weak with Andrew and I agree; but what can I do at present? Mary lent us Bedales' Jubilee book. E thinks Margaret might get a lot out of it and he said they could both go to the junior school if necessary and as soon as need be.

Raper (who flew over from Belfast for the AGM on Sunday) came to see me on Friday morning. He and Mrs Raper had spent Christmas in Dublin, expensively at the Gresham, but sumptuous. His account of the food was mouth-watering. Still, we did well this weekend: oranges and lemons in addition, and Margot got some marmalade oranges yesterday which are having their preliminary boil at the moment.

Monday 22nd January 1945

It got milder last week but on Thursday there was a gale and by yesterday it was as cold as ever. Yesterday was brilliant sun and cold NW wind. We had a good walk over the downs. I was surprised to find when I got out at Surbiton that it had snowed again. Purley had 2 or 3 inches this morning and I have been colder in the office than on any day, I think. I ached, especially when it blew and rained straight in. I had neuralgia in my head and eyes, but today I have been numb and aching, although I had more clothes on than in the street.

Rosa was better and the twins were in good form, though Andrew had burnt his hand on the hot plate and was wearing a bandage and bag. He awoke with a dream at 6.10 yesterday crying—demanding, to go into Nannie's bed. When he realised I was there, he elected to come into mine and fell asleep at once, but the disturbance woke Nim, who didn't sleep again but sang to herself 'Yankee Doodle' over and over again. She is asking Why? questions: "Why hasn't Bill come to see me? Why must Andrew take care of your watch?" Andrew remarked about a lemon skin Hobday was rubbing on her hands—"The lemon hurts my nose." We had Glitterwax. Margaret gets intense satisfaction as she manipulates it. She made Finn the puppy—just a long sausage with 2 eyes at one end! I took her a new yellow and rust jersey which she pounced on before I unpacked it!

Rockets were rarer last week till Friday. We had 3 or 4 in the night and 2 on Saturday morning. Margot stayed at Purley at the weekend and said there were several. I heard 2 today and 1 at 5.15, of which I felt the blast. I was on the way to the station. A window was blown in near me. It was just south of the river between Tower and London Bridge.

I lunched with Oades on Thursday. On Friday, we read 'The Circle'. I was astonished at the disapproval evoked by the ending. I can understand Rosa's horrors at the neighbours finding out about the twins.

Monday 5th March 1945

It turned colder with sharp morning frosts before the weekend but spring continues to advance. Mauve, white, purple and yellow crocuses; pink, red and yellow primroses, anemones; snowdrops in the garden, violets, Arabis and primroses at Purley, with the almond blossom showing pink.

I went down on Saturday in record time: Andover 2.13, Collingbourne 2.55. They hadn't reached the station. Nim thought my train must be a Marlboro train, but Andrew said it was from Andover. He had bites which kept us both awake till after 1.30. I am nearly certain I heard a very distant siren. It was a lively weekend in London. Alerts on Sat afternoon and Sunday morning; flying bomb by East Dulwich station and a bomb on Jamaica St, Bermondsey. We had an alert on Friday night and I heard several rockets—all distant. We didn't hear anything in the alert but they heard a flying bomb at Dulwich. 2 Alerts this morning in the office. There is a suggestion that the Germans are sending flying bombs from Holland. If so we can expect a few in daylight. It is lucky Rosa didn't come back last week. Lloyd (of the Thames Steam Tug) phoned and apologised for delay. His house in Ilford had been destroyed by a rocket which fell 20 yards away, last Wednesday week. His wife slightly hurt. At Collingbourne, they have threshed the rick at the bottom of the path and there is a lovely sweet-smelling pile of chaff, which the twins loved. It was almost like sand.

Wednesday 7th March 1945

I had supper with Ella. She is much better and enjoying working in the city. She is to learn all branches of publishing and finds it stimulating and much less wearing than teaching. She likes unacademic people for a change.

Monday 12th March 1945

We have had no rain to speak of for a month and there is a shortage of water at Collingbourne—one butt empty, one two thirds empty. The twins were very lively and spending most of the weekend in the garden in the sun. I did some gardening and helped Hobday to fix the gate—she had made it quite effective. Margaret describing how they saw rowing on the river: "the boats did swim in the garden with their water brushes."

Rockets have been frequent. The worst I have heard was on Smithfield Market on Thursday about 11.00. It blew my mirror off the wall. E said he was told 90 bodies had been taken out; 70 still missing; 347 detained in Barts. I also heard of one on Tooting Broadway and one at Camberwell, one at Thornton Heath, one at Long Lane between Elmers End and Woodside, 70 still missing.

One day last week we got back and found the glass had been put back into our broken windows and the glazier was storing his gear in the garage.

Monday 19th March 1945

This evening it is blowing and raining after another dry and sunny week. The Collingbourne people went to Salisbury last Tuesday and Rosa bought a new coat. The twins enjoyed the cattle market. They had Geoffrey to tea on Friday and told me all about it. He had washed his face and hands, had on his best shoes, sat next to Nim while Andrew sat round the corner; he had 2 buns and some treacle sandwiches. Nim played the bells yesterday, rattling them and banging them hideously till I asked if she knew how they should be played—with the little hammer, one at a time. I suggested that she played each one in order. She tried and was charmed with the result. I had a tummy upset and retired to bed with a hottie and recovered sufficiently to come home in the evening but I have still felt shaky today. I seem to get one small ailment after another—I suppose I need a holiday. Margot has renewed her cold somehow. On Friday, we went to the youth club who were having a Brains Trust. It wasn't bad—I have heard worse on the radio. I liked best a man called Hawkins who is something legal. His little girl and boy with their mother were sitting just ahead as I found later and I had been admiring the girl—a charming little thing like Alice, but less pushing.

I hope to get the bungalow painted and the gardener is coming to dig and plant potatoes next Saturday.

Rockets continued last week but I heard fewer and more distant—though last night one noisy one woke me with a jump. I have heard of them falling at Crystal Palace, Upton Park, Long Lane and yesterday, at 9.00 am, where the soap boxes are in Hyde Park. We had 2 alerts last week, one at 5.30 am and one for which I heard an All Clear as I was crossing London Bridge. I didn't hear any flying bombs but the typists said there was an Imminent in the second. I have heard various scare rumours about gas and about the Germans sending by radio their obsolete bombers to crash in London. It is a weary business, though we continue to make progress everywhere except Italy. Food and clothes are to be scarcer than ever.

Monday 26th March 1945

Last week was perfect—sunny days and frosty mornings first and gradually warming up till Saturday was the warmest March day for 50 years. Things are growing too fast; tulips out, grape hyacinths, forget me nots, flowering currants, cherry and plum, violets and primroses; even a cowslip on the downs. The hawthorns are green. And at the weekend and today we have had soft mild rain to fill the water butts.

Rockets have continued and we have had 3 alerts. On Saturday morning at 7.55, I looked out of the kitchen door to see a flying bomb zooming through the blue a mile or so south, from east to west. I had not expected to see another so clearly. E said there was one in Leinster Square. I get a bit edgy even when we don't get a near or loud rocket and I persuaded Margot to come down for the weekend to relax. It is pleasant to enjoy the country and know that the bangs (frequent) and droning (continual) mean nothing sinister. The twins came to meet us and Andrew looked at the unexpected Margot in ecstasy, as at heaven opened! They pointed out some fluffy yellow chickens in the field and then a calf we found was a day old 'just out of his mother's tummy', said Nim. They took us round the garden showing us all new flowers. Later Andrew said, "Gip Harsit—Nimmie can't know it." We cudgelled our brains as to what he meant till I said, "Grape hyacinth?" So it was. It is difficult to make any headway over the downs as they have to keep stopping to pick daisies and hate to be left behind. I have never seen Andrew eat a better dinner—a small piece of roast pork, roast potatoes, broccoli and gravy, and a second helping of all except pork, 2 wedges of jam tart, a hunk of roll (which Rosa had made for him to cook) and butter and a cup of tea. Margot took mustard and cress and they had some for tea, eating each bit separately. Nim had 2 helpings. We went to church yesterday morning. Andrew sang 'Pilgrim' and 'Now the day is over' high, on his own when we were singing psalms, but Margaret watched and joined the congregation quite creditably. Andrew drew a schema of a cat and a station, signals and lines.

Tuesday 3rd April 1945

As was to be expected the weather broke for Easter and March went out like a lion. A cold wind, grey skies, scudding clouds with showers and sun patches made it pleasanter indoors. So we went on Saturday to Andover to the cinema and saw George Formby in 'He Snoops To Conquer', a slightly propaganda film about town planning and public opinion polls. It was better than I expected from the title. I don't approve of the twins going but they seemed to suffer no ill effects. Andrew said, "That man snatched the letter—he was rude. Why did he snatch?" and he was scared when George F drove the lorry and couldn't stop it.

On Sunday morning, we went to church and the twins sang lustily, and in the afternoon we played Snap. They have both quite seen the point but might be quicker with their 'snaps'. Andrew sees 2 alike and just looks at me with a brilliant smile and says, "What now?"—which is what I said when I taught him. It just proves that example is stronger than precept. Nim is apt to get distracted by the pictures. Yesterday morning I gardened—the gardener can't come so we have to dig the garden. I found a ladybird and the twins played with it for a long time, very gently, being careful not to hurt it. In the afternoon, we went to the wood and picked primroses, anemones and violets. It was exquisite and the twins loved it except when they got scratched by brambles.

Andrew surprised me by drawing letters quite confidently and well. A,M,N,Y,L,F. He can't manage curved letters. He copied a square as a good oblong and made a fair attempt at a triangle (mosaic). In the bus on Saturday: "I saw a phone. Mummy, did you miss it? Someone was phoning—I saw a coat so there must have been someone, mustn't there?"

No rockets or fly bombs since Thursday! The Germans are pulling out of Holland. No one is making rash statements but we all hope they are finished. I felt excited last week at the news; one felt that anything could happen. Now I think it will still take a few weeks. The Russians are nearly at Vienna and the Germans intend to defend it. Such a pity! It seems incredible that it may end soon. Rosa is probably coming home on Thursday.

Tuesday 10th April 1945

Rosa came home on Thursday. She didn't sleep well at first, but in the absence of rockets this is improving. E came down for the weekend and the twins gave him a great welcome. Saturday was dull and bleak but Sunday was sunny by noon and we all went to the wood. The blackthorn is out as well as the anemones, primroses and violets in the wood. The country looked exquisite and E said Purley wouldn't be so lovely for the twins. When we reached the wood, Andrew complained of a pain in his tummy and looked pale. Margaret was sweet to him—"It's alright Andrew," she said, and rubbed his tummy for him. She picked him a bunch of flowers and gradually he improved. E collected some wood and we 3 had primroses etc. They had good meals and behaved very well.

E gave them his belated presents: round bricks, train and number book and signal for Margaret; big bricks, round bricks, '10 Little N***** Boys' and signal for Andrew. He longed to play with her train and tackled her with great skill. He asked her when she would lend it to him. She said, "Tomorrow" (Sunday); then on Sunday morning she said, "Afternoon"; after dinner she said, "before tea." But he laid his hands on it by inviting her to use the station he had made from his new big bricks. He was very thrilled with the N***** Boys and E was impressed with his accuracy counting. He is quite safe up to 13. Margaret impressed him when she showed him the garden—"A red tulip," said E. "Oh, no, an anemone," said Margaret. Not at all suggestible, as it looked like a tulip and was growing by itself. We had a lovely time on Sat night, after so long—and may have started a baby.

Monday 16th April 1945

The great news—greater than the advance in Germany—was the death of Roosevelt last Thursday. Its suddenness made it incredible. It darkened the glorious weather of the last few days. I felt we had better spared Churchill as Roosevelt was the greater and wider statesman—more vital to the peace negotiation than anyone else. It is an irreparable loss. Even if Truman is as great there is the loss of knowledge and experience—the gradual building up of friendship, especially with Churchill and Stalin.

The weekend was perfect. It was sad to leave Collingbourne at 4.30 yesterday. This spring is perfect except that it is passing so quickly. Already the plum, pear and cherry blossom is fallen or falling. The apples are still at their zenith. The cottage garden is a picture with saxifrage, polyanthus, grape hyacinth, forget me not, daffodil, narcissus and tulip. The gooseberries and currants are covered with blossom and on Sat evening we had the first asparagus. The twins were in fine fettle, Margaret brown and rosy, Andrew pink, with gold tanned forehead. We went over the downs yesterday morning and picked cowslips. Andrew squeaked with excitement and Margaret was blandly maternal, showing him where to pick. Hobday sent hers to Rosa who had sent her down a lemon curd tart. I spent what time I could digging the potato patch but it is hard work, though satisfactory. Digging up the dandelions is particularly good, the grass less so as it is just a heavy mat. Andrew helped me dig, using the small fork while I used the big. He wrote 3 letters—one to me, one to Bill, one to Margot. He is getting good at capital letters but makes them sideways or upside down as easily as the normal way. He has quite mastered the number book. He said, "I can't count the eggs now there are 12!" He has become nervous of bees (I think from the N***** Boys—'6 little n***** boys playing with a hive, A bee stung one and then there were 5'). He is also most cautious with flowers he isn't used to; I gave him a piece of cow parsley, just out. "Will it prick me?" he asked, before he would take it. He built a very good signal box by himself and wanted a pointed roof. Hobday said they had flat roofs (easier), but he looked up his train book and found the signal box in the picture had a pointed roof. E marked Margaret's round blocks with an 'M' to distinguish them from Andrew's. Yesterday Margaret said, "Will you lend me your pencil?" I said, "What for?" She said, "I want an 'M' on this brick." I think she was quite innocent.

Tuesday 17th April 1945

Still a heat wave. Lilac, laburnum, chestnut all in flower. The faint yet heavy, slightly sickly, sweet scent of apple blossom came over in waves as I passed The Spinney. Even the beech leaves are unfolding; the elms are quite green.

I listened to Truman last night and was favourably impressed. A letter from de Ploeg in Holland this morning—"We had a bad 4 years, very many men were moved to Germany to work there in the factories and others were put in prison and many were killed. There was great want of food and of all things and still it is bad. But we enjoy our greater liberty." It is cheering to see people re-emerging as the floods recede. I managed to get 6lbs of potatoes; all last week I could get none, though I queried once.

Tuesday 24th April 1945

It turned colder at the weekend with a strong north wind. Sunday was brilliant from morning and we went to the wood with the twins. It was a paradise—a few last anemones, primroses, violets, bugle, garlic, celandine, dead nettle, crab apple, what seemed to be wild columbine and wild gladiolus and cowslips on the downs. E had studied the map so we walked back to Ludgershall via the Sheans and a path. It took us as long as the main road but was pleasanter. I saw a swallow and at least 4 hares in a field of springing corn round which we had to walk as the path had been ploughed up, butterflies—orange tip, blue, painted lady, tortoiseshell. The train was packed and we stood to Surbiton. Going down we went to Woking and changed, where we got a seat. Hobday and the twins met us at Andover. They had been wearing sun suits the week before and were quite brown. Andrew said to E, "I've got a little boy (meaning Pink Bear) and you've got a little boy" (meaning himself). Margaret is very sweet. She gave me 3d, putting it in my bag loose. When E gave them 6d each, she said at once, "Now I can get you a hankie for your birthday."

Margot came back from Spicelands on Saturday looking very brown. She had enjoyed it and not worked too hard. Rosa and I went to the Benbows on Friday to read 'The Critic'. It is astonishingly good and alive. We talked about the war and the Germans in the interval. No hope of curing the 12—20s, said Mr Benbow—segregate them all in Siberia and just make them work. The vicar was hopeless about them all—even the babies—"in the blood," he said. I felt terribly depressed.

Tuesday 1st May 1945

It has been bitterly cold with NW wind, snow flurries, white frost, grey sky. I went to Collingbourne Kingston on Sunday and gave a bottle of blood. People said, "Perhaps this is the last time." It was the second time the village had contributed—130 in Oct and 161 last Sunday—mainly women. Margaret was willing to come too 'and help a wounded soldier's leg to get better'. I took the twins for a short walk around the green road for the first time. When we reached the Ludgershall road, Margaret recognised it and said Rosa had taken them there. I was wearing shoes they hadn't seen and she saw them at once and said I was wearing Rosa's shoes. Hobday said she remembered, and mentioned, the pink may tree in the front garden at Addiscombe. This is remarkable as she hasn't seen it in blossom since she was 18 months old. Andrew wants his train painted green, like the (SR) London trains at Andover. He said he hadn't seen a train all different colours. There was a lovely example of Susan Isaac's 'cosy places': Margaret was hoeing and made a shallow hole. She was delighted with it and got in, calling to Andrew to come too 'into this dear little hole'. They both squatted down together in it with evident pleasure. On Saturday, they were both stitching small canvas mats with wool. Margaret is more adept and can even thread a needle with the wool. Andrew is interested in the process and counts the stitches on each side, pokes the needle in and tries to capture the exact moment when the stitch is created.

The great question is: when will VE day be declared? On my birthday we went to the Classic and saw an old Ginger Rogers film, 'The Major and the Minor'. The Newsreel showed some concentration camp photographs. The corpses were less awful than the people who could still just move. Some of our own prisoners were shown too. It was very moving. Mussolini is dead, shot, as was fitting by the Italians. It seems so simple, so natural, now. If it had happened 10 or 20 years ago…

Wednesday 2nd May 1945

It is bewildering. This morning we were told Hitler was dead—killed in Berlin—and had been succeeded by Admiral Doenitz. Nothing of Himmler. No one knows if it's true. Tonight we heard that the Germans in Italy had surrendered. Things move so fast that it seems ages ago that we heard Hitler had been killed. Meantime, of the important things like St Francisco, we hear little. Mussolini was killed on Sunday or Monday and now Hitler. So they disappear, almost as if predestined, till one remembers 1940.

Friday 11th May 1945

I have got badly behind. All last weekend we were in a kind of suspended animation, waiting for VE day. It was most humbugging. E and I went to Collingbourne. I stayed till Monday morning but all we knew was that it would be before Thursday, so I came back. We did little work and flags began to appear. On Monday afternoon, I had 4 phone talks about my Modiano conference, fixed for Tuesday at 4.00. We arranged what to do in any event. I would have preferred to keep it but EA was against it. I forgot to let E know and he thought I was working on Tuesday. In fact, we heard the announcement that Tues and Wed would be holidays at 7.00 on Monday, so I just caught the 9.00 train down to Andover, caught a bus to Ludgershall and walked from there. I was tired when I got there at 12.00 but they were very welcoming. It poured thunder rain after dinner and we listened to Churchill while the twins played with plasticine. Margaret made umbrellas, little pigs and a 3-legged stool. Andrew made trains, a 4-legged stool and boys and girls. Then Margaret and I went to the church to see when there was a service, but there was no sign of one. The men were ringing the bells but Margaret was not interested. She looked for the choir and said, "Where is the song?" There were flags, including hammer and sickle, on the Blue Lion and many coronation flags. I even saw a woman on the bus with an Edward VIII coronation flag.

Thursday 24th May 1945

It seems weeks and weeks since I last wrote. Things have crowded on each other. On the 12th, Rosa and Margot went to see London flood lit and I went alone to see the twins. I can't remember much about the weekend except that we all went to church for thanksgiving and the lovely old church was full for once, yet the vicar was as poor as usual. It was an opportunity lost. Yet today we hear he has been made a Canon of Salisbury—why? The Land Girls and Observer Corps and Home Guard came to church in uniform. The Home Guard quite moved me; such odd-looking yet ordinary men—elderly or very young—completely resisting the tendency to be reduced to uniformity by their uniform. They looked completely individual and knobby. The twins were good and sang lustily. Andrew sang 'Praise Him, praise Him' on his own most suitably. Margaret was conscious of her new viyella frock.

On the 15th, Tuesday evening, May phoned from Plymouth to say Auntie Paul[64] had had a stroke. Rosa and I went to Plymouth on the 12.50 the next day after I had had a hectic morning at the office. Rosa got corner seats and I caught the train with 3 minutes to spare. It was a comfortable but slow journey. It seemed queer not to get out at Andover. At Salisbury, I jumped out and got cups of tea and a sandwich for Rosa who had had nothing but some rice pudding before she started. I have never seen richer colouring than in the country just beyond Exeter—the deep blue sky, fresh new green of corn and grass, deep and vivid red of bare earth—it was unbelievable. The route, new to me as I have previously gone Great Western, was lovely. It almost touches Dartmoor round Okehampton, Lydford and Tavistock, with wide views south; then the Tamar with its 2 bridges, the exciting run into Devonport and Plymouth, roaring through short tunnels and cuttings at the water's edge and finally through the grey, steep streets. We were not more than 10 minutes late and May[65] met us. We had a meal and then Luce and I went to Peverel to sit up with Auntie Paul.

I had never seen anyone with a stroke and she was not so altered as I expected. Her right arm and leg were paralysed; she breathed heavily and quickly; she was quite unconscious, but she might have been in a heavy sleep. I found the breathing trying all night. One listened and listened; couldn't get the sound out of one's head. Once she stopped for perhaps 3 or 4 breaths before resuming the rhythmic snore. I got one and a half hours sleep and Luce dozed

---

[64] Rosa's sister
[65] May and her sister Luce were Rosa's nieces

perhaps the same time, sitting up. She went back at 6.30 and I watched alone till 9.15 when a girl came to relieve me and the Dr came. He couldn't tell. I returned to Auntie Bess[66] for breakfast about 10.30 and slept for one and a half hours which seemed like 12, and got up to dinner. It was a lovely sunny day after a cold grey morning when I couldn't stop shivering so I suggested to Rosa that we should go to look at the sea.

It was my first visit since Christmas 1940 and I hadn't seen the effects of the blitz. On the whole, I don't think it is worse than the City, but there just isn't any of the shopping centre left. One can see one's way about and the general layout as never before. St Andrew's has lost its roof and windows, but the pillars with their lovely delicate capitals still stand and the floor is grass. It was as lovely to me as before, but then I always see more beauty in a roofless church—Tintern Abbey and St Swithuns, Cannon St, for example. I like the way they are using it for services too and growing flowers. The Hoe was lovely as ever. When I was a child, I took it for granted but with wider knowledge I can see its individual beauty overlooking perhaps the loveliest port in the world with the sparkling busy sea, the unspoilt green slopes of Mount Edgecumbe Park and the rugged rocks of Penlee beyond on the one side, balanced by the sweep of Mount Batten and the point on the opposite side, with Drake's Island in the foreground to break the line. Glorious! A look at old Drake where he has stood all through the blitz ministering to Plymouth's superstitious faith and we turned back. Rosa caught her toe on a blitzed pavement and fell full length, banging her knee very badly, so I could just get her to a bus and indoors where Luce rendered first aid. After tea, I went back to Auntie Paul who hadn't changed. The district nurse came to wash her, etc. and her friend Miss Prideaux kept me company—a simple soul who, at my invitation, told me about her 9 years' stay in China where she went as a children's nurse.

May joined me about 7.00 and the night nurse was coming about 9.00. We left Lily in charge for 30 minutes and went back discussing the administration. There was some clash of opinion as to whether Luce should sit up for a third night. She insisted because she did not want Auntie Paul to be quite without her own people if by some chance she did regain consciousness. She had hardly started when the nurse phoned to say Auntie Paul had died—just 3 gasps and she was gone. It was midnight before we went to bed having fixed the funeral, phoned Roy etc. I left the next morning by the 8.15 train for Andover. When I

---

[66] Rosa's eldest sister and May's and Luce's mother

got to Collingbourne, Andrew had a running cold, with streaming eyes and nose. I suspected measles at once. On Sunday morning, he developed the spots. All day he was miserably ill, and at night his temperature was 104. Hobday sat up with him. On Monday morning, it was down to 102 and during the day he visibly improved and began to take an interest in things, had some rice pudding I had made him, objecting to the 'icing sugar' (glucose) on it, wanted to get up, had his bricks on a tray. The doctor came on Sunday morning and said, "A moderate attack with no bronchitis." Margaret was very well all the weekend and good as gold. The weather was poor, though I did do a little gardening on 3 evenings.

E took Margaret out one morning; they got drenched. It was pleasant to have a Whitsun with him after so long and we loved on Friday evening and shortly and fiercely on Saturday evening. ("Why do you provoke me?" he said.) On Sunday evening, I was worried about Andrew and just cried and cried. It was partly coming from Auntie Paul, who was dying, to him when he was so ill with the fever. It was futile to tell myself how different their cases were. Of course, his improvement on Monday cheered me up and I stopped worrying. This morning I heard from Hobday that he was going on all right.

Wednesday 30th May 1945

It has been chilly and unsettled for at least a fortnight and I can't shake off the cold I had when I went to Plymouth. I went down to Collingbourne on my own at the weekend and found Andrew much better, looking taller but very thin and in good spirits with good appetite. Margaret, quite fit, came on her own to meet me as far as the bridge. Andrew got up for the first time on Saturday and was weak on his legs. He got up to dinner on Sunday and was much better. He built a complicated house with covered sidewalk and garden and 2 storeys. We all had breakfast in bed as Hobday was depressed and tired. I put some more potatoes in. Margaret had no cold or watery eyes but she had a temperature of 100.2 on Saturday night. Was this measles, so light as not to notice or was it just the beginning of them? Mr Hobday is due back on leave on June 8th so I shall have to have a week's leave.

The 7.44 from Andover was punctual. I went with Oades and his colleague Kendal to a meeting of the Royal Statistical Society. It was above my head, but it is pleasant to see a subject just thrashed out thoroughly—all terms defined and every statement examined. What a contrast to newspapers. Afterwards I had dinner with Oades at Bertorelli's where I hadn't been for years. He can't find anywhere to live. EA went to City 18 yesterday and Pole arrived at City 6. He seems pleasant.

Tuesday 5th June 1945

It was a lovely weekend in some ways, though it was a bit spoilt because Margot got a cold and wouldn't come down when she knew E was coming. He had offered not to come as we should be crowded. Rosa knew he was there and was upset again. Still, even so, it was lovely. Margaret's measles were nearly gone but she had a disturbing cough. E suggested going for a walk and we went up towards Collingbourne Woods. There was a stormy red sunset. As it got twilight he left the path, to my surprise, and under a beech we loved. Like a saraband. It was queer to be in the air, under a tree again. In the middle, we heard a nightingale. Not full, as it was past its peak (2nd June), but lovely, the first time we have had both together. There were several, and also corncrakes, and as we reached the road planes were flying high, leaving white paths, and two flares lit up the hulls.

Andrew was in good form, still pleased to be better and enjoying Margaret's toys while she was in bed. He helped me sow potatoes; cut up rhubarb; picked gooseberries and topped and tailed them; built complicated houses.

Andrew: "Where are my cotton reel bricks?"

E: "You ought to know. There were 12 altogether."

Andrew: "And how many were there not altogether?" He noticed a photograph of an engine with only one big wheel. E is sure he is reasoning out the meaning of multiplication.

Raper phoned me yesterday and I lunched with him today. He is at Somerset House devilling for AG Roberts. He is optimistic about finding a house. He has realised £300 by selling surplus furniture, including a fridge, which cost £60 7 or 8 years ago, for £132. This morning Reen phoned, up at the Albert Hall for the day with a WI conference. She may stand for the local council in the autumn. We heard Churchill last night and thought him very poor and cheap. Atlee was better tonight but lacks drive and incisiveness.

Monday 18th June 1945

I came back last night after a week's leave. Mr Hobday came on the 7th and returned yesterday, hence I let Hobday have half her summer holiday. They did not get their plans settled until I arrived on Sat so it was difficult for me to fix,

194

especially as they were coming and going all the week. He went to Devon on the Sat and she met him in Andover and they went up to town in the evening, returning to Wilts on Tuesday evening. He went to Devizes on Wed and she went to her sister who came for the night. They were married on Thursday and went to Bridport on Friday morning and came back on Sunday evening.

It wasn't so bad for me as this sounds, though the wedding and its preparations were trying, especially confetti in the garden and bedroom, which really did annoy me as it is so difficult to clear up. Between times I enjoyed myself and the twins and I had quiet hours which were lovely. Margot came down for the first weekend and they gave her a great welcome. The weather was bad but it was lovely to be on our own. And we did just manage to go for a short walk. It was a pity she couldn't stay a day or two. On Monday, the weather was bad. We walked to the wood in a lull in the rain and found 2 strawberries which Andrew liked, but we got wet against the wind coming back. Tuesday was better and we went to Salisbury for market day. I looked at St Thomas for the first time and admired the huge Doom (restored) over the chancel arch. There was a good Children's Corner with books to look at. The market was great entertainment— pigs, calves, hens, rabbits, geese (very unpopular), ducks and ducklings (Nim wanted to bring one of these home—"We can give it water from the water butt"), sheep, turkeys, and, finally, a man speaking for the Liberals. In the afternoon, I sat in the Close admiring the sun on the old houses and the perfect pattern of the cathedral while the twins picked daisies and played 'leaves' and danced round the tree. It clouded over and we went for tea just as it rained, but it was a shower. Just as we reached Tidworth a storm cloud blew up and when we got out at Ludgershall the rain was as heavy as I have ever seen. It didn't last long but I had to take Margaret to do a wee at the station, leaving Andrew in a shop. He was quite unconcerned when I returned for him.

Wed was a lovely day. We spent the morning in the garden and the afternoon on the downs (after haircuts). We were two and a half hours and they flew. Wild roses, rock roses, lady's slipper, elder blossom, honeysuckle predominated. We got back at 5.30 to tea and found that the Hobdays and his sister had arrived. They all went out later and left me to put the twins to bed in peace. After they were asleep, I sat drinking my coffee and reading Eiluned Lewis' 'The Captain's Wife', and looking from the open door, filled with a great contentment, in a mood of surprising serenity. It was a golden evening, the sun shimmering the silver birches, a blackbird calling, a lark singing, 2 goldfinches twittering, Mr

Blackmore's hoe crunching. A short half hour containing the essence of Collingbourne at its best. I love being alone with the twins, awake or asleep.

By contrast, Thurs was awful. The rush to catch the 8.29 to Devizes, a piercing cold wind and grey sky (though it didn't rain). The twins in coats and complaining; Nim cried because she wanted her coat off; Andrew cried because he poked his eye against a pram. We had 2 coffees to pass the time till 11.00. It was market day but there was nothing but calves and a few hens to see. The ceremony was short and unimpressive. I signed the register as a witness and it was over, with an hour till the train home. While the others sought a drink, I took the twins to St John's again and soothed myself in admiration of the hard Norman tower and graceful Perpendicular chapel, and the twins recovered their spirits picking daisies. I took them on to the footbridge over the railway and said, "Look."

"Tunnels," said Andrew.

"Poppies," said Margaret. So typical! We returned in a car from Savernake, getting back at 1.30 and had lunch—tongue and salad (the twins had theirs on their blue table and went on to rice pudding and gooseberry juice; they helped themselves and almost finished it), cake and cocktail. I was glad when they caught the 4.14 and I could peacefully bath the twins.

On Sat, I did the chores in the morning and we met E at 3.00 and went for a walk over the downs. The Hobdays came back at 8.15 just as we had finished supper (including the asparagus). E and I walked to Everleigh. There was one bunting after another, all the way, sitting on the wires. I got rather tired and so had less energy than often for loving. It was very pleasant just being passive. Curiously, I found I had slipped into a trance of ecstasy. Not the unconsciousness I used to fear in our early days, and at concerts, with some music, but a profound, still kind of ecstasy which left me feeling like Keats—"Now more than ever seems it rich to die, To fade upon the midnight with no sound." E said the transfiguration story described it better—the natural but vain wish to dwell upon the mountain top for ever.

Sunday was the finest weather, a brilliant cold morning, getting hotter as the sun gained power. It was the beginning of the best spell since early May. We were in the garden nearly all day till just before tea we took the twins round the green road. So my week's holiday ended.

Tuesday 19th June 1945

Today I phoned Mary. She told me of a house at Denmark Hill to be auctioned on Thurs so we went to look at it. It is lovely but too big and I am sure will be too expensive.

Monday 25th June 1945

E went to the auction of the Dulwich house which began at £3,000 and went for £4,375. We had decided to go to £2,000!

It was a real midsummer weekend. Hobday took me and the twins to tea at Sally Lunn and we had strawberries and Ideal milk in their garden. They are selling the business from 1/8/45 and going to Beaminster; very business-like, as Collingbourne will decline with the departure of the Americans. Their new place is to be The Greenwood Tree.

Yesterday I got up early after Margaret woke me at 6.00, gave Hobday her breakfast in bed and picked blackcurrants from 9.45 to 12.00 and from 12.15 to 12.35—about 7 lbs. Andrew helped me steadily till 12.00. Margaret got tired after half an hour and said it made her hand hurt! She walked round the garden in the sun and when I enquired what she was doing she replied, "Smelling the flowers." The garden looked lovely in spite of the weeds with delphiniums, sweet Williams, white campanula, pink, white, mauve and purple Canterbury bells and honeysuckle. Hobday picked and bottled 5 jars of gooseberries. I had a hasty salad lunch and left at ten to one to walk to Ludgershall. I was just climbing the slope of the Devizes Rd when a farmer in a van overtook me and gave me a lift to Weyhill. He said they had to cut the hay before it got old, and from that to artificial manures—"like giving a sick man nothing but brandy." I caught a bus to Andover and reached the station at 10 to 2, caught a non-stop train to Waterloo and had one and a half minutes to catch the Purley train. I arrived at 4.40 worn out and very hot to find Hartlcpool[67] having tea. We all went to church for the dedication of Wyndham's memorial[68], which looked lovely. The vicar did very nicely and we were all gratified. The road turned up for the occasion and pleased Rosa. I was still tired today and woke with a headache but it was better this evening, and I made 10lbs of blackcurrant jam.

The twins were looking fine. Even Andrew was brown. He builds complicated stations with footbridges and steps, waiting room, and name of

---

[67] A friend of Margot's

[68] A stone sculpture by Rosa of St Francis

station; and houses with stairs, coalhouse, WC (separate!) and garden with privet trees. He was asleep in 5 minutes on Sat night but Margaret took longer and sang a 'fairy song' that was lovely and long, which she invented. They both ask questions about the songs they choose: "Why was Boney sent away?"/"Why was the elephant stuck in the door?"

Thursday 28th June 1945

It has turned bleak and grey and chilly and wet—2 miserable days. E thinks he has flu. Yesterday we went to see the new Tate pictures at the National Gallery from 5.00 to 6.00. We just began to see them. I wasted too much time in the first room wondering why they had acquired some of the 19th Century ones. A group of small bronze studies by Henry Moore of Madonna and Child and the family were lovely. I couldn't appreciate The Bridge of Stanley Spencer but found The Roundabout rather exciting. Gwen John's Self Portrait is lovely. I liked two Matthew Smiths (a still life and portrait). Harness on a Wooden Chest was the most realistic painting of wood I have seen. I was interested in Duncan Grant's portrait of Vanessa Bell and liked a great chalk cliff by Wm Rothenstein. But we hardly saw the Blakes and would have gone again today but for E's flu.

Margot and I went to Michael Astor's meeting this evening. It was packed. He is young. The only good idea was to have fixed times for consulting his constituents if he is elected. Otherwise it was the same one-sided picture running everyone else down, appealing to nothing but self-interest and personal preferences. I shan't vote for him. Questions were lively and the meeting was alive.

Tuesday 3rd July 1945

It was a mild weekend. All day Sunday we picked fruit—blackcurrants, red currants, gooseberries, a few raspberries while the sun shone, and rushed indoors during the downpours. We didn't go out and we hardly sat down. The twins were in good form. Margaret eating tomatoes, lettuce and radish and Andrew raw carrot and lettuce. E took him a name for his station which he had made which pleased him much. We had a wakeful but enchanting night. He had had a chill on Thursday and I was doubtful whether he'd be well enough to come, let alone love. But he was. On Sat evening, Hobday and I went to the school for an hour to hear the Conservative candidate, Squadron Leader Hollis. He wasted no time and did not rake up the past except when driven to by questions. The school was full and I didn't get a question in. Last night I went with Mrs Benbow and Margot to hear Major Weaver. We preferred the Chairman but Weaver was quite good and one felt his confidence in tackling questions, and also his sincerity. The Chairman was excellent and kept the crowded meeting in a good temper. The opposition came more from Liberals than Conservatives.

Monday 9th July 1945

A lovely but strenuous weekend. Mary came down and it was the best weather since April, so we tried to do too much. We took her for a walk over the downs on Sat afternoon. Sat night was disturbed by Nim, who had a chill which hurt her to wee. Sunday morning I did some washing for Hobday (who had cut her left forefinger with a bill hook) and some weeding. We had an early dinner and caught the 12.55 to Marlborough.

The twins were good and Mary saw a great change, especially in Andrew, since last year. She recommends Marlborough College where her cousin went, a boy of rather similar temperament, and was very happy. Nim was slightly shy at first but very friendly later. In fact, she explained, "I couldn't speak to you at first because you had your hat on." Sometimes she hits on a phrase almost of poetry. The onions had died down and she said, "Look, the onions have gone back to winter."

Tuesday 17th July 1945

I begin this new book at Yeovil where I arrived for 3 weeks yesterday. I was doubtful if I should be able to come as on Friday evening, when I got in after having dinner with Mary and Dorothy in Soho, Hobday had wired that Margaret was ill. "Come as soon as you can." The wire had been phoned and Rosa hadn't understood all of it so I didn't know what the trouble was and I was very worried. E had had to cancel the weekend as K was sick and we phoned him. I was distracted and would have given much for a car. As it was I caught the 7.20 from Waterloo and caught a bus to Ludgershall, had to walk from there as I couldn't get a car, and arrived just before 11.00. She had had cystitis, an infection of the bladder and very painful, with high temps of 105° and 106°. Hadn't had anything to eat since Tuesday. Wed and Thurs were the worst days and the doctor came every day. He was a locum and the best I had seen down there. Not brilliant but careful and painstaking. She liked him. She had had M&B but there was nothing to be done for the pain. He said her heart and lungs were sound and there was no sign of appendicitis. He had suspected stone but it did not materialise. I could see she was past the worst when I arrived and on Monday she was much better—temp normal and very little pain. It was very hot and I took a pre-war bottle of lavender water which she much appreciated, and the illustrated Alice book. It was a great relief.

Andrew had been very good and was full of life. I was not over-anxious at leaving her as the doctor wasn't coming today. Rosa was sweet and Margot was a great help. I phoned from Collingbourne Kingston on Sat evening and was told the line was out of order but I got E who said he would let them know. On Sunday evening, his line was off so I wired Purley. The damage was due to terrific thunderstorms at the weekend. I came on here yesterday by the 2.16. The Dr gave me a lift to Ludgershall. He talked history, medicine, international relations, politics and economics with me!

The Evens welcomed me last night, though I am sleeping downstairs owing to the approaching visit of an aunt. The old lady was 81 on 25/6. They have a nice little girl from Wilton living there, dispenser to a Dr.

Last Wed I met Ella. E and I looked at the rest of the Tate pictures (especially the Blakes) first, so I was late. We had dinner and tried to see 'The Skin of Our Teeth' but it was full. So we went across the road to the Tatler to see Lemontev, which is the first Soviet film I have seen with absolutely no propaganda. It had the good acting and imaginative photography of many Russian and French films. A man next to me asked if I understood Russian, and learning that I didn't he produced a running commentary for the evening which included even more, such as "Ah! The street where I was born" (in Petersburg)! The shorts were all good, one a re-construction of S Italy—bullocks pulling ploughs and women carrying baskets of stones to men mending bridges. One on Jan Mayen island, all huskies and pack ice and fog coming down on snowy mountains. One Ministry of Information film on the rescue of the 900 partisans from Yugoslavia. A pleasant change from the common round.

Thursday 19th July 1945

Pouring with rain and blowing a gale. I have worked till between 8 and 9 each night and done 101 accounts in 3 days, but it gets boring.

Letters from Margot, Rosa, Elsie and E today. K is getting better very slowly and he is doubtful about the weekend. Margot heard yesterday morning that she had got the £200 scholarship and added a postscript. A long letter of congratulations from Carr Saunders. It is lovely and I hope she has an interesting time. Maybe she will get a line on research and meet some stimulating people. The cross-examinations and hectic letter writing were worth the effort.

Yeovil is as enervating as before. I suffer from sleepiness and thick head and do nothing but work, eat and sleep. I have a room to myself downstairs while Whiting is away, and the birds are lovely—warblers, tits, blackbirds.

Tuesday 24th July 1945

I went to Collingbourne on the 5.35 on Friday and came back yesterday morning. The weekend was fine with a few showers and a lot of wind. Margaret got up for an hour on Thurs and for 2 or 3 on Friday. On Sat, she got up at 12.45 and joined Andrew and me in the garden where we were weeding groundsel. The sun was out but there was some wind. She had a good dinner but in the afternoon she had pain. She slept a little and was comfortable under the eiderdown and got up to play Snap with gusto and seemed better. We couldn't get her off after I picked her up at 9.30 and she had a bad night, though no temperature. Yesterday morning I left her in bed but better and in good spirits. But I arranged for the doctor to come because we must find the cause of the trouble. The only thing we could think of was the wind for 10 mins. Andrew was a dear, helping with the weeding, fetching and carrying for Margaret. He has a passion for cabbage now. Picks, washes, cuts, salts and put in the pan and then invites you to have some of his cabbage. They both progress with writing more than reading (though A can read 'On' and 'Off' on the electric stove). They do Ms and Ns and W upside down. They have no idea of position. Andrew said he wrote Bill 'LLLBI'. A great development with Snap, which we haven't played since the summer. Margaret is quite competitive. Andrew sees as quickly as she does but can't say 'Snap'—has a kind of inhibition and merely looks and says, "Oooooh!"

Tuesday 31st July 1945

We are still very anxious about Margaret. Last Friday I had a phone message from Hobday and caught the 1.30 train, getting to Twinpath about 4.30. She had been running high temperatures and was feeble, had had nothing to eat since Monday. No pain again. The doctor seemed unable to find what the trouble was so Hobday was very blunt with him. He said he would arrange for her to go to Savernake Hospital for observation. E came down on Friday night so we both saw him on Sat morning. She had had a full course of M and B (she had half

201

doses before). He said the M and B might clear it up if it was a local and temporary infection. If it wasn't, it might be a stone (he didn't think so) or it might be some congenital kidney trouble. Must be bladder or kidney infection. We took her to hospital on Sat afternoon and went to see her on Sunday. They had stopped M and B and her temp was then normal. The first urine analysis was satisfactory. They seemed to be taking her seriously. The Dr had seen her Sat evening and was to see her Sunday evening. I am hoping for a phone report when Hobday has seen her tomorrow. She seemed quiet but not unhappy, though she cried when I went on Sunday. Hobday was very upset about her. They seem certain it isn't appendicitis. She has been sick only once (after M and B). She had half an orange for tea on Sunday and enjoyed it. But she seemed so small to be uprooted and put among strangers. Andrew enjoyed his visit to the hospital— inspected the sandpit, rocking horse etc. He looked anxious till he saw her and then beamed and bothered no more. Reen came over on Saturday and told me all she knew about the hospital. It seems one must watch them and insist on everything being done so I told sister she was to have a specialist if they had the slightest doubt.

It is extraordinary how, in spite of the anxiety which we both felt, we yet had lovely fucks on Friday and Sat nights, Sat especially, when E got a marvellous slow movement like the slow movement of a symphony. Just at the climax—the peak of the last Vivace movement, Andrew woke up and wanted to wee. It didn't matter—as E said when we resumed, "Quite different but very nice." I wonder whether we started a baby, though we didn't intend to. We shall see. He has gone to Wales till Friday week.

Heyhoe has gone on leave. I have worked 284 accounts up to now and there are still plenty.

Tuesday 7th August 1945

Last Wed Hobday phoned me after seeing Margaret in hospital. They could find nothing wrong and she was eating well and quite happy. I saw her on Sat, Sunday and Monday. She cried when we left her but seemed quite contented. She would volunteer little but we learnt that she had had a bath in the big bath, had had meat, gravy and potatoes for dinner. She had milk pudding each day. She had evidently had some communications with other children. She said a little boy broke her yellow pencil! She had played dolls with Thelma. She had good teas each day—ate a whole orange on Sat, a boiled egg on Sunday and one orange plus a quarter of Andrew's yesterday. Sister said they were sending a urine specimen for further analysis to Salisbury yesterday and if the report was satisfactory she could soon come home.

Tuesday 14th August 1945

On Sat, we saw Mrs Blackmore at Collingbourne and learnt that Margaret was coming home that afternoon, so we went on and E got out at Collingbourne Kingston and phoned the hospital to tell Hobday to meet me with the car at the Newbury Rd turn. The doctor reported nothing wrong, though she is very wobbly after being in bed so long, and looks pale. She has an excellent appetite. Hobday borrowed a pushchair so we took her on the downs on Sunday after it was hot. She loved it, and picked flowers with evident joy. Andrew loved pushing her on the level road all by himself. He is just beginning to show some understanding of reading—chose a story with only 2 pictures, and those dull, but attended entirely to the words, found 'on' and 'off' (which he knows) and then 'on' in 'ribbons'.

Wednesday 15th August 1945

Having got up to go to the office as usual this morning I learnt that today is VJ day. I had arranged to go with Nancy to the Prom. We were just in time to hear the National Anthem. To our sorrow (as we couldn't stay until the end) Sir Adrian stopped the Jupiter after the first movement for the King's speech. It was an experience to hear it in the packed Albert Hall, though there were many calls to the conductor to carry on. Coming back there were fireworks and a big bonfire at the fountain and reflections of bonfires around.

Monday 20th August 1945

Margaret seemed to be getting on well at the weekend, though she is still wobbly and complains that her leg and ankle ache at times. Hobday has been keeping her in bed to breakfast. Her appetite is excellent. She still wets her bed badly. She wants a nightie case like Margot's (embroidered) for Christmas. Andrew can almost tell the time. He put every one of his toys away last night before we went to the station. He is fascinated with the growing acorns.

Wednesday 22nd August 1945

It has rained heavily at times but I have been lucky except after lunch. This afternoon an interview with 2 men from Deloittes on Wearnes of Singapore. The Senior remembered seeing me 5 years ago at City10 on a Tea Co.

Went with Nancy to the Prom. The Bach was perfect, exquisite form and precision. The Mahler (Song of the Earth) a lyrical thing in bits and pieces.

Thursday 30th August 1945

A crowded week so I am very tired. Last Thursday Rosa, Margot and I went to see the film based on Enid Bagnold's novel 'National Velvet'. Made in Hollywood and containing queer mistakes (e.g. lilac in blossom when the Grand National is run), and over-bright technicolour, but the quality of the book comes through. There is far more character than in most films. The child's parents, the lad who helps deliver and trains the Pie, even oddments like the doctor, a sightseer, the village people, etc. are alive. And the story, like a fairy tale, is thrilling. All comes right in the end. It is charming to see Velvet (played by an English child evacuee) refuse offers to film with the Pie.

Unexpectedly, the weekend turned out perfect weather. Lovely sunsets, sparkly, dewy mornings, blazing sun at noon, still and misty starlight till the waning moon rose gold over the hedge. E came down on Sunday. We went over the downs and Andrew and I picked blackberries while E and Margaret sat on logs. On Monday, we took a day's leave and went to Marlboro' and, after coffee and some delay waiting for a bus, to Martinsell. E hadn't been before and was overcome by its beauty. We had only an hour before the bus took us back to Marlboro' for lunch at the British Restaurant. Andrew begins to put letters together to form words. Margaret really looked herself for the first time for 7 weeks. The hollow rings round her eyes had gone and she seemed quite herself.

Last night I went with Nancy to the Prom—Mozart and Haydn, and the interludes from Britten's Peter Grimes, which impressed me. I want to hear the whole opera. Most enjoyable. I saw Sir Wm Beveridge there. (He didn't remember giving me my degree 17 years ago!)

Monday 4th September 1945

A lovely weekend with the twins on my own. Andrew was very good. I took them the script letters and he loved them. Apart from 20 minutes for tea he played with them on Sat from 3.20 till bedtime, just putting them in rows, exchanging with Margaret, making words or just putting them away in the box—all the 'e's and all the 'n's, etc. on top of each other. The weather was bad but we managed to go out twice on Sunday.

In the afternoon, we went on the downs and it rained as we walked into the wind and we sheltered under an oat rick. It was half thatched and a ladder was lying by it on which we sat. When the rain abated, I wanted to look for mushrooms but Andrew didn't enjoy the wind. I suggested that he should stay under the rick and was surprised when he agreed. Even then, when Margaret and I went off, I wondered how he would feel alone and didn't stay more than 10 minutes or a quarter of an hour. When we got back and Margaret took him some acorns and a pink mallow flower, he was fine. I found about half a dozen small mushrooms. It was a sign of his growing independence.

English is difficult; a sentence of Margaret, while we were walking: "I must go in front of you. I want to catch one another."

I asked her if she had had a letter from me. "Yes."

"What was drawn on it?"

She replied, "You know. You saw it before you put it in the envelope."

I wrote 6 letters about houses on Sat and had one reply this morning and E phoned about 4, all of which were sold.

I went to UCH this evening to give blood, 420cc. They kept me waiting half an hour.

Friday 7th September 1945

Have been most depressed about finding a reasonable house. Rosa went to Seaford on Wed and said the house for £1,200 was awful. She looked at a few more and got details of one that sounded promising, but dear at £1,675. She got back worn out. I went to Caterham. The house was built 1898, had been re-decorated inoffensively and had adequate rooms. But the place was appalling—children with sores playing in the road and screaming, an utter slum. I couldn't take the twins there; £1,000. I phoned the agent at East Grinstead. He had one £1,050 but a near-council house in an estate. All the others were sold or no reply. I felt the twins would just have to go to boarding school. I phoned Killick this morning to ask him if he could send the Croydon Advertiser. He said he could sell dozens more, but if he had one owing to holidays he would send it. Have answered 2 ads of House Keepers.

Went to the Prom tonight with Nancy and it was just heaven. Beethoven Violin Concerto with Ida Haendel. She played it as well as I have ever heard it and how lovely it is. The first and second movements seem perfect and the Finale, for all its repetition, had glorious spirit and verve. I was ready to come home after that but the 4th symphony is a light one and I just listened without attending to it.

Tuesday 18th September 1945

I have been rushing about looking at houses and at last succeeded in finding one—Woodcot, Holland, Oxted, £950, with the upper part occupied by Miss Bannister, a retired LCC nurse. I went to see the owner, Mr Wood, of Caterham last Wed. He took me to see it in his car. Miss B said she would give up one room, which leaves me 2 rooms and a kitchen downstairs and one room up, and we must just manage. E and I went to see it in pouring rain on Friday and she liked him—"a very nice gentleman." I wired him on Sat that I would see him yesterday and Mary and I called last night. He was then out, phoning some people who wanted it but hadn't ready cash so Mary and I jumped in and paid him £95 subject to survey and war damage claim for some cracks. It is a relief not to have to search everywhere. I also looked at one at Elmers End (£1,300, badly blasted and very poor back) and E and I went to Dorking on Thursday to see one built 1863 with 8 rooms (£1,500). I was so tired that day that I didn't know how I should get home. Tonight I played the piano for the first time since last Thurs week!

We had a good weekend of the 8/9. E said it was the most artistic love we had ever had and remarked that it was strange that 'an artistic performance' should leave one more satisfied—like music again. He mended Andrew's wheelbarrow and we went over the downs and picked mushrooms and blackberries, also hips and haws, guelder rose, acorns etc. Last weekend Margaret kept her bed dry and also 4 nights during the week. They both seemed very well. We had chicken (Joan Blackmore has moved and killed her chickens). Andrew said he liked it better than meat. I brought one home the previous weekend and we had Mary to dinner. Rosa liked her very much and they discussed Alexander (technique).

Last Tuesday Rosa and I went to 'Lady Windermere's Fan'—entertaining, witty but nothing solid. The people are cardboard pegs to hang the wit on. The dresses are a feast.

Monday 24th September 1945

Rosa, Margot and I went to Collingbourne on Sat and Hobday is away at Bridport for a week's holiday. Rosa and Margot are staying till Wed evening and I am taking 3 days' leave. I daren't risk taking more. That leaves me with 10 and a half for the move to Oxted and the changeover from Hobday to her successor. The twins were in good form. Margaret cross-examined Rosa. She would soon be 4. Did Rosa know Mummy when she was 4? Where did Margot come from? How many was Mummy now? How many was Margot now? She made her own (dry) bed, shook the mats, swept the floor and when I appeared to dust the bedroom said, "Thank you very much for bringing me the duster, Mummy!" Andrew built a house—'like Woodcot', complete with 2 storeys and stairs inside and windows, and trees in the front garden. They played Snap and Margaret was very keen and won easily. Andrew doesn't mind handing cards over but she doesn't like losing! They both like Rosa and twist her round their fingers. She draws letters for them, makes them jam tarts, lets them cook, makes them slippers etc. She wants to move mainly so that they can come and stay with her. We have decided to use E's name in spite of immediate complications with ration books etc. Margot came to Hurst Green (Holland) to see the house and liked it. Mary phoned me on Thursday and said she had got the surveyor to do it on Friday, but we haven't heard the report yet. He was going away on Sat but fitted it in as he lives at Oxted.

There are rumours of re-organisation (at work). Technical and clerical are to be combined. Also rumours of new salary scales. SI max £1,300, HG max £950. Oh, for equal pay! E says the equivalent for women will be £775. Still, I shall get 5/- per week less tax, say 2/6d for Margaret next year! If the allowances are increased it will be still easier. Margot is to get her full salary on condition that she refunds to the council her Fellowship less fees, which leaves her just as she is. Quite ingenious of the LCC.

A mishap on the train last night: we had left Ludgershall station and were backing to pick up something, very slowly. There was a bang and a terrific jerk. The parachute men on the train jumped out. The line was broken, the point lever was snapped, bits dropped off the train we had crashed into, and we had broken the buffers. I guessed it would be a long job anyway so I jumped down, walked back along the line to the station and caught a bus. I reached Andover at 10 to 7 and got my connection which left at 7.25. There was no sign of the train then.

Tuesday 2nd October 1945

The weekend weather was perfect. Misty shining morning with slight frost and sun, warm mellow noon, starry night with milky way. Rosa and Margot stayed with the twins till Wed evening. Margaret was unwell on Wed so the plan to meet me in Andover with them was abandoned. On Monday, they all went to Salisbury and on Tues over the downs. E wired that he 'can come' on Thurs. We shopped in the morning and I made my first steak and kidney pudding. In the afternoon, we picked mushrooms on the downs. On Friday, Andrew was sleepy and couldn't eat so I stayed with him and turned out the cupboard and E and Margaret went to Avebury, getting back at 4.14. Andrew was alright on Sat, in fact he had his usual piece of chocolate and had supper of bread and butter and marmalade and milk in bed. We intended to go to Pewsey to the Food Office to see about the changed name and call on Reen but the bus at 10.00 didn't run so we walked along the road as far as Eastern Royal, picking huge blackberries. Andrew grudged everyone eating a single one—he wanted them all for blackberry jelly! He can forego the immediate pleasure for a greater remote enjoyment! So we arrived at Pewsey at 12.15 to find the office closed at 12.00. We couldn't get lunch in Pewsey so we went by bus to Marlboro' and lunched at the British Restaurant. We walked down to the river and came back to catch the 2.50 bus, only to find it was 2.10 on Saturday! The weather was so lovely that it didn't matter. On Sunday, we cleaned up the cottage but managed to walk over the downs after dinner. Margaret had a slight cold. It was lovely to be on our own with the twins for the first time. E couldn't get any French letters so we could only play. Hobday was back for tea after a good week and thrilled to see the twins.

The surveyor's report on the house is satisfactory, though he says it has unquestionably suffered blast. We now await the result of the WD claim. Apart from this there is only the conveyance before we can move in. I am meeting Mrs Harper (possible Housekeeper) in Brighton tomorrow.

Monday 8th October 1945

The weather has continued beautiful, golden and sunny with misty mornings. We had a lovely weekend with the twins. It was their birthday on Friday and they had a party. Hobday made them 2 cakes, Andrew's in the form of a train and Margaret's a house. We went to Gamage's on Friday to look at utility furniture and toys and E bought them a metal spade each and solid mosaic bricks for

Andrew and a doll's cot with adjustable side for Margaret. They were thrilled and went straight out in the sunshine to dig. E remarked that Andrew at once handles his spade like a man. He was in fine form. Yesterday morning we all walked over the downs. At the gate, Margaret went back with Hobday and Andrew (who had protested against going out because he wanted to play) came with us. We walked through Collingbourne Woods, at least 5 miles and he walked well, never complaining, but I thought he would be finished. But he ate a good dinner ("I like cabbage and that was nice meat!"), ate all his own Yorkshire pudding and some of mine and then scraped the dish. Then immediately played trains with great vigour and spent the rest of the afternoon digging potatoes and finished by coming to see us off and carrying my torch. Margaret was good too but had been slightly sick owing to excitement and injudicious food.

I met Mrs Harper on Wed. She brought Patsy, a plain and quite attractive child of 2 and a half, neatly dressed. Mrs Harper is Irish and I was on the whole favourably impressed. I wrote on Friday offering her the job on trial but haven't heard yet.

Tuesday 16th October 1945

The weather continues remarkably fine, sunny and golden, warm with misty mornings. It is quite hot in the day. Last week we had one day when it was 73° in London. We lunched with Mary on Thursday and I spent Sunday night with her after coming back to Paddington (train packed and 50 minutes late). The twins were fine. We took them to Marlborough Fair on Sat afternoon. Hobday took Margaret on the roundabouts and she loved it. Andrew stayed with me but enjoyed watching, and the lights—"so many that you can't count them." Mary gave me some oddments for curtains and a quilt. E (in spite of a cold) went to Oxted on Sat afternoon to look round but couldn't find a school. Yesterday I had to give the typists their Grade I test and I am still spending three quarters of an hour a day trying to work up their speed for the proficiency test on Sat.

Sunday 28th October 1945

We have moved. I had a day's leave on Friday and superintended Skinner's move from Purley with beds, bureau, sheets, clothes etc. The Collingbourne stuff with Nannie, twins and Sallie arrived about 3.00, having waited 2 hours in the hope that the rain would cease. It poured all the morning so most of the things got wet, especially a parcel of books that fell to pieces on the front path. It wasn't so bad at Purley, though we did have spatters. The twins were very good and enjoyed the whole thing—journey, packing, unpacking. E came down on the 5.12 and stayed till this morning. Margot came over to tea. I have been appalled at the number of things to do, much increased nowadays. Just buying the house, insurance of house and contents, fuel registration and fuel order (Hall's delivered some coal, fortunately), electricity, bulbs, and palavers about points and wiring the stove, gas and asking for a point in the dining room, re-registering all the rations and, most important, milk supplies, utility furniture, sheets etc. There was one casualty—the teapot! We couldn't get one in Oxted so I am still using a jug. But to celebrate the housewarming I bought a new ordnance map of Guildford, and Trevelyan's 'English Social History' and E and I unexpectedly had a lovely fuck last night. Rosa has told all the neighbours that I have been married some time and have twins but had to keep it dark because of the job. An awkward job for her and Margot. I shall tell the relations.

Reen came for the night on Thursday, an inconvenient visit, but I owed her a lot. We had dinner at the Brasserie and then caught the 9.20 to Riddlesdown. We lunched with Elsie who has given up the Passport Office and is on holiday till she gets another job.

Tuesday 6th November 1945

The weekend was lovely, mild and sunny apart from some rain on Sunday morning. Margot came on Sat morning but caught the 2.50 train back. E came for the weekend. Margot took the twins for a walk and E and I took them to Eastbourne on Sunday. They both, but Andrew in particular, loved the journey. We reached Eastbourne about 12.00 and had lunch at Lyons. Soup and potato for the twins and Andrew had a whole piece of cheese and half a roll and orange juice. Then we walked down the road to the sea. Margaret was pleased with the shops and Andrew with the traffic lights and one toy shop. Then they saw the sea and both ran down the steps to the beach. Andrew loved the pebbles and threw huge stones into the waves. It was high tide with big waves, but they were not nervous. Margaret said, "Don't let the sea go in Andrew's eyes!" Andrew stood at the edge and said, "It comes up and then it goes back. Go back, sea!" We had difficulty in persuading him to leave the beach even to go by bus to Beachy head. We climbed nearly to the top and sat on the square seat to eat chocolate and an apple, and I remembered sitting there twice with E before the war. They loved rolling down, and rolled down the steepest slopes. Margaret noticed the resemblance to Collingbourne downs—being chalk hills. She hurt her knee on a cinder path but didn't cry. She was much taken with the sea's changing colour, and by seaweed, but Andrew's ambition was to make enough holes in the sand to hold all the stones. There was a mistake about meeting—Mrs Harper went to Brighton by mistake. Margaret and I went to South St where she was staying and discovered this. The lovely crimson and mauve sunset kept her going, and also walking in the gutter, full of fallen leaves, but she was tired when we re-joined E and Andrew. We went to have tea and were joined by Mrs Harper and Patsy, who had rushed back from Brighton. Patsy was most demonstrative and the twins didn't quite know what to do. We got back just before 9.00. They slept between Eastbourne and Lewes but not afterwards, as they played with the blinds of the carriage.

Hobday has got the radio to work and distempered the kitchen.

Thursday 8th November 1945

18 years ago today I began work at Croydon 2. I had half a day's leave and met Hobday and the twins at Charing Cross and we went to the zoo. They had caught the 9.49 to London Bridge and Andrew kept them 50 mins on the bridge while he enjoyed the spectacle—ships unloading Billingsgate fish, a family of swans, speedboats in the Pool, Tower Bridge all contributed. They enjoyed the traffic and the crowds and the bus ride. In the zoo, Margaret loved the little animals—squirrels, rabbits, guinea pigs. Andrew liked birds—ducks, flamingos, owls (which he recognised). They both loved the bears and monkeys. Margaret liked the colours of the parrots but Andrew hated the noise and wouldn't stay. They liked bison (a woolly cow!) and donkeys (Margaret had a ride) and zebra. Andrew asked once, "Is it alive?" They loved feeding animals.

Wednesday 14th November 1945

The weekend was sunny with a cold wind. Hobday went to Kennington and Margot and Rosa took the twins to Peter Robinson's to buy them new winter outfits—Nim's crimson and Andrew's yellow. They wore them at once and when I met them at 1.15 they looked quite transformed. Margot had a conference so Rosa and I took them to the Victoria and Albert as we wanted to see the exhibition of sculpture from Westminster Abbey. They were well shown and most impressive and included the royal effigies, the figures from the Henry V

Chapel (rather mouldered) and those from the Henry VII Chapel which were numerous, well-preserved and lovely. A whole range of 15th and 16th Century people. The faces were astonishingly similar to ours and the hats most astonishing. We went back to tea for an hour at Purley. On Sunday, it was brilliant and the twins were in the garden while I cooked the dinner. After dinner, we walked south to Hatchetts Wood—oaks and beeches. It was like Savernake in that one had to keep to the road because of ammunition dumps. Margaret began to like it and said, "I shall call this Collingbourne Woods." Andrew has grown crazy about trees. Oaks are still his favourite, but he looks at the Puffin tree book and then at actual trees. They grow almost to the favour of trains. On Saturday what he liked best were the plane trees in Kensington with their peeling bark and spiky round fruits. Hobday took them to see Rosa today. Yesterday she distempered the front room. Today she got me an ARP rug for 2/6 pence and 2 damaged ones for 6 pence each. Margaret broke wind noisily as she was going to sleep in the afternoon on Tuesday. Hobday said, "What do you say?" meaning, "Excuse me." She said, "I don't say anything. That's the 2 o'clock hooter!"

Tuesday 20th November 1945

Hobday has gone and Mrs Harper, 'Dorothy', has arrived with Patsy. So far she seems satisfactory and an improvement so far as cleanliness and spick and span is concerned—a good cook and a pleasant, unobtrusive person. Used to play piano and fiddle—has begun James Joyce's 'Dubliners'—read The Observer diligently. Margaret says she likes her voice. Patsy is attractive when she is a rogue and enjoys the twins' company. They have been very good so far eating their meals like models (unlike Patsy), treating her with consideration and justice. She has a tricycle which the twins are enjoying while Patsy likes the pram and cot. E and Margaret went to meet them but they went on to Oxted (thinking Hurst Green Halt was Monk's Lane Halt), so they missed them. They arrived to find me and Andrew, which prevented Andrew hiding behind Margaret. He found Patsy some toys and welcomed her very nicely. I am very pleased with them both and I think Patsy will respond well to a wider environment. Yesterday afternoon we went to Oxted to the Food Office after I had cut down daisies and had a great bonfire. Today there was a damp mist and I took the twins to see Rosa which they enjoyed. I had a headache. I have heard from Miss Pace of Dunrobin School and fixed an appointment for Monday evening. We couldn't visit it this morning owing to gym. There may be a vacancy in January, certainly in May, and it is a real nursery school. Miss Pace on the phone sounded nice but rather like the skit on rhythm teaching by Stephen Potter.

Wednesday 28th November 1945

A miserable cold. I have tottered to the office but felt very queer. It developed on Monday when I had 3 interviews (Felton and Gregson, egg merchants; Mark Fawdry, advertising agents; and New Sylhet, tea estates). I went to bed early with aspirin. Yesterday I felt dopey—saw everything flat! Caught the 4.20 home, a very good train. Today an interview with Consters about Stephen Poteras, a Greek. The train up broke down at Oxted—25 minutes late. Train back also 25 minutes late. Margaret has had a cold but it is going. The weather has been bitter—the sharpest frost this morning—though lovely and sunny.

Things continue satisfactory. Patsy seems very happy. I took the three for a walk on Sunday picking up sticks and she was as good as gold. I gave Andrew one and a half reading lessons on Sunday. He was very quick and last night remembered the words well. On Monday (with a cold), I called by appointment at Dunrobin. I liked the head, who didn't seem snobbish. She showed me the school, but it is the company that the twins want. She is to try to fix up with a Mrs Monk to take them by car which would be ideal. They are very interested. Margaret said, "I know all the letters and numbers so I don't know what I shall do at school!" Andrew's repeated remark when he feels affectionate: "I will cut off your head and throw you away"—but last night when Patsy 'shot' me and said, "Bang—you're dead now" Andrew came to me after 3 or 4 minutes and said, "You are not really dead, are you?" and put his face against mine. He is putting his bricks away beautifully at present and building the tunnels on the way to Riddlesdown (he has switched from Andover Junction—a little). Today Dorothy said he put rolls of paper in all his cotton reels and made a forest. Margaret, apropos of nothing—"Do the lambs and sheep die when we take their wool?" Andrew: "So why don't we say tenteen?"

I have applied to be considered for one of the 10 posts as principal! So has the rest of the HG!

Tuesday 4th December 1945

Lunched with Auntie Katie[69] today and told her I was married and we had the twins. She was very pleased! Wrote to the Reynolds yesterday the same. I

---

[69] The eldest of several paternal aunts of Doreen's

hate this—though it is a very small line between, all the essentials being true. E came for the weekend, though I still had my cold. The twins went to Purley in the morning and we brought them back on our train. We went to Oxted in the afternoon to buy Christmas presents, E having given them 10 shillings each. Andrew bought Margot some cigarettes and Rosa ink, on my advice. Margaret refused to consider stockings for Margot but insisted on an oilskin scarf in yellow. Sunday was wet, though we were able to go out in the afternoon. Margaret took Patsy upstairs to wash her and did so rather too thoroughly. She was restless last night and was awake till 2.45 while I had a headache, so she has been half asleep all day, though her appetite was OK. She was better this evening. Andrew has been very good looking after her.

Monday 10th December 1945

Nim isn't too well. She hates the bitter weather and grizzled half the time we were out yesterday even though the sun shone and there was no wind. She seems paralysed by the cold. She is resentful and yesterday I had several crying fits to cope with. She is good with Dorothy but seems to play me up. This evening she worked herself up over nothing so I took her up to bed protesting and screaming. After a few minutes, she came down quite calm and made peace. She is still missing Nannie and seems a bit jealous of Andrew and Patsy. Dorothy said they all played a complicated make believe of going to Collingbourne by train to see Nannie. Margaret was Nannie and Patsy Sandra and they had tea still being unusually good. Andrew seems to do well under Dorothy's less harassing rule. We played Snap yesterday. I was reduced to one card—a ship. He said, "When I see a ship I will turn my head away and you must say Snap and you will get a lot of cards." Margaret's nice phrase: "I've got the lottest!"

Margot took them up to town on Saturday and I brought them back to Rosa's from Victoria. We walked through St James Park and they loved the ducks. Margaret said she saw a dog 'in a glass box' that was dead. "It couldn't bark and it couldn't go." She is quite preoccupied with death: "When are you going to bed?"

"After the news."

"What time is the news?"

"9 o'clock."

"What time is the news tomorrow?"

"9 o'clock."

"Will it be 9 o'clock every day till we go to God?"

We picked holly yesterday morning. Andrew's appetite is marvellous. Miss Bannister is still in Godalming Hospital but hates it as she is hungry and cold. Had letters from Luce and Auntie Bess—very friendly, but May had an attack while she was writing—it sounds serious; speech incoherent and just wants to sleep. Dr says her brain is tired.

Reading C.V. Wedgwood's 'William the Silent'—a lovely book. I should be proud to have written it.

Sunday 30ᵗʰ December 1945

After a cold downpour yesterday morning when I walked miserably to the station, the weather improved. It turned colder with blue sky and sunshine— frosty starlight. "We are going home in the light of the stars"—a favourite phrase of Nim's. Today has been cloudless and drier with sun really warm on the back. I took all 3 children for an hour and a half's walk this morning that was a delight. The hills in mist, the furrows still frosty where the sun had not touched; the pools, still frozen, but the sun warm to the feel so that Nim (who feels the slightest cold) discarded first her gloves and then her hat. They have all been peaceful and happy today. Andrew built a house with his new bricks. They all did their jigsaws. We walked and came home hungry (Margaret had a roast potato, lamb and cabbage followed by a big dish of apples and custard, more custard, a cup of tea and an oat biscuit—and chocolate cream. Andrew had 1 roast potato, Yorkshire pudding, lamb, cabbage, Christmas pudding and custard, tea, oat biscuit and chocolate cream.) In bed this morning, I read the school book to Nim and Andrew read his number book. Margaret said, "Why does Andrew want all those numbers? They don't make anything!" She was maternal with Patsy for three quarters of the week, talking to her and holding her hand. They enjoyed having the tree for tea and Margaret made the toast. We played Snap and Andrew won. Margaret was a little put out but wouldn't concentrate enough to beat him. Once he said, "Next time you say Snap," and prompted her at the right moment. Yesterday I took them to Oxted and we walked all the road part of the Woldingham Rd and met Rosa and Margot at the old farmhouse and came back to tea at Bobbies. Listened to the second part of Bach's Christmas Oratorio.

1946

Andrew and Margaret with Bill at Perranporth
in Summer

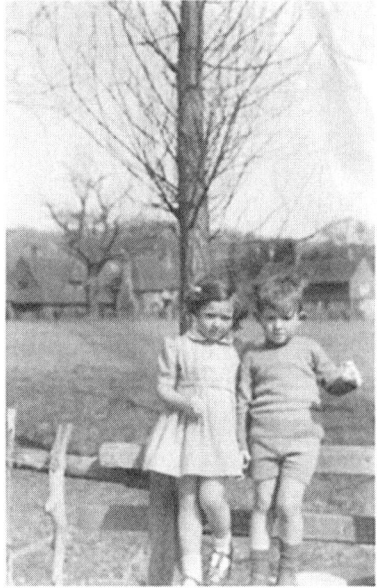

Andrew and Margaret at Oxted in Autumn

Tuesday 29th January 1946

Andrew has been exceedingly good since Dorothy came—cooperative, thoughtful, eats his meals easily and expeditiously, goes for walks, plays, and gets out of the bath quickly, puts his toys away, is ready to lend his books and toys, is long-suffering with Ivan[70]—in fact I wonder what he is working up for. He is beginning to control his tempers at the start. E brought him some wood blocks last Saturday and their relations were very good all the weekend. He has been very well too.

Monday 4th February 1946

Yesterday was Patsy's birthday. We had a party for her—our 3; Roy and Marjorie brought (big) Peter; Jock brought her nephew (little) Peter and Margot came—Jock, Margot and little Peter came to dinner, the others rather late to tea. Little Peter was an angel; a stolid little fellow without a tear all day. He ate well (including Andrew's peas,) and loved books, plasticine and John Brown's

---

[70] Boy living next door

knapsack. Big Peter looks 6 and one was surprised not to find him more sensible as he is so tall. He can't count to 10 but writes well. He gets excited and foolish due to not being used to playing with other children. He badly needs companionship. Dorothy made a fine cake and we had chocolate biscuits and I think it went quite well though Dorothy and I were dead tired afterwards. Anyway, little Peter didn't want to go and the twins liked both Peters. I gave them a lesson in knot-tying one evening and they loved it.

Very busy at the office—EPT post-war refunds. Everyone is annoyed. Why should we offer them? They can't be spent now. But anyone who can use them for reconstruction could claim. Everyone is furious at dried egg running out. I have never heard so much discontent. We have no dollars for dried egg but we can import US films. Food (apart from oranges) is worse than ever. No pork sausages, no more dried egg or milk, bacon being cut to 2 oz. Last week we were one meat ration short.

Marjorie Rogers has got her Senior Inspector—a pioneer again, and with no bother.

Monday 11th February 1946

E is back after 9 days away with flu and now K has it and prevented him from coming this weekend. He came back rather feeble on Thursday. I suffer from exasperation when he is ill, a sort of mixed frustration; partly anxiety and missing him; mainly envy that someone else is looking after him, and annoyance that he is piling up obligations and has been careless enough to catch it again! However, I went with Margot to see the Old Vic Company do Sophocles', 'Oedipus' and 'The Critic' at the New Theatre on Wednesday evening. We booked a month before for three and six pence and had excellent seats. We enjoyed both plays. The Greek is fine and touches very deep feelings. Laurence Olivier was excellent (also Sybil Thorndike). But he enjoyed himself exuberantly as Puff in The Critic. I missed the last half hour but it was a lively thing to take one's mind off Oedipus. Curiously enough I felt much better after it.

The twins are lovely. Andrew is still very good. They play shops together in the morning.

Andrew: "It's your turn—just skip along the road."

Margaret skips by, rattling the cot. Andrew: "Yes Madam—what do you want?"

Margaret: "I want some shoes for my little girl. Have you got any?"

Andrew: "These are 10 shillings—they are too big for her. I've got some socks though."

Margaret: "How much are they?"

Andrew (looking at imaginary ticket): "This one is ten and seven pence and this one is ten and six pence."

I wish I could put it down in shorthand. Margaret is better and is much healthier psychologically. She has had several dry nights and doesn't mind talking about it. Andrew asked her this morning if her bed was dry. "No—Oh, never mind, I try every night." She was talking to him about the hospital this morning—small details. She can turn a somersault perfectly—which the other 2 can't do. They went to Purley on Saturday morning and I also took them yesterday afternoon by bus (4 buses) which they enjoyed. We had the gramophone and singing and dancing to the piano. They can go to school in May—the problem now is transport. Miss Bannister had her operation and is getting better and is happier in hospital this time.

Sunday 17th February 1946

A spring day of sleepy sun and misty hills, swelling buds and active birds—so heavenly after a week of dull, damp dark but mild days.

On Tuesday, I had a day's leave and went to Brighton by train with Rosa and the twins. We looked at the shops first. I had got my curtain coupons but saw nothing attractive enough to pay the huge prices. We bought the twins a pair of wooden-soled sandals each and I did manage to get some green walking shoes although nearly all the shops had sold their quota. After lunch, we went on the beach and the twins had a lovely time throwing stones in the sea etc. After a good tea at Clarks, we caught the 4.24 electric train to East Croydon where we picked up Patsy to let Dorothy go to the Empire to see a man she knew in the RAF and met (by chance) Margot on the 5.50. Yesterday I took the twins to Purley and Margot and Rosa brought them to town in the afternoon to see the Klees. It was very hot and crowded but they liked them for a while. Margaret was fascinated by the Death of St Francis (she has a queer morbid strain of interest in death). We walked through St James Park but found the lake still empty and unexploded bomb notices. Five minutes before the 5.50 went out from Victoria the lights went out. I found out from the 9.00 news that there was a serious fire and only one line was running. All the electric trains were disorganised. I explained what happened to Andrew this morning and later found him playing stations and diverting the buses and cars from the yard owing to the fire.

Tuesday 26th February 1946

A busy week. E and I were on leave last Tuesday to Friday. I worked on Saturday morning and he stayed till Sunday evening—the longest spell he has had with the twins. Last Tuesday we met him at Victoria and went to the newly opened Science Museum. They both loved it. We went to the children's gallery where the train which goes over the bridge was the greatest thrill—though the rainbow, the series of indoor lighting, the street lighting, clocks, the water-using series, transport—all attracted them. We had lunch and then back to the engines and they both pushed knobs and E turned handles with enthusiasm. Andrew was there from 11.15 to 3.20 (less an hour) but Margaret and I went to Kensington Gardens to feed the ducks at 2.30. Since then Andrew has taken Pink Bear by my morning train, changing at East Croydon for Victoria, to the museum! On Thursday morning we took the twins to Oxted to the school. They were both shy and said little or nothing. Margaret sat with her hands on her knees and put her gloves under her coat. Andrew turned his back on Miss Pace—but they liked it and tried the posting box. Andrew noticed the piano. We have made arrangements about transport which I hope will work. Mrs Hartley is to bring them back to the Post Office Tuesday to Friday.

E had bought a Meccano each so they had great fun working it. Andrew is better at grasping the design, but Margaret is much better at the mechanical and manual side—putting in screws etc. They made trucks first and then Andrew had a trolley bus and Margaret a crane which are still in play. He contemplates—she puts together and takes apart.

On Sunday morning, we went for a walk to Itchingwood Common—brilliant sunshine but cold wind. In the afternoon, I taught Margaret to do double crochet. She got on very well. She is quite adept at chain and can do it quickly and evenly. Yesterday Mrs Parsons sent us a dozen eggs—a marvellous present. Margaret had one fried and Andrew one scrambled for breakfast. Today on the worst day for the winter I had half a day's leave and met E at 2.00 at Burlington House to look at the Greek Art Exhibition. We stayed 2 hours. It was lovely. It was like past lives, a change to be just ourselves. E said Margaret would certainly have remarked on the tassels of the Apollos if she had been at the exhibition! We had

2 lovely loves last week especially the second when I told E I didn't like modern music—not enough variety—all loud and deafening and he translated the music I do like into other forms. Though we do it so seldom it is important—"the mortar" he suggested. It was lovely to have him so long and see him so easy with the twins. They both loved seeing him. He made Andrew a tray for his bricks.

Monday 4th March 1946

I took the twins to Purley on Saturday. Andrew played with his letters from 3.45 till 6.30 with an interval for tea—making words. When he saw the similarity between van, can, and man and deduced P.A.N. "Pan," he crowed with triumph. Margaret practised double crochet after a week's interval. The maturation after her first lesson was very clear. She was more skilful when she resumed than when she ceased. Andrew drew two diagrams on Saturday, one of 'Rosa's house' with every room except the sewing machine room (which he remembered afterwards) and great detail down to rosaries on the bed and the telephone wire; the other of Riddlesdown Station with train, signal, lamp, lines, platform, guard waving flag, Andrew, Mummy and Margaret running down the approach.

Very busy at the office with EPT refunds—the rest piles up. Elsie has a temporary job with Odhams to run their modern homes exhibition at Dorland Hall. We listened to the 'The Trojan Women'. It is not dramatic as I know it—but painful and pitiful. Yes, it takes a long time to say what seems obvious—that war is a pointless and brutal activity. Attlee last night. His speech was reasoned and sensible and necessary but he scorns rhetoric—for which I respect him, but he hasn't the emotional pull.

Monday 11th March 1946

The children have all been full of life the last few days with good appetites. Margaret has a vitamin sweet now as I told her it would help her to keep warm. Dorothy reported that they listened with great interest to a schools broadcast for under-7s last week. Margaret is odd in her mistakes—a natural Mrs Malaprop. About Andrew practising on Patsy's tricycle: "Andrew is putting his feet on the pebbles now!"/"Shall we hear the Weathercast?" She is most mature in her attitude to the other two. Yesterday morning we were all in bed together and Patsy (who wasn't, and felt out of things) wanted to go down. Margaret without a word got up and opened the door (which sticks). She plays mother to them— feeds them, tucks them up, reads to them, etc. Andrew took his Meccano trolleybus to pieces and he and E made a railway crane. E said he had developed a lot in a fortnight though he hasn't done a thing except play with the trolley bus. They went to Purley on Saturday morning and had a marvellous cooking game.

Still busy with post-war EPT refunds. We have broken its back.

Friday 15th March 1946

On Wednesday morning, Andrew counted 20 backwards carefully but with no great effort, no difficulty. This morning he said he would sleep with me 'when he was as big as Bill'. He also expressed the first idea of what he would be when he grew up—a policeman. I wondered why and soon learnt. He had watched a policeman on point duty by Kensington Gardens with great pleasure—"When he lifts up his hand all the buses stop and when he puts it down they go." He built a factory today. Margaret is worse than ever at wetting. She has already wetted two sheets and nighties (11.15) and another 2 sheets at 40 winks and a pair of knicks today. She has been bad all the week—It may be that she has been excited and very lively. On Tuesday, Dorothy had 2 teeth out so I brought all three home from Oxted and put them to bed. Margaret undressed Patsy and cut her bread and butter up for her and undressed herself altogether. Tonight she also folded up her clothes without being asked.

Tuesday 19th March 1946

At last, the weather is spring-like. It turned milder on Sunday morning which was sunny with SE wind. In the afternoon, it drizzled a little. Today has been lovely. The children played in the garden all day. It is like a release after three and a half weeks unbroken cold.

On Sunday, we saw tits (Margaret said, "He was near enough to see his blue tail!") thrushes, blackbirds, chaffinches, rooks, two magpies and a green woodpecker. We picked some reddish catkins (?alder) which have come out beautifully. Margot brought some almond blossom when she came over in the afternoon and I picked five chestnut buds at Purley on Saturday. The children go mad when she comes, especially Patsy, who regards her as a party in herself. We played Snap and mulberry bush. On Saturday, it was bitterly cold and I took the twins to Purley for the day. Margaret broke her sequence of wettings by being dry all day and at 40 winks (in Margot's bed). Since then she has been dry all day and last night was only a little wet! This morning she was in my bed and said, "Do you love me when you're in London? When you're in the train? When

I'm asleep?" And then a pause, "Do you still love me when I'm naughty?" Andrew was amusing in his identification with E on Saturday. They had their hair cut and when Margaret was having hers cut he was chatting—"What colour is your hair?" Answering himself, "Grey"; "Margot's?" "Brown"; "Rosa's?" "Grey"; "Nimmy's?" "Brown"; "Mine?" "Red"; "Patsy's?" "Fair"; "Bill's?" "Red." Then on the way home: "Bill's got braces—I've got braces—I'm Bill." His conversation sounds oddly mature in some ways. He had a good breakfast this morning and was reflecting on it. "I had my cracklepops and then my bacon and fried bread. I saw the crust and said I'd have it. I didn't realise I wanted it till I saw it."

I have been terribly tired today. Pole told me in confidence on Saturday that Craddock had been asked for a considered report on me—and I'd better see to my arrears cases. A nasty thought. E reckons that to get S.I. would make £4000 difference. Put like that it sounds impressive but I hate the idea of striving for it. I'd rather have another baby. Reading Rieu's translation of 'The Odyssey'. It is good and how lovely to read—so simple a life. One knew what was right and wrong. Also V. Woolf's 'Common Reader'. And Gow's 'Letter from Cambridge'—the fascinating university background and so quietly written. He is nice.

Monday 25th March 1946

It has been real spring at last. Saturday and today have been continuous sunshine.

E came for the weekend and yesterday morning we caught the 10.16 with Dorothy and Patsy (who were going to Woodford Green for the day). We got out at Woldingham and walked back to Old Oxted—about 4 miles through Marden Park. The twins loved it especially when we sat down to look at the view and they had orange juice and bread and butter and biscuit (picnic) and then ran down the hill and found primroses in the copses at the bottom. Margaret didn't like the wet path—she sat on it once and fell down on it later and cut her knee but Andrew didn't mind. He said once, "Is this the country?" and said he wanted to do this walk again before the primroses finish and when the bluebells and cowslips are out. He was very hungry. In his spare time, he took his crane to pieces and made (with E's help) a signal that he took to pieces and made buffers. Mrs Blackmore has offered to buy Twinpath for £275. It is now just a question of completing and getting the Hobdays out.

Wednesday 27th March 1946

The lovely sunny weather continues. 64 degrees in London today. I wore my new green tweed costume with silk blouse and new green shoes to have lunch with Auntie Katie—she is coming to lunch on Saturday week. The children play all day in the garden and begin to look sunburned. They all asked for water to drink today. Margaret still has difficulty in remembering words correctly. She sang yesterday morning—"Little boy kneels at the foot of the bed, Loops on his little hands little gold head" and in the evening seeing a silver and black moth— "See this dear little mosk!" Dorothy went to the dentist and I put the children to bed. Margaret undressed Patsy completely, gave her her supper and supervised my putting her to bed.

Monday 1st April 1946

The fine sunny weather has continued without a break. It is fresh at night and morning with a breeze all day, but hot at midday so that the children can play in the garden all day.

On Saturday, the twins went to Purley. We hadn't time (owing to someone ahead trying to book to Barnes for the boat race) to get tickets so I gave 1/8d to Margaret and told her if she saw the man to ask for 2 half returns from Hurst Green. She managed it beautifully. He gave her a 'special' ticket and told her to take care of it. In the evening, we got back to the Halt about 7.20, nearly dark. Margaret wanted to go the short cut but I said it was dark. Andrew wanted to go across the green. Margaret said she would go by herself. I agreed, thinking she would change her mind. She didn't and a train came the other way. I was alarmed, thinking she might panic by herself so I took Andrew quickly after her. We couldn't see her; we called—no answer till we were again across the railway. Then we found she had got to the road and had walked down to meet us cool as a cucumber. She is growing up. And yet she wetted her bed at Rosa's, and her knicks yesterday morning and today. E thinks it may be anxiety about death. Unconsciously she may want to stay a baby to avoid death. She is certainly preoccupied with it. She produced the reincarnation idea yesterday—"after I die, then I'll be a little baby again."

On Saturday afternoon, I mowed the grass for 30 minutes. They picked the daisies just in front of the mower and then collected the grass cuttings. Then we went with Rosa over Riddlesdown to the far wood to pick anemones and saw the other end of the tunnel coming back. Their energy, and especially Andrew's, is colossal. Rosa gave him a note case and I gave him a new halfpenny to put in it. Yesterday he was sliding it up and down and said it was his sun going up and down and shining. He loves the sun, moon and stars. He admired the glowing sky after the sunset this evening, cloudless except for a tangle of pinky-gold cloud. "It looks like a scribble—the sun has scribbled on the sky," he said. E has taken the WEA[71] secretaryship—it will be good for him. Elsie came yesterday and was impressed with the twins and liked Dorothy.

Tuesday 9th April 1946

All last week was sunny but not heavy, although it was hot—one day it was 80 in London. Long cloudless days with fresh mornings and evenings, except Friday when it rained all day. After that, the heat wave broke and, although it hasn't rained since, there has been a north wind which has made it cold even when the sun was high. But Sunday was perfect—fresh and sunny with orange after-glow and cool evening star as I went to the station with E. The hedges are green, the trees are budding—even oak, while ash has fans at all its twig tips. We began digging at the weekend and E said he had never met such heavy digging. Still, we managed a walk on Sunday morning to let the children pick flowers. Miss B came back on Saturday and has (we think) cracked the lavatory basin so that it leaks.

Mrs Blackmore has paid her deposit and I had to write to her and the solicitor at the weekend. The twins went to Purley on Saturday morning and helped Margot cut grass. Margot mentioned to Nim a 'rock cake'—Nim, "Does it rock?" I am reading Alice to them—we have got to page 30 and they like it and take it in (mostly). E heard Margaret telling the story in detail to Patsy on Sunday when they were out. She showed her books to the children next door on Sunday—quite unselfconscious and not shy at all, but rather managing: "Ann can look at it when Ivan has finished."

Tuesday 16th April 1946

The marvellous weather has continued. Margaret is quite brown and Andrew has had midge bites.

Margot came to tea on Sunday and we went for a walk to Itchingwood Common and got some primroses etc. The children were trying on Sunday—perhaps the weather makes them too active and they find it difficult to sleep.

---

[71] Workers' Educational Association

Margaret wouldn't lie down for her midday rest let alone sleep. When I remonstrated, she screamed. After dinner, she said she was, "Auntie Joan" come for a cup of tea. She couldn't leave her baby long as it was screaming! She would spank it. I said I had a little girl who screamed—What did Auntie Joan advise? Margaret saw the point quite clearly and said, "You should beat her—find a stick—like the clothes prop and beat her on the bottom with it!"

Andrew has eaten half the bananas and Patsy the other half. Margaret had gooseberries on Sunday and 7 prunes today. Her wetting is as bad as ever both in the day and at night. Andrew has a collection of milk tops (192 last count) and match boxes, and begins to want to climb trees. Last Saturday E went to Chichester—his uncle is dying at 83—it may interfere with Easter!

Monday 22nd April 1946

Easter has been lovely—no rain, a lot of sunshine with pink sunsets and white or pale grey clouds sweeping the blue sky, a north wind which tempered the sunshine and made the nights cold.

Old Uncle Chichester died on Tuesday and E had to go to his cremation on Saturday so he couldn't come till Saturday afternoon. So on Friday, as Margot was at a retreat, I took the twins to Upper Warlingham and we walked over the downs to Rosa's and spent the day. It was very pleasant; we saw a blue butterfly and I cut some of the grass. Rosa made small steak pies and the twins enjoyed them very much. I went to the office on Saturday morning and met Auntie Katie who came down for the afternoon. Everything seemed to go off all right. E arrived at 4.30 and saw her off at the station. Margaret was perfectly behaved and looked sweet. Andrew was rather obstinate over his dinner and washing his hands for tea but she thought he was a regular boy. Yesterday the children had their presents. E gave Andrew a cooking set and the girls a tea set each. They were all thrilled with them and spent every available minute playing with them. Dorothy and I took Margaret and Patsy to church yesterday afternoon but Andrew stayed at home and played with his cooking set and E said that he was completely absorbed for 2 hours. He didn't go out at all, all day.

Today we all picnicked at Crowhurst. The walk was lovely—footpath first and then very quiet road with copses full of bluebells and primroses, celandines, anemones and cuckoo flowers. Almost as good as Collingbourne Wood as even E admitted, and there were some special things—another blue butterfly, cuckoos, the first swallows I have seen swooping round Crowhurst church, my first lambs, a herd of young Friesian cattle and most remarkable of all a sheet of golden kingcups which I left the party to pick. I gathered a big bunch, too big to hold in one hand. We all looked at the oldest living yew in England in Crowhurst churchyard with a cannon ball in its hollowed trunk. The church was a good one but restored with wooden belfry spire (a 'spower', as Margaret called it!), 3 or 4 good brasses, a pleasant wooden roof.

The nights were lovely. On Saturday, E was dead tired but said in a little while 'I'm getting stirred up!' Last night was lovelier still—I was tired, so sleepy that I almost slept before he came but he just deliberately took me and it was sweet. I cannot think it is wrong to cooperate in such joy. On Saturday night when I let Sallie out I heard a nightingale, not at its fullest but quite clearly, and yet the night was cold.

Last Wednesday I had a day's leave and Margot and Rosa and I took the twins to the zoo. We saw an elephant for the first time. "Is that his tail end?" said Margaret. They both loved the bears, and Andrew liked the monkeys—best, he said. Margaret said she liked all the monkeys except those that were fighting. I tried unsuccessfully to get Andrew some sandals and a shirt. Rosa went to the Abbey for the Maundy service and much enjoyed it.

Friday 26th April 1946

It rained nearly all day yesterday when I reached 40. Time is inexorable though my only regret is that there is so little time to do all there is to do—having children, rearing them, travelling, reading books, listening to music, gardening, watching birds, flowers, trees, doing research, teaching, writing—and all the hosts of things I want to do. As it is I pick superficially at a few of them but spend most of my time earning a good-ish salary.

It rained today but it was milder and drier this evening and the walk from the station by the short cut through the fields was lovely. I couldn't live away from England, I think. I am getting to love this place, though I must always be at least 12 months before I begin to root. I planted spinach seed after dinner when I had hoe-ed the bed I dug at the weekend. E was right, the rain had broken down the lumps. It begins to look cultivated at last. On Tuesday, I took the twins to Reigate to meet Rosa and Margot and we had a picnic on Colley Hill. We found a sheltered sunny corner and Margaret and Rosa stayed there. Margot, Andrew and I walked across the hill. He finished up with 9 branches of beech, chestnut, oak, laurel, wild cherry and box! He had 2 bananas altogether and a good lot of cheese. Dorothy said he was tiresome today, probably due to anxiety about school.

This afternoon Dorothy says Andrew played on his own at the sink with his cooking set and Margaret's tea set. The girls painted on the hall floor. They went to school and Mrs O'Hanlon brought them all the way back in her car. They said little about what they did—especially Andrew, who is never communicative. It is difficult to tell what they think. Margaret told Margot the tale of how I left her at home to go for a walk. She said she didn't think we would all go out and leave her, but she went indoors and found we had—but there were Ann and Ivan and Ivan's mummy so she didn't cry at all. She appeared quite unconcerned when I turned back, wondering if she were upset. Their appetites are fine and they are both getting tanned.

Tuesday April 30th 1946

The twins went to Purley on Saturday morning, all alone from the station. I went to dinner and took them down to Purley in the afternoon and bought Andrew a shirt at his request. We missed the 6.43 train and he said at once, "We shall have to sleep at Rosa's." Both of them were thrilled and went back very pleased. Rosa said they could stay and also for Sunday, and Dorothy and Patsy could come to tea. Margaret was very excited at the idea and said she would show Patsy the downs, the garden, the house, the gramophone and the piano— all in 2 hours. They were as good as gold. Margaret and I met Dorothy and Patsy, although it was raining. Margaret and Patsy went under Margot's umbrella and Margaret took her all over the house, ending in the 'Piano Room', where they all sat themselves and demanded that I should play. Andrew sings best to the piano and gramophone but they all joined in. We caught the 7.18 after a good party. Rosa was very pleased and made a potato cake and a sandwich with egg and chocolate filling. They start school on Thursday.

Tuesday 7th May 1946

The great plunge has been taken. Margaret is sailing like a duck in water— wants to go to school in the afternoons. "Mrs Marsh picked me up today."

"Why?"

"Because she likes me." She has been highly commended for crayon work— colouring a picture without any whiskers—very good for her age. She has learnt jumping exercises, had swings, rides on the rocking horse, climbed the climbing frame, knows lots of children's names, fell down and cut her knee—"It bleeded a lot—and made drops on the floor—but I didn't cry"—and came home very pleased with the patch. Andrew was more doubtful, he says, though without much conviction, "Don't want to go to school" but goes without trouble—has not cried at all either at home or school (except from over-tiredness on Sunday). He can recount the story he hears and correct Margaret, notices everything there but was inclined not to join in or to sit silent or play (with dominoes). Today he was good—had climbed on the frame, had swings, talked to Sarah, etc. and was in obvious good spirits. He gave the impression that he was adjusting—that it wasn't as awful as he expected—that a weight had been lifted from his mind.

I had a day off last Thursday and took them and fetched them. They did not make any fuss when I went and seemed quite OK at 12.00. In the afternoon, we walked to the stream, threw dandelions in to watch them float under the bridge, then Andrew picked a big bunch of bluebells—"my hand looks all blue." On Friday, Dorothy took them all the way and Mrs Hartley brought them back. Yesterday I walked with them in pouring rain against a north wind and caught the 9.26. Dorothy met them and they couldn't get on the bus so didn't get home till 1.30. Today Dorothy took them and got taken on to Lingfield coming back! The bus and train are bad—buses are packed and few—trains are almost non-existent. Nothing between 8.30 and 9.47. Tomorrow Dorothy intends to put them on the bus and leave them to go on their own.

On Saturday, E took them to Oxted (at least he took Andrew and I had to follow by bus with Margaret as she wouldn't rest) to get me a birthday present. Andrew got the new book about trees which is lovely. He was just radiant. Margaret got a flower bowl—wooden with a glass lining. They love to give. We found a fair in full swing and met Dorothy and Patsy. The girls went on a roundabout and then Andrew ventured on a bus top. He liked it so much that he went twice more and wanted to go again. He wanted to try every seat on the bus, his first venture at a fair; he is coming on.

On Sunday, it was chilly and grey with showers in the afternoon. We (without Patsy) went to Woldingham and walked to Old Oxted. The twins did marvellously, especially the last mile and we caught the 12.34 bus with 2 minutes to spare. They loved it. We picked big bunches of cowslips, I have never seen them finer. In the afternoon, Margot came to tea. Dorothy made her a birthday cake.

There is too much to do and see and think about, I get quite breathless and find the office quite a relaxation! On Saturday night I was dead tired but we had a marvellous love—the best managed climax I think he has ever done, If only I could convey so that even just I could understand the loveliness—but words just mean nothing—but it isn't just greedy grasping, much less regret. It is a deep instinct to want to make something permanent of a supreme experience—well I must give it up. It can't be done.

Tuesday 14th May 1946

It has remained cold for at least a fortnight—not heavy frosts but a strong north wind with grey skies except for periods when the sun made it warm in sheltered places.

The twins have had nearly 2 weeks at school and seem to be settling down well. Dorothy called for them yesterday and Mrs Marsh said that they were 'surprisingly' advanced for their age. They both like colouring and today drew and coloured trains. Andrew is keen on the climbing frame and yesterday said he got to the top—taller than Bill. Margaret practices jumping, hopping, pirouetting etc. Dorothy said yesterday Andrew was quite engrossed with looking at something on the floor with other children. I took him a piece of plane tree from Trinity Square today and he was entranced. We have just finished reading Alice in bed in the mornings. They loved the songs particularly.

On Saturday, they went to Purley in the morning and then to Kew with Margot and Rosa. I got Andrew some sandals at Clapham Junction at Saxone. They enjoyed Kew. We had sunshine and it is sheltered. It was difficult to get Andrew to leave the water with weeping willows, geese and three tiny goslings, ducks and ducklings, coot and babies, moorhens and babies. The rhododendrons, azaleas, tulips, and bluebells were the high spots. Neither liked the hothouse.

In fact, Andrew wouldn't stay, even to see a banana tree. They saw some fish coming up for crumbs. Andrew loved the trees, especially under a dark holly. He took a dead oak leaf, very big. Coming back Margaret made friends with a parson—gave him a silver paper bookmark and then a lot more tiny paper ones. Finally, he taught her to wink. We had to move to the front coach—Andrew said, "Very smoky, I think it comes from those cigarettes."

Margaret: "Perhaps it is coming in the windows from the engine."

Andrew: "No, we aren't going." On Sunday morning, they washed dolls' clothes and then I took them all out by footpath to Itchingwood Common and back. In the afternoon, we went for a short walk with Dorothy but Margaret wouldn't come and stayed by herself for 40 minutes, playing in the garden. On Saturday night, Sallie had 7 pups of which we have kept 3; 2 black and white and 1 black and brown.

Monday 20th May 1946

Yesterday morning it poured but cleared to a perfect day after dinner—one of the loveliest evenings I remember—golden and cloudless. We went for a walk to West Heath near Limpsfield Common. It is sandy and the children had a marvellous time playing in the sand and a muddy pool. E and I walked ahead and left them with Dorothy playing and Margaret told Dorothy she didn't want us to come back as she wanted to stay there. Andrew had a slight cold and was rather crotchety—we had a job to get him out, and a job to get him along as he wanted to stop and pick daisies. Finally he loved the sand.

Tuesday 28th May 1946

I am so tired and ought to sleep. I spent the morning on interviews—a long congenial one with Lloyds on Thames Steam Tug and a short uncongenial one with Dodds about a 37/38 arrear. Margaret is as wet as ever and has even slightly dirtied her knicks. Perhaps due to her cold. Yet she shows no other signs of anxiety. She is keener than Andrew on the physical skills they are learning— hand stands, hopping, skipping, etc. and practices all day. He gave me a long and detailed account of the story they had on Friday.

Sunday was a miserable grey heavy day with slight drizzle which turned into a downpour in the evening. I did some digging and sowed beans, and cress on flannel in the morning and we all went to play with sand at West Heath in the afternoon. The children loved it but Dorothy and I got bitten. Last night I went to Purley for dinner as Stuart[72] was coming. He has a scheme to go in with another man on printing textiles and had an idea of running the agencies in with it using the company. It sounds promising and doesn't mean risking much, as he proposes to start in a small way. He has a boy five last January and a girl ten and a half months. I like him best of the Bates cousins.

---

[72] A cousin of Doreen's who was previously in business with Wyndham and was starting his own company

Tuesday 4th June1946

E came for the weekend. It poured with rain coming back from the station on Saturday and we didn't go out again. We had Patsy as Dorothy was having her hair permed. The twins played with Meccano after 40 winks. Andrew made a trolleybus again and Margaret a swing which she likes and has played with more than anything else. We went to bed earlier than usual and had a lovely hour with the light on for the last part. It makes it much sweeter for me if we can see. E said, "Exquisite" afterwards. Sunday was unsettled with sun and heavy showers. We took the children for a walk and picked moon daisies and a few wild roses. On the road back, we saw butterflies and Andrew caught 3 in his hand but let them go without hurting them. Patsy and E were ahead and Sallie found a newt. After 40 winks, E and I dug in the garden and I found 6 small blue dragonflies. Margaret and Patsy dug too but Andrew played with his cooking set at the sink.

Today I have lunched with Oades. He recently went to Blyth and back in a collier and loved it and he hopes to go to Gothenburg for his summer holiday if he can get Ellermans to fix it. E and I have arranged to take a 'hut' at Perranporth for the first fortnight in September at 3 guineas a week. A friend of Margot took it for 4 weeks but can only use 2. E is coming for a week. It is right on the sandy beach and there are rocks and pools—but it is a journey. We must work it out. Very busy at the office. E's general inspection today. We lunched with Mary on Friday.

Tuesday 11th June 1946

The weather over Whitsun was unsettled with downpours of rain on Saturday and Monday, thunderstorms and gales and cooler than March. Sunday was the best day after Friday, when we thought there might be a heat wave.

We went to Purley for the day on Friday as the Oxted school children were having a free film show—too old for the twins. In the afternoon, I left the twins with Margot and took Rosa up to Paddington on the first stage of her journey to St Ives for a month. There were crowds and the direct entrance was closed. When we managed to get to her train she got a seat. On Saturday morning, E arrived at 11.00. We listened off and on to the V celebrations but saw nothing of them except some boys with torches about 7.00 which pleased the twins. We didn't go out all day. On Sunday, Margot came and we met her at 9.30 and went to West Heath for the children to play in the sand. Margaret made 'meals' and 'cooked'. Andrew made an elaborate railway system with 10 level crossings, a tunnel (E helped with this), a station, 2 signals, etc. He logically made the sleepers before the line. Patsy picked grasses and played with the sand very little. Andrew had a bunch of green ash seeds which pleased him very much. In the afternoon, we did some gardening and Andrew played with his cooking set at the sink. Margaret had God save the King for her bed song. She was surprised at 'Long to rain over us'. We had elaborate pretend school 3 times, with Andrew as Mrs Marsh beginning with hymn, register ("Yes, Miss Pace"), marching out, writing, break with milk, toys ("too wet to go out") and story. He sustained the part well, playing the piano (desk) and singing at the top of his voice.

Thursday 13th June 1946

Today has been sunnier than any day for 6 weeks and warmer out than indoors. Dorothy and the children were gardening all the afternoon. They were looking out of the stair window for me when I came home and were jubilant. We heard from Rosa yesterday that she had a good journey, though slow, and was settling in at St Ives. The twins returned happily to school yesterday. They have to queue at 8.45 to get on the 9.00 bus. I wrote to the company about the intolerable position between 8.30 and 9.30 and Dorothy said there was an inspector there yesterday, when the facts supported all I had said.

Tuesday 18th June 1946

Far too much this time. Mary spent Friday night with us and brought me some chocolates, Margaret a baby doll, Andrew a 'book' of sweets and Patsy a book. Margot came to dinner and we talked about the business. Dorothy awoke with a bad throat and by the evening was quite finished though she managed to cook us a nice dinner. It must have been a kind of flu. She was in bed all day Saturday. Margot came over in the morning and cooked the dinner. I made marmalade in the evening. On Sunday, Dorothy began to improve and got up about 10.45 and went to bed at 9.00. Margot came for the day. After supper, I had to go to see Mrs Sharpe to find out about the twins coming home on Monday. The children were very good all the weekend. The twins played with their tea and cooking set all Sunday morning. Andrew cooked his bacon and fried bread in his frying pan and was thrilled. In the afternoon, Margot and I and the twins went out for an hour and picked wild roses, honeysuckle, maple, ash and oak.

We took Margot to see the mill. Last night I went to Purley to share Margot's Sunday dinner. It was lovely to play and sing afterwards and finally I collected the minute book, share register and accounts of the company.

Andrew was sweet this evening. He came up with me to take off my green costume and shoes and was far more ready to talk of school than I have ever seen him. He said that there was a boy of six called Richard who plays with him. At playtime, "We make a little gang in the corner." They were going to climb on the frame but it was full so they waited. They saw some children having a pretend picnic and joined in. Then the bell rang and they all ran in for their story—a bit of 'Jennifer goes to school'.

I omitted to note that at Whitsun E and I had two lovely nights. The second one was fiercer than I ever remember him—He hurt me and yet I said without meaning to 'Go on!' and he laughed. How sweet! How mysterious! I want another baby very much. Against all reason! I am reading Mauriac's 'Woman of the Pharisees'. It is very good. Reminds me of French histories—so clear and logical and detached and easy that one hardly realises its profundity and subtlety. I would give much to have their power.

Friday 28th June 1946

Very busy. Last Friday Ella spent the night with me. She may spend August also as she probably hasn't anywhere to stay. Ella hopes to go to South Africa for 6 months in October. Staples has an editorial job for her on her return. The weekend was lovely—almost a little heat wave, the best two days in all May and June. Took the twins to St James at Riddlesdown. The vicar saw them and chatted and they enjoyed the service though Andrew made many enquiries in a piercing whisper. We had breakfast, dinner and tea in the garden and they had their 40 winks under the silver poplar. I was very strict at the start and they lay quiet without talking and both slept. They loved it.

Margot came to us for Monday, Tuesday and Thursday nights much to the twins' delight and she took them to school today. She was doing her exam and found it a strain. On Wednesday, she went to a party at L.S.E. and I took the dogs to meet her in Oxted at 11.23 but she missed the train. It was a lovely evening, warm and bright and one could tell all the flowers by their smell—elder, wild rose, honeysuckle, syringa. It was very dark and sinister under the trees and I was glad to have the dogs. She got a police message through to me. We have also been hectic over the company. Stuart phoned me last Friday that they had got hold of some material and wanted a bank reference. E gave me a cheque for £300 and we re-opened an account for the company. Margot and I met Stuart and Dudley Smith last night. They want two thirds of the shares and control or nothing, and they want us to put up £400—interest and dividends to be paid and a small directors' fee. We lunched with Mary and E and ended with a resolve to let Rosa meet Dudley Smith. We are doubtful about accounts and financial experience and knowledge.

The twins are sweet. Early in the morning they let out some odd remarks. There were some small flies on the curtains. Andrew killed one and Margaret caught one, "I'm the fly deading man," said Andrew.

"And I'm the fly caught girl," said Margaret. Margaret said they both had brown eyes because I had brown eyes and they were my little babies. From which they turned to death.

Andrew said, "After I'm dead I shall be meat!" There followed discussion as to why we eat some animals and not others. He thought we ate dogs. They went to tea with Sarah Sharpe on Tuesday, the first time on their own. Andrew kept saying, "Don't want to go out to tea," but he went and enjoyed Sarah's sand pit.

I have had a polite if pompous letter from the bus company saying they can't do anything but will see in the winter. Bread rationing starts on the 21st. It is just awful. It isn't so much the restriction—bread will be ample, but we shall miss flour for cake and puddings, pastry and the 101 things one uses it for. Who would think we'd won the war? I know there is more to it, but I think it could have been avoided.

Wednesday 3rd July 1946

At last, we are having summer—87° in London yesterday and nearly as hot today. It is difficult to work and I am so glad the children are in the country. They have worn sun-suits and find it difficult to sleep before 9.00 or 10.00. I took the dogs on Monday evening and there was a flaming red sunset and a thin crescent moon with the evening star just beneath, so cool and clear. Tonight there is sheet lightning in the east. I have never been able to see the beauty of lightning before, as I have been afraid. The wild roses are lovely this year. I never remember so many. E came for the weekend and did a lot of gardening so we were both too tired on Saturday night for anything. He came up to the sand on Sunday afternoon for half an hour. Margot came over on Saturday afternoon to say goodbye and went to Edinburgh on Sunday, going on to Aberdeen on Monday. I have had a card from her to say she had a comfortable journey. I called on Mrs Sharpe on Sunday and arranged about transfer as Mrs Hartley can't bring the twins any more. She kept me half an hour and said Sarah is worrying about death—doesn't want to go up from the Kindies next term. She was reading Trevelyan's 'Social History' and Mr S said they read all Trollope in the blitz. The twins went to tea yesterday and she gave them strawberries. Andrew is improving—he likes mint sauce and strawberries under protest.

Thursday 11th July 1946

We have had a heat wave since last week—the children are getting brown and wear sun-suits every afternoon. I took the twins to Purley last weekend as Rosa was coming home on Saturday. We caught the 2.51 and got there at 3.30, went to Purley to fetch the meat and have my haircut (Andrew refused to have his cut!) and then went back to tea and bath and Rosa arrived. She was brown and very pleased to see us. On Sunday, Margaret wanted to go to church so I took her. Andrew stayed at home to cook with Rosa. They had their sleep in the garden and both slept but were disturbed by a plane. On Monday, Stuart phoned and arranged to meet on Tuesday. Mr Oxborrow came over on Monday evening and I went over to see him too. He was very kind but too optimistic about the shares. On Tuesday, Rosa came up to town to see Dudley Smith. Her impressions resembled mine—that he was honest, energetic, ambitious, impatient and too confident. She agreed to transfer 80% of the shares for a nominal sum, say £20, and not put any money in, she to get a dividend when possible. It is not good but it is more than one would have thought possible at one time and she doesn't risk any more capital and it satisfies them without harassing us. It remains to put it into operation.

Friday 12th July 1946

The twins chose to talk at bedtime instead of having their usual songs or hymns (Andrew: 'Now the day is over'; Margaret: either 'We plough the fields and scatter' or 'Through the night of doubt and sorrow', or 'Water is wide' or 'Cuckoo' or 'God Save the King'). Andrew gave me a detailed account of his day. At playtime, he played buses on the climbing frame—Graham was driver, Gillian Hartley conductor. Andrew and Jimmie and Philip were passengers. He was going to West Croydon. Was Margaret in the bus? Oh no, she was up there practising handstands with Sarah. After 4.00, they were in the garden with Anne and Ivan (from next door) and took off their shoes on condition that they played on the grass. Andrew, "I put my shoes on to go to the shed for my bucket and spade and a piece of brown carpet—so then I had a pretend picnic. I went to Woldingham and walked to Old Oxted to catch the bus" (he has done this twice). He had a piece of bread and butter and a cress sandwich (Margaret had a tomato too) for tea, and a mug of milk and another of milk and tea. Margaret told me a long fantasy, which she called a dream, about Jimmie in hospital (who never stopped crying 'Jim wants Mum' in reality). The twins know Big Ben on the radio and also in the flesh and call any other chiming clock 'Little Ben'. Andrew said that at school today they had 'rhythm' and 'rat-a-tat-tat'.

Monday 15th July 1946

The heat wave finished yesterday. Today was 23 degrees colder than Saturday—a day of showers and blue sky (the pines were dazzling this morning in the early sunshine); so was yesterday. I picked raspberries in a mac while the rain poured on the dry earth. In the afternoon, there was one clap of thunder. As we went up to bath Margaret said, "It is the sort of day when we might see a rainbow." They hurried out of the bath to see a faint one. As I came back from seeing E off there was a heavy shower—like diamonds in the sunshine and a high bright rainbow! I ran home to tell Margaret but it had faded. Still, she had heard the rain and saw the sun and crept down to the stair window and saw it.

We celebrated E's birthday this weekend. On Saturday afternoon, we went to Oxted and Margaret got him some green pyjamas and Andrew a set of chess men. I showed them to him and he told Dorothy he had got him a game with the top of a lamp post and a horse. He also got him a card with the Southern Belle. Margaret got Margot a card with a bowl of roses. E got No 5 Meccano and Andrew bought himself a toy jeep (3/2d). His taste is good—it was the best model. E gave the 3 children their books, though Andrew said quickly, "I can't read yet." Then we went to the fair and E took them on swings. Margaret was nervous and wouldn't go high but Andrew wanted to go higher and higher. I managed to redeem an old promise to give Margaret an ice. On the way back (very late, as the train was half an hour late and we hadn't had tea) Andrew said, "I've had a lovely day!" So he did yesterday, spending every spare minute making (with E's help) an engine with the new Meccano.

Monday 29th July 1946

A long interval because Ella came to stay from the 16th of July to last Saturday (27th July) and I had no opportunity to write in bed. It was pleasant to have her and it seemed a nice long time to talk, but it has just slipped by and we haven't nearly finished, as always. Although the bedroom is so cramped, I think she enjoyed it and the children liked her. Andrew called her Ellie—a sure sign of acceptance—and got up when she did at 7.00 and he liked her to do his hair. The twins were much impressed when at my request she played the comb to them. It was so different from her speaking voice that they fled from her, shocked, at the first note. I read and enjoyed the first 3 sections of her novel, tentatively called, "If This be Error." I think it is her best thing so far and a good story. One wants to know what happens and I like it for its background, geographical (Norfolk) and philosophical. On Saturday, she gave me a lovely surprise by giving me an electric kettle—a most extravagant present.

A landmark yesterday, 28 July: Margaret tied a bow without any help at all. She was thrilled. E came for the weekend and had a busy time. He finished Andrew's engine with Meccano—at 11.50 on Saturday and helped Andrew make a truck yesterday. He did some digging on Saturday and yesterday morning and in the afternoon he began to teach Andrew chess and made me play one game. I hated it, though I should love to practise hard and beat him! Odd! So odd that I surprise myself. I went to the children's sports and was pleased to see Andrew sitting on a form with the others, hobnobbing with a small boy next him. They both seemed so self-possessed and independent. Andrew won a prize—so did Patsy as a 'small visitor'. I didn't and Margaret didn't. The children all went to tea with Sarah last week. Margaret hasn't been improved by Sarah who is rather defiant and shows off. Still, we can't insulate them and I expect Mrs Sharpe says the same about the twins.

Wednesday 7th August 1946

We had another short heat wave at the weekend rising to sun suits on Monday. Sunday was very hot. Monday was hotter. Yesterday was cooler and windy. Today it has rained.

A lovely weekend. Where to begin? E might have gone to Axmouth with K up to the last minute, then she was ill on Friday—but he phoned on Saturday morning to say he could come. In the afternoon, we went to Oxted. He took Andrew to watch the cricket match. I took Margaret to get her hair cut and to buy wool and buttons. We all met for tea at Bobby's and then watched cricket for half an hour. Andrew clapped the good bits. Margaret practised handstands on the grass.

On Sunday, we all caught the 9.31 to Forest Row. We crossed the Medway ('Meadow Way', Andrew called it). They dallied on the children's swings for a quarter of an hour. Then we climbed up to the golf course and walked two and a half miles over gorse, heather and bracken and then through forest. First it was misty and damp but at 12.00 it cleared and the sun blazed. We walked to the road from Wych Cross where ages ago Margot practised driving. There, by the road, we made a fire and boiled a kettle for tea and it was delicious. Every few minutes we heard a woodpecker yaffle. The view was beautiful—north to the downs behind Maidstone, with fields glowing gold to contrast with sombre summer green of the trees. Near at hand heather, ling, centaury and hairbells. The children had 40 winks with a prize for the first to sleep. They were all so good that they each had a prize when we got home. We walked back easily with time for more swings and caught the train which gets to Hurst Green at 4.43. Margaret and Patsy had a boiled egg for tea.

After this excitement, we had a quiet day on Monday—It was very hot and airless, we just walked to Itchingwood Common in the morning. I found some of the magenta spire flowers that grow on the Kennet Canal and loveliest of all, musk, which I haven't picked since I was working at Newbury. E took 2 roots for his ponds. There was also ragged robin and meadowsweet, and at last the limes are in flower by the railway gate. I picked a little this evening and it is scenting the dining room.

The children were lovely. E was surprised to find Margaret playing air raids. "We'll have another war, a German one I think. Now we'll bomb the children." Imitation siren—"Everyone go to the shelter" bang, etc. She was too realistic for Andrew who retired to help me sweep the bedroom. Two malapropisms: in difficulty with her egg shell she said, "Mummy, will you help me to coat (cope) with it?"; telling a long tale about a butterfly, "it was a broomstone." Andrew regularly chooses 'I shall lift up mine eyes unto the hills' and 'Onward Christian Soldiers'. The latter is far too great a favourite. I usually have to sing it twice.

I bought 1lb of mushrooms last night. Margaret was concerned—"You must send some to Bill—you ought to have told him to wait." Dorothy gave them a book each of flower outlines to colour and these are so popular that they have stopped bedtime stories for the last few days. They have no horror of insects etc.

Andrew woke me one morning. "There is something on my pillow. Will you take it away?" I found it was a huge spider but he was not unduly concerned. Margaret was about to pick up a good-sized frog in the road to put it in the ditch away from cars. Their reports came yesterday. Margaret seemed quite intrigued when I read it to her especially at, "She will soon read."

We had two lovely nights. On Saturday, he said, "Seeing you standing with nothing on has made me like this." Sunday, so hot that we needed no covering, was sweeter still. "The best for a long time" he said. We are fortunate—such joy in spite of K and Rosa.

Wednesday 14th August 1946

I took the twins to Purley on Saturday morning for the day as I was going to spend the afternoon with the Oades. I intended them both to stay the night but Nim wouldn't stay without me. Andrew stayed and Nim and I caught the 10.16 on Sunday for the day. Andrew decided to stay till Monday and I called for him on the way back. He was quite good on his own and thanked Rosa for 'my little holiday'—In the train coming home he seemed much more grown-up. He observed, "You are less interested in trains than I am, Mummy."

Last night I went to the Prom with Nancy. Mozart and Schubert. I was very tired, and caught the 9.20 but it was lovely. It is impossible to get anything much to eat as there is a gas strike. Dorothy went to Oxted to change our 67 surplus bread units yesterday and found they had run out of points—so they had in the city today. E has gone to Hastings for a fortnight with K—in the nature of a penance, but she insisted.

A rumour that the Treasury's new leave scheme is not more than 36 days plus every other Saturday which would suit me. Margot is due back today. This is very scrappy, but Margaret is sleeping with me as she has pain again which even a hottie didn't soothe.

Monday 19th August 1946

I forget if I noted Margaret's spontaneous raising of the problem that baffles science about three weeks ago. Going to Torr at Riddlesdown she saw a cat and said, "I expect it was a kitten first and came out of its Mummy's tummy—all kittens do. But where did the first kitten come from?"

Last week was too hectic. On Wednesday, the only day I caught my early train home I went to Edenbridge by mistake. The train went at the right time but must have been the one before, 20 minutes late. Another man did the same. We had 45 minutes to wait for one back. I had a look at the church. I went to Purley on Thursday. Margot had got back from Shetland and Orkney and had much to say and some rum to present. It was delicious. On Saturday, I took the twins to Purley and stayed the afternoon. Today I went to Heal's to look at a carpet and liked it—Axminster, green with small design of squares of brown and fawn, nearly £20, 9 by 12. We are getting one to be delivered next month.

Tuesday 27th August 1946

A rather hectic week packing and planning (a) for a week in Purley (b) for a fortnight in Cornwall. The food problems are endless. We got emergency coupons including priority milk but (1) the milkman doesn't deliver emergency priority milk (2) we have to go to the shop for it one mile away. They won't supply it without empty bottles. We have to keep these from the man to carry them a mile to the shop! Yesterday after learning all this I took 2 half pint bottles to the dairy which supplies the office in the city and got two and a half pints in the bottles plus one pint in a carton which I had to bring home.

The twins are enjoying themselves at Purley and being very good. Dorothy reported that they acted Patsy Podger all through, with Andrew as the scarecrow. Today I had half a day and joined the others at Kew. A small child of 2 had joined the twins and Andrew, particularly, was liking her. We walked to the water and looked at the water-lilies. The twins lay on their tummies and dabbled their hands in the water. We had tea at Zeetas, Richmond, including ices for Nim and Rosa and then came home. Rosa and Margot took the twins to see Uncle Bill and Auntie Milly[73] on Friday and it was very successful. They were very good and Rosa liked showing them off. E was back yesterday.

Monday 23rd September 1946

The holidays have come and gone. On the whole successful. The twins loved the sand and pools and paddling in the sea. Andrew was efficient at climbing over the rocks and got right up a fairly easy cliff. Margaret was bolder in the sea. At first, they played in the sand individually but in the second week they began to cooperate. They found a big hole and embellished it—playing that it was a nest—Margaret the mother bird and Andrew the baby. Andrew was more sociable and played with at least 3 other boys. They were interested, but nervous

---

[73] Uncle Bill was Rosa's only brother and Millie was his wife

of a little crab, but amused by the sand hoppers. Andrew loved the two or three days when it was warm enough for his red knicks only and Margaret (who had a slight cold) envied him. They loved running up and down the sandhills barefoot.

Managed to see Crantock church (where E told Margaret the story of the Good Samaritan from a window) and East Newlyn church (with medieval bench ends, old pulpit,15th century transept roof, Norman font and coloured medieval choir screen). The vicar was charming, and the twins took to him. There was a cloudburst so we stayed a long time in the church. We had an afternoon in Truro (where Andrew liked the Tudor font decorated with acorns in the 15th Century Parish church incorporated in the cathedral), another in Newquay where we saw boats for the first time. I took them for the day to Falmouth and across in the ferry to Flushing, their only boat trip, which they loved. The sea at Perranporth was lovely and more sand than I have seen anywhere. The granite cliffs and fantastic caves and tunnels prevent it from being insipid. With the sun shining and a strong wind high tide is glorious—indigo and green-blue sea with spray dashed high over the rocks.

The journey was good to Plymouth. We caught the 9.00 from Waterloo and met Nannie at Andover and taxied to Hatherden for dinner with her and her family. The twins were thrilled and she thought Margaret as sweet as ever and Andrew much improved. He played with the boys without trouble and traded some old bus tickets for 3/4d with Michael. We caught the 2.14 to Plymouth. Neither slept and we had tea on the train much to their satisfaction. It was raining and Andrew said, "Look at the rain, but we are all right having tea in the train!" We reached Plymouth to time and May met us with the car. Andrew took to it. They were very good though the Reynolds made a great fuss of them. Auntie Bess gave Margaret a baby doll, Elizabeth, to which she is devoted. E came through the night and Margaret and I met him in the morning. Luce took us round Plymouth and we caught the 12.50 to Perranporth. It was so full we could hardly squeeze into the corridor.

Tuesday 24th September 1946

E went back on the 8 September—i.e. he had 8 days at Perranporth. It was lovely to be a family and I enjoyed housekeeping and giving them what they liked—pancakes and dumplings and mushrooms and tomatoes. The bed was uncomfortable but we slept all right. We had 4 lovely nights. I still want another baby but E keeps evading and it is easy for him to do so. He came this weekend and was busy every minute. He did the garden and I took the twins blackberrying. I have never seen such mud. They wore their boots but got stuck more than once. At Jincocks Farm, Margaret and Patsy were carried by a land girl and farm boy. We picked a good lot and they were nice ones. It was fine and the sun came out. We saw dragonflies and what Margaret called 'yellow bottles'. They go back to school tomorrow. Andrew is keen: "I've had enough holidays," but Margaret says she doesn't want to go. I suspect that at bottom this is due to the story of the old man and the sack, told her by another child. It is difficult to counter-suggest it.

I phoned Miss Pace last night and asked whether she could suggest any solution of the going home problem. She was cordial—said they were sweet and so sensible.

Craddock came down in August and looked at four of my cases to make a 'considered report', but I need a move to get promotion and I would rather stay as I am and have a baby.

Elsie's job finished on Saturday. She has a temporary job at the Britain Can Make It exhibition. Stuart is doing some business but the Board of Trade does its best to stop people. He had a difficult job to get a licence to pay purchase tax! Ella goes to South Africa on Thursday thanks to Oades, who got the Union Castle moving. A man Rosa has seen twice, whom she met at the Dowsers Garden Party, proposed to her when he called last week. He has 14 factories doing something with tin! Two years a widower and all she said was, "Let's talk of your wife!" Went to the Prom with Nancy last Wednesday. 'Belshazzar's Feast' overwhelmed me but gave me the authentic tingle.

Tuesday 2nd October 1946

The twins returned to school last Wednesday and the problem of fetching them was solved by putting them in 'transition'—i.e. skipping kindergarten and going straight up from nursery class. They must be the smallest children in it. Now they have real lessons—reading, writing, 'sums', 'grown up story'—which is rudimentary history—'about the cavemen'. Mrs Marsh sent me a message yesterday that they were holding their own well. Andrew will soon read—had read a whole page with only one or two prompts but had he learnt it by heart? I wondered. They have started on Ballard's arithmetic. They aren't allowed the climbing frame now, which is hard. They go to school all by themselves now, but today Margaret only gave the conductor two pence instead of four pence.

Dorothy and Mrs Sharpe share the fetching. Andrew was very sick last Friday. We don't know whether it was the change in routine—over excitement—the heat—or over fatigue. He slept with me and we both had a disturbed night. He was all right by Sunday but is still very tired by the evening. He needs watching but is full of energy by day.

Whitton retired yesterday with quite a ceremony when Pole handed over the trays we gave him. Very tired—two interviews, one on Adam brothers and one on Modiano. On Monday morning, I caught the 7.47 and went to Nicholsons to queue for utility bed linen off dockets. It took till 10.30 and I got one linen sheet (25/3d), one blanket (for Nim, 24/10d), 2 pillow cases (1/8d each compared with 7/2d I paid for the others, no better). It was well organised and two flashlight photographs were taken, but the queue was enormous. I was worn out after it, but it was worth it even for the sheet and if they hadn't limited each person I shouldn't have got any.

Tuesday 8th October 1946

The twins were 5 on Saturday. They went to Purley in the morning after waking at 6.00—back with E and me to dinner when E gave Andrew his Lotts bricks and Margaret a scooter. Between 3 and 3.30 the 'party' arrived—Sarah Sharpe, Graham Edmonds and Ann and Ivan Humphries. Rosa sent some paper tea napkins which were very popular. Dorothy made Andrew an engine cake and Margaret a house and they had candles. Margot went to Edenbridge by mistake but arrived about 4.30.

Sunday was brilliant and E and I took the children to Oxted church for harvest festival. We had 'Praise my soul' and 'I will lift up mine eyes unto the hills' but not 'We plough the fields'. We walked back and in Oxted saw a swallow's nest with the parents still feeding 2 young ones. After dinner, I picked blackberries and Margaret came with me with her scooter. Andrew and E spent every minute building—a house in the morning and a station in the afternoon. The twins continue to enjoy school. Margaret said today she had been doing adding up sums with counters. Yesterday they had singing—Andrew sang by himself, a scale, I think. Margaret is getting on very well with reading phonetically—she gets the Beacon and reads the lists of words at any spare minute and has done it instead of a story several times. She says Andrew is further on than she, but he won't divulge.

Tuesday 15th October 1946

The main event has been Dorothy's decision to join her cousin as partner in the guest house at Ballina. She seemed sorry and said but for this offer she would have stayed for years or as long as I needed her. It is a good thing for her, though not, I think, so good for Patsy. I have got to find someone else but I can hardly expect to find anyone so good in every way. I have written five letters already.

The twins continue to enjoy school. Margaret has read all through the introductory book but I suspect from the way Andrew helps her when she hesitates that he can read as well or better, but he doesn't read at home. On Friday, he did his sums so well that Mrs Marsh said he could play with the doll's house by himself. Margaret had a good Malapropism on Saturday. She said, "I saw the corn being put on a rick and threshed. There was an alligator (elevator) working." One of them on the fine weather: "We've had a shower of sunny days." Andrew, about giving up the return halves of their tickets at the station: "Can I give her coming back's tickets?"

Yesterday morning I met Rosa on the 7.58 and we went to the Britain Can Make It exhibition. It was lovely to see the china, shoes, towels, stoves and kitchen equipment, furnishing fabrics, etc., but I was unimpressed with the fashions (mainly evening and day frocks and suits and coats—not tailor-mades and tweeds), which aped Paris—not much impressed with furniture and children's toys and things. The greatest weakness is that no indication of cost whatever is given. Elsie got us in with no queuing which was a boon. We saw it at leisure and did not get tired before we began. Pleasant, but I got a headache and was amazed to find it was 12.15. I took Rosa to the Venice and then went to the office. I should have taken the whole day but for the need to save all the leave I have to work in the new House Keeper.

Tuesday 22nd October 1946

The dry spell broke on Saturday afternoon when we had heavy rain about 4.30 but the most brilliant rainbow I have ever seen. It was dazzling and yet solid and lasted 15 minutes. Andrew and I were walking from Riddlesdown Station. We walked backwards so as to watch it. He had had a slight chill on Friday evident from his loss of appetite and desire to sleep. He was better on Saturday but I decided after some hesitation that he couldn't go to Brighton with Rosa and Nim. He was furious but Dorothy let him have his new bricks and he built a station from the diagram with only one suggestion from her. I took him to Purley in the afternoon and we stayed over till Sunday evening. Margot took Margaret and me to church but Andrew stayed home. She ate an enormous dinner and tea. His appetite needed persuading. By yesterday, it had recovered. Two enquiries—Margaret at the weekend: "Who looked after the first man when he was a baby?" Andrew, this morning before getting up: "How do the things we think about come into our heads?—out of the air?"

When I got back last night a woman with a boy of four was waiting. She is Irish with traces of Cockney—a difficult mixture—has been in service all her life—is giving up her present job with a school teacher because she can't cope with a boy of 7. I think she is kind but uncouth; is ready to work hard, but hasn't high standards; would do her best but has a weak character. I can hardly be lucky again, but don't know what to do. Andrew took to the boy.

Monday 28ᵗʰ October 1946

I heard from Miss Fray on Saturday—a social worker—about a woman of 37 with a boy of four and three quarters who wants a job as House Keeper. I went to see her today and liked her very much—in fact invited her out if Mrs Pearce came to me. Mrs Pearce sounds promising—quiet, neat, clean—"superior domestic type"—has had unfortunate jobs, the worst an old man of 80 who hated children and never spoke to the boy. Her only weakness according to Miss Fray is that she is not 'very jolly'—just beginning to be sorry for herself. Miss F evidently thought it a suitable job for her. The snag is that she is now near Falmouth and I don't want to be definite without seeing her. Miss F, perhaps 45–50, talked of her own contemporaries—70 girls to one man after the 14–18 war. Some felt deprived of children very badly and she herself feels out of touch with the young. What an appalling waste of potentiality!

E came for the weekend which was wet. He played with Andrew on Saturday and I took Margaret to Oxted to meet Margot and bought some paint and a Puffin (Plants) and a Penguin (E. Bowen—'To the North'). On Sunday, E and Andrew built a moot hall and in the afternoon we all played Snap (when Andrew won) and then E and Andrew chess, which E won. Margaret is getting on with her reading though I still guess Andrew is even better but he won't read to me! An air-mail from Ella—it sounds delightful—jacaranda trees and deckchairs.

Thursday 7th November 1946

I heard from Mrs Pearce that she can't face two children so I have arranged for Mrs O'Leary to come tomorrow. Dorothy is crossing to Dublin tomorrow night We enjoyed the weekend at Purley. Margaret combed all our hair and produced another 'howler'—'Hairy grip'—Kirby grip—hair grip.

Tuesday 12th November 1946

Dorothy went off on Friday with some regret. They had a car at 2.30. Mrs O'Leary (Mary Josephine) arrived about 11.00 with John and a lorry load of baggage. So far, so good. She seems determined to like it. I think she is clean and neat. The sink is nice and this is a good test. She is charmed with the kitchen, the gas copper and the gas poker. She likes the electric stove though she hasn't cooked with electricity before. She made an excellent cake on Saturday and a loaf on Sunday. She says she likes cooking and washing and all domestic jobs. The twins seem to have taken to her and John, and John likes them. She is Roman Catholic and her speech is a queer blend of Cockney and Irish. E came for the weekend and liked her cooking. We took all the children for a walk on Sunday morning and Margaret took her scooter.

I called for the twins on Friday and saw Mrs Marsh for 2 minutes. She said Andrew was 'definitely bright'—his reading was good. She supposed I helped him at home and was astonished to hear that he had always refused to read to me. She said he had an excellent memory and learnt by heart with no effort at all—could recite strings of poetry to order. (I knew nothing of this, but persuaded Margaret to say some AA Milne next morning and Andrew said the last verse and helped her!) Apart from snuffles they seem all right. Andrew is most diplomatic with John, "I'm afraid you can't have that John, but would you like this"—Mary says, "Quite the little gentry!" Tonight he asked Margaret to look at a photograph of an old engine and she said, "No Andrew. I'm not interested in engines!" Yesterday was half term and they spent the day with Rosa. She took them to Croydon to see the shops and they enjoyed Kennards—Roundabouts—Old King Cole—pets corner etc. I called for them in the evening and just saw Margot.

E and I painted the back door on Sunday afternoon although I had a bad cold. He was sweet on Saturday night. I rarely remember such ecstasy. It changed key in the middle—"modulation" he said—into a kind of holy rapture—like Pentecost. He exhibited a strength and tenderness more than usual—or was it just that I was more perceptive? I don't know, but I can still feel the afterglow and so I think can he.

Wednesday 20th November 1946

The twins are flourishing and like Mary. They are eating a lot. Margaret's knicks have been dry since last Monday week and her bed for 5 nights running. Such queer twisty minds we have, even at 5! What has caused the slight hitch in her environment which makes it easier for her? I don't know. Mary is more demonstrative than Dorothy but not kinder. She is more like Nannie. John occasionally wets his bed. Anyway, there is a clear improvement. On Sunday, Mary asked me if she could have a friend to tea—an Austrian who married an Englishman and had a little girl now six and a half. He was killed on a motorcycle going to work. She hasn't seen her family since before 1937. She can't decide whether to stay (she is in domestic work) or go back to her family and leave the child here to her grandparents. She was impressed with Andrew's singing. He just sang one thing after another.

Monday 25th November 1946

Another wet weekend—we are getting 2 months rain in one after a dry October. Last week the pond at the corner overflowed. In between, there are short periods when the dark sky twinkles fiercely with stars—or huge clouds sail across the pale blue driven by the gales. One day was utterly Shelley's West Wind—even to thunder and lightning, black rain and hail.

E came for the weekend and was very busy. We went shopping on Saturday afternoon in the rain and the twins bought Christmas presents—Margaret a writing pad for Auntie Bess; cold cream for Rosa; one book for Margot. Andrew envelopes for Auntie Bess; saucepan for Rosa; book for Margot etc. E got another box of Meccano, a Hornby train set for Andrew—Andrew got a calendar for me and a train book for himself too. E also got a second-hand Children's Encyclopaedia at Wilson's (Canadian Edition) for £9 and I am bringing it home two volumes at a time. Yesterday it rained all day though Margaret took her scooter out in the afternoon with me to post letters.

Andrew had his prize for dressing himself quickly—a signal with 2 arms and played trains in the morning. Before tea, we did a play—'The Billy Goats Gruff'. It was the first attempt at dramatics and I was astonished at the twins' ability. Margaret just took to it with no effort. Andrew had one attack of hesitation and reluctance but then wanted it all over again! It will do him good. E helped. We did 'The Three Bears' too. John enjoyed it but at times thought it was real. A most successful experiment. I was awfully tired all the weekend.

Monday 2nd December 1946

It has been cold and wet. It was the worst walk from the station I remember and with the twins. Margaret cried and said, "If you were sensible, Mummy, you would get a car." During the last week we have all been sick except John. Margaret began on Wednesday night. I kept her home on Thursday although she was clearly better in the morning eating an egg with pleasure; Andrew on Friday night so that I was very doubtful about taking them to Peter's birthday party on Saturday afternoon. Although he didn't eat any breakfast and little dinner, he was in good spirits.

It wasn't raining and they were both keen so I took them by train to East Croydon. An old lady who got in at Oxted said just before we got out—"Excuse me, how old are they? Twins—I have never heard such charming children—so intelligent!" We had 35 minutes to wait for a train, so, to the twins' joy, I took them by tram. Andrew especially was thrilled with buses, trams, trolley buses etc—but as we approached Norbury—"There seems to be only houses" was his reaction to a dormitory suburb. The tram stopped and I lifted Margaret out—several people were waiting to get on and the tram went on before I could get Andrew. One of the people waiting grabbed him but not before Margaret had seen the situation and panicked. It upset her because last night she had a terror dream about it. I had to wake her up to show her Andrew sleeping safely with his pinafore over his face! When we reached the house Margaret said, "What a little tiny garden!" They loved the party and Andrew ate an enormous tea. He was fascinated with Peter's trains and lines. There were 8 children including 2 girls. Peter goes to a prep school in South Croydon for Whitgift. He goes all day and Saturday morning and plays football but he doesn't seem to be making so much progress in learning as the twins. He is much improved from mixing with children. The twins each won a prize, Margaret a doll's knife, fork and spoon and Andrew a gun from which he fired burnt matches with the gusto of one who has never had a military toy. Roy brought us all the way to Purley. Stuart was still there and Margaret took to him—"I like his face and the way he does his hair!"

Friday 13th December 1946

A long gap, partly due to Andrew having another chill and partly to me having another cold.

It has been bitterly cold all the week. This morning was like a Christmas card here, glittery frost and sun but by Oxted it was fog. The Southern Rail has been running a fog service since yesterday. Nights glitter beautifully and the weather is perfect here but for the cold. Mary took the children to the school play yesterday and they all enjoyed it and the twins want to go to a 'real' pantomime. E had relaxed to the length of Jean Stirling McKinley, but I lean to Toynbee Hall 'Pinocchio' in the absence of 'Hansel and Gretel'.

Margaret is proud of her 'silver tooth', a minute stopping she had done last Saturday. She was very good though it didn't hurt her and the dentist was tactful and explained everything as he did it and even gave her a bit of silver. I bought a winter coat last week when I had a day's leave and went to town shopping with Rosa and to see the King's Pictures. We got a party frock (pink) for Margaret and had a large lunch at Flemings including for Rosa a glass of stout. Thus strengthened we spent one and a half hours at the pictures. For sheer enjoyment, I preferred the Dutch—2 de Hoochs and a Vermeer, the Rembrandts, especially the Epiphany which is never adequately conveyed in reproductions—the mysterious starlight glinting on the Kings' jewels and focussed on the child— these were the highlights. The royal portraits have an interest apart from the painting and there are isolated things—a holy family especially—which fascinated Rosa—the child about 3 with a cradle of carved wood, too small. A well-filled day with good weather and no mishaps.

When we were in Oxted on Saturday, E got Margaret a second-hand dolls house for £7.10 complete with furniture. It came on Wednesday. She has been agitating for one but doesn't know for certain whether she will get one or not. Andrew was smitten with desire for one when he saw hers in the shop. It is sweet inside with stairs and a bathroom and a standard and real lights. Mrs Parsons sent me 10 shillings for them and I got A an aeroplane and M some furniture units to make (15/4d altogether!). I heard from Dorothy this week, they are getting a quarter of a pound of sugar per week only. She offered to try to send a turkey so I said yes. Mary's sister-in law intends to send some more meat.

Wednesday 18th December 1946

On Saturday afternoon, it turned cold and it has been bitter ever since with a strong E or NE wind cutting one in two. Monday was the worst day because it was grey. Tuesday and today have been sunny, in fact this morning was beautiful with a clear pale blue sky and a red gold sun, white frost and robins. Traditional Christmas weather. But it is uncomfortable and I am glad the living room and my bedroom face west. Miss Bannister's room and Mary's room are bitter.

Andrew was well enough to go to Purley on Saturday morning and the weekend there did him good. Both ate big dinners. We had separate steak pies on Saturday and Andrew ate all his, the carrot from Margaret's and then scraped my dish! He was very good all the time though Margaret was querulous on Saturday. Andrew was quite himself on Monday and went back to school. I had brought them home and Margot and Margaret went round to pick holly. She is standing up to the cold much better this year. Today was the party at the Hoskyns Arms and I called for the twins and Sara; I had a job to find them and then had to get them ready so we missed the bus. We caught the train and I took Sara home. Andrew was very tired so I was very pleased to see a bus which brought us to the corner of Mill Lane. They enjoyed themselves very much, though Andrew was diffident at first. Margaret was in her element in her new party frock which she took great care of.

I lunched with Auntie Katie who sent them a book and was very cordial. It took me half an hour to get there. On the way back, I got a pair of red suede shoes at Le Pied after trying in vain at all the shoe shops in Strand and Holborn. Margot wanted blue or black but the ones I got are nice and she may take to them.

Milner went to Somerset House this week and is on instructions! Butler came today and seems to be trying. Lloyd called this afternoon on, I think, a mere pretext and brought me 2 boxes of cigarettes. I was overcome.

Tuesday 31st December 1946

Nearly a fortnight and what a full fortnight. Christmas has come and gone with its excitement and weariness though we still have the tree and the paper chains, the Christmas cards and the lanterns. E came from last Saturday week and stayed till Christmas night. Margaret had a slight chill with no appetite and a pain in her tummy when she went out so we had to abandon our plan to shop altogether on Saturday afternoon. E stayed and dug up the Christmas tree. Margaret retired to her cot with a hot water bottle; Andrew and I went to Oxted for last minute shopping. It was bitterly cold and we were glad to catch the earliest bus with Mary and John. On Sunday, it was damp and milder. Margaret refused to let E and me go for a walk to Limpsfield as he suggested. Neither he nor I could prevail and as she wasn't well I stayed except for a short walk round the P.O. with him.

We tied the parcels on the tree and on Monday the children were all speculating about them. I went to the office but caught the 4.20 down, meeting E and the twins at Oxted where they had been shopping. E had got me an electric clock and Margaret had got me a toast rack. They went to bed early, as we were treating it as Christmas Eve. I had the first symptoms of a chill. We still had a lot to do including the socks and E unpacked Margaret's dolls' house which was much finer than I remembered. In fact, the furniture inside was worth a lot. There were 2 dolls and a baby doll, exquisitely made, and electric lights in the kitchen and living room. I was so thrilled with it that I felt quite sick. Andrew woke me up at 2.00 am and kept asking to see his presents at intervals till, at 6.0 am, we gave in and turned on the light and the electric fire. They played happily till tea arrived. John came up to show us what he had. We had breakfast in a state of mounting excitement. Mary put the pudding on to boil and Miss Bannister came down at 10.00 and E began distributing the presents from the tree. It lasted for 2 hours with an interval for orange juice. The boys got very excited, especially John. Andrew had attention for little but his Hornby train which he received in bits. He could hardly be distracted from it even to receive other things like another Meccano. Margaret was quite calm and self-possessed but was clearly thrilled with her dolls house, the last present to be given. She took everything out at once and had 'tea in the garden'. John kept clamouring for his constructional train to be made for him and tried, rather unsuccessfully, to build a house with his new bricks. Dinner was much enjoyed and we sent some up to Miss B. We had roast pork and Christmas pudding. Andrew had the first 6d in the pudding and J had 2 helpings to get another. I gave mine to Margaret.

Andrew played with his train in the afternoon and we had the tree lights and lanterns for tea. Margot had meant to come and Margaret, E, John and I went to meet her—a cold sunny afternoon with red orange sunset—but she wired to say she had a bad chill. Miss B came down and we had candles on the cake; so our Christmas Day ended. I felt queer in the evening. Mary and John went off on Christmas morning to Mrs Jarrett and we had a lovely quiet day on our own which I should have loved if I hadn't been feeling very queer and I shivered all day. At 11.30, the turkey arrived from Eire but it was too late for dinner and I felt unequal to tackling it. We had cold pork, Christmas pudding and mince pies. After dinner, Andrew did his jigsaw (from Nannie) as it was the Silver Link. He was surprisingly good at it—lucky, or a very good quick eye? We were both impressed. After tea, he did the other smaller one from Auntie Bess, but most of his energy went on his train. Margaret and I sang carols and we had just the tree lights and lanterns.

Suddenly I felt quite overwhelmed with happiness—seeing Andrew and his father crawling about the floor—Margaret with her bright face in the glow of the lights and Sallie on the floor. The whole scene fixed itself on my mind and I watched. I knew I should look back on it in the future as one of the loveliest moments in my life. And then it dissolved like a cloud picture—E went off on the train; the twins were tired and I put them to bed.

Epilogue

Doreen continued to write her diary, but with increasingly long gaps between the entries, until the twins left school for university. At that point, when she was nearing retirement, she took a law degree and read for the bar. She then acted as an adviser on taxation to two commercial firms and wrote a monthly column on pension taxation for a journal, after having spent a long spell as an adviser to firms setting up pension funds while in the Inland Revenue. Earlier, when he retired, E undertook a course leading to a diploma in archaeology. They both met up frequently to attend concerts, plays and lectures at the Royal Institution and elsewhere in London, and went on residential courses arranged by London University at Westonbirt School in the summer, until E died in 1974.

They both took delight in becoming grandparents. Doreen also helped Margot look after their mother, Rosa, as she became older (she died in 1972, aged 92), and they went on many holidays abroad together, satisfying their interest in travel. This included a visit to Australia when Doreen was in her early 80s, to visit Andrew and his wife and their young family when they were living there. Doreen died in 1994, a few weeks after meeting her first great grandchild. Margot lived on for a further ten years, spending many weekends, full of pleasure, with her great nieces and nephews, before dying in 2004.